INTEREST GROUPS AND JUDICIAL FEDERALISM

INTEREST GROUPS AND JUDICIAL FEDERALISM

Organizational Litigation in State Judiciaries

DONALD J. FAROLE, Jr.

PRAEGER

Westport, Connecticut
London

Library of Congress Cataloging-in-Publication Data

Farole, Donald J., 1969–
Interest groups and judicial federalism : organizational litigation in state judiciaries / Donald J. Farole, Jr.
p. cm.
Includes bibliographical references and index.
ISBN 0–275–96067–6 (alk. paper)
1. Citizen suits (Civil procedure)—United States—States.
2. Pressure groups—United States—States. I. Title.
KF8896.5.Z95F37 1998
347.73′53—dc21 97–34751

British Library Cataloguing in Publication Data is available.

Library of Congress Catalog Card Number: 97–34751
ISBN: 0–275–96067–6

First published in 1998

Praeger Publishers, 88 Post Road West, Westport, CT 06881
An imprint of Greenwood Publishing Group, Inc.

Printed in the United States of America

The paper used in this book complies with the Permanent Paper Standard issued by the National Information Standards Organization (Z39.48–1984).

10 9 8 7 6 5 4 3 2 1

Copyright Acknowledgment

The author and publisher gratefully acknowledge permission to use quotes from interviews with Trish Jerman (July 1995) and Jane Bell (August 1995) and from a letter from Richard P. Kleeman (August 1995).

To my parents,
Cathleen A. Farole and Donald J. Farole, Sr.
for their many sacrifices

Contents

Tables and Figures

TABLES

FIGURES

Preface

Interest Groups, Rights Litigation, and Judicial Federalism

This is a study about interest groups, rights litigation, and judicial federalism. A number of the most important rights developments in this century are the result of litigation campaigns by organized interest groups. The most well-known example is when the National Association for the Advancement of Colored People (NAACP) Legal Defense Fund financed, organized, and argued the most important civil rights cases before the Supreme Court (Greenberg 1994; Kluger 1976; Vose 1959). These efforts eventually led to the desegregation of schools and public accommodations, and to the removal of racial barriers to voting. Prompted by the NAACP's success, other groups turned to the courts to pursue their goals. The American Civil Liberties Union (ACLU) was instrumental in the development of many areas of constitutional rights (Walker 1990). Groups and their attorneys were also essential in litigation on women's rights (O'Connor 1980) and religious freedom (Sorauf 1976).

Organized interest groups play an important role in the American judicial process. Since courts are largely passive institutions that do not actively seek out cases to decide, they depend on others to bring matters to their attention. Most cases reach the courts through citizen-initiated suits, a process known as legal mobilization (Black 1973). By bringing cases, litigants make demands on the courts and set the judiciary's agenda (Zemans 1983).

But not all litigants are equal. In the courts, resources matter. Access to the judiciary requires money, time, and legal expertise that many individuals, especially the poor, do not possess. And while resources may bar litigants from initially entering the courts, fewer still are able to pursue litigation at the appellate level. Appellate courts most directly affect the "rules of the game" by expounding on legal doctrine. Without sympathetic lawyers and the money to finance appellate litigation, it is little more than a fiction for most citizens to proclaim that "I will fight this all the way to the Supreme Court if I have to."

However, some litigants, such as business corporations and many interest groups, can and do turn to the courts on a regular basis. Marc Galanter (1974) asserted that these "repeat players" fare much better in courts and are better able to influence legal change than "one-shotters." Repeat players are able to structure their interactions with the courts by carefully selecting cases to pursue and developing favorable legal precedents. As the state of the law evolves, it reflects the interests of repeat players, and they win more often than one-shot litigants in the courts.[1]

While barriers to the courtroom suggest that meaningful legal change is difficult to achieve, interest groups and other repeat players are favorably positioned to seek legal change and to influence legal doctrine in ways that further their members' interests. By representing the interests of one-shot litigants, interest groups can help to bridge the gap between repeat players and one-shotters.[2] Groups can offer to individuals the resources and expertise necessary for success in the courts. An organization can bring cases that individual litigants might not pursue due to a lack of resources or incentives.

Of course, organizational litigants[3] do not solely represent the interests of the "have-nots" in society. Corporations, trade associations, businesses, and other presumably "advantaged" interests also turn to the courts to advance legal claims. Whichever interests they represent, however, organized litigants occupy a central role in affecting the types of cases that courts hear and the ways they resolve legal questions.[4]

This study examines the participation of major litigating groups, not in the U.S. Supreme Court, but rather in state judiciaries. In the wake of the Warren Court's liberal activism of the 1960s, state courts have reemerged as more prominent actors in the American judiciary. Republican control of the presidency (and, more recently, Congress) has resulted in the appointment of ideologically conservative judges to the Supreme Court and other federal courts. The more conservative Court has discouraged the use of federal court forums, relegating cases increasingly to state judiciaries. In addition, the Supreme Court has been less willing to protect many rights. It has issued numerous decisions in many areas of law, most notably criminal law, that have restricted the scope of protection under the federal Constitution. In response, advocates of the "new judicial federalism"[5] have encouraged litigants to continue the rights revolution in state courts by seeking broader protection for rights based on state constitutions than the Supreme Court recognizes under federal constitutional standards.

As a result of these changes in the federal courts, battles over rights increasingly are fought at the state level. In this context, what I call a *decentralized litigation environment*, interest groups appear to have greater incentive to litigate rights cases in state courts. One would expect interest groups to adapt to the changing trends in judicial federalism, but scholarly studies have not directly examined this important and timely question. I rely on the lesson of previous studies of group litigation to identify concepts that help me to examine the willingness and ability of interest groups to litigate in state courts. Specifically, I ask two questions. First, under what conditions are interest groups, particularly major litigating organizations, likely to participate in state litigation? Despite documented trends of increased rates of group litigation in state courts (Epstein 1994), I find that many groups did not litigate on a regular basis. Why? One possibility is that groups did not view state courts as important enough to justify their litigation efforts. Since state court precedents directly affect only one state, these decisions do not have the potentially broad nationwide implications that Supreme Court decisions can have.

But there is another possible explanation. Many groups may not have the resources to litigate consistently in state courts. If this is true, then these groups do not choose to avoid state court litigation; they simply lack the capacity to shift their focus from one Supreme Court to the much more numerous state courts. Thus, a thorough understanding of *why* groups do or do not enter state courts allows us to understand more completely organizational litigation in state judiciaries.

Second, when groups do litigate in state courts, what legal arguments do they offer? Of particular interest is the willingness of interest groups to assert rights claims based on state constitutional law. Since state courts may interpret their constitutions to provide greater (but not less) protection for rights than that available under parallel provisions of the federal Constitution, a central component of the new judicial federalism has been the use of state constitutions to preserve rights that have been restricted by the Supreme Court's interpretations of the federal Constitution (Linde 1980; Brennan 1977). Do interest groups turn to state courts to seek broader protections? This research will explore the extent to which they have attempted to further their policy goals by mobilizing state constitutional law.

I base my analysis on a comparative study of group litigation in eminent domain (takings) and obscenity law in five states (Colorado, Indiana, Minnesota, New Jersey, and South Carolina) between the years of 1960 and 1994. The comparative design of the study allows me to assess the importance of the legal context in which groups make litigation decisions. In obscenity, the Supreme Court, in its landmark decision in *Miller v. California* (1973), provided clear incentives to litigate in state courts. *Miller* issued a more expansive definition of "obscenity"—it gave governments greater leeway to restrict sexual material—and also indicated the Court's unwillingness to continually review state convictions. In contrast, the Supreme Court has not provided such clear incentives for groups to participate in state court takings cases. Since the late 1970s, the Court has become more attentive and receptive to rights claims in takings law. This analysis helps us to understand how legal incentives influence groups' litigation behavior and strategies.

The project proceeds as follows. The next chapter sets the context in which the empirical analysis takes place. It examines in more detail changing trends in judicial federalism, documents the growing importance of state courts as policy makers, and considers the implications of these trends for the judicial protection of rights. Chapter 2 briefly reviews previous studies of interest group litigation, and based on the lessons of these studies, develops the concepts and analytic framework that guides the analysis of group litigation in state courts. Chapters 3 and 4 examine takings law. I argue in Chapter 3 that the Supreme Court has not provided interest groups with strong incentives to litigate takings claims in state courts, and in Chapter 4, I attempt to explain patterns of takings litigation by interest groups in the five states. Chapters 5, 6, and 7 examine obscenity law. I argue in Chapter 5 that the Supreme Court's decision in *Miller v. California* (1973) provided groups with clear incentives to litigate at the state level. Chapters 6 and 7 examine the empirical evidence and explain the impact of *Miller* on group participation in state litigation. Finally, in Chapter 8, I evaluate my findings and consider their implications. Analysis of why the interest groups did and did not litigate provides insight into the role of organized litigants in the new judicial federalism. It allows for a better understanding of the conditions under which interest groups turn to state courts and seek protection for rights based on state constitutions. The analysis also allows for an assessment of prospects for the continued politicization of state courts, and for a more complete understanding of the complex relationship between federalism and rights.

Finally, I wish to acknowledge a number of people without whose support I would have been unable to complete this project. This book began as my dissertation at Indiana University. I owe a great intellectual debt to Marjorie R. Hershey, whose advice and encouragement were crucial at all stages of my research. Leroy Rieselbach, John T. Williams, and Jeffrey Stake, all of Indiana University, provided comments and feedback on early versions of the manuscript. I am especially grateful to my good friend Charles Epp of the University of Kansas, whose criticisms and insights were absolutely essential not only to this project but also to my academic development. My colleagues and students and the University of North Carolina at Greensboro make work fun and stimulating. Finally, I thank my wife, Rebecca Roberts, for her love, patience, and constant encouragement. If not for her many, many sacrifices, I would never have written a page of this book.

NOTES

1. Not all interest groups are repeat players. Some organized interests rarely, if ever, go to court. Others, such as the American Civil Liberties Union (ACLU), devote a significant percentage of their resources to litigation. This study examines major litigating organizations that certainly deserve the status of "repeat players."

2. Galanter (1974, 150) notes that "if rules are the most abundant resource for reformers, parties capable of pursuing long-range strategies are the rarest." In addition to interest group litigation, other mechanisms such as legal services and class action suits may also be used to improve the status of disadvantaged litigants.

3. Throughout this book, the terms "interest group," "organizational litigant," "organized interest," and "group" are used interchangeably, and varied solely for stylistic purposes.

4. Chapter 2 addresses in more detail the ability of interest groups to affect judicial agendas and legal change.

5. The new judicial federalism refers to the "renewed willingness of state courts to rely on their own law, especially state constitutional law, in order to decide questions involving individual rights" (Abrahamson and Gutman 1987, 89).

Abbreviations

AAP	Association of American Publishers
ABA	American Booksellers Association
ACLU	American Civil Liberties Union
AFBF	American Farm Bureau Federation
ALA	American Library Association
CDL	Citizens for Decency through Law
CPDA	Council for Periodical Distributors Association
ICLU	Indiana Civil Liberties Union
IPDA	International Periodical Distributors Association
LDF	Legal Defense Fund
MC	Media Coalition
MCLU	Minnesota Civil Liberties Union
MM	Morality in Media
MPBA	Mountains and Plains Booksellers Association
MSLF	Mountain States Legal Foundation
NFLF	National Family Legal Foundation
NLCPI	National Legal Center for the Public Interest
NLD	National Legion for Decency
NODL	National Office for Decent Literature
NOLC	National Obscenity Law Center
NWF	National Wildlife Federation
PLF	Pacific Legal Foundation
SCFBF	South Carolina Farm Bureau Federation
UMBA	Upper Midwest Booksellers Association

INTEREST GROUPS AND JUDICIAL FEDERALISM

1

State Courts, Federalism, and Rights

> It is doubtful that our differences can be fully explained on the comparatively neutral grounds that we are divided over the proper role of the states (and state courts) in American society. The battle is not over the better structure for preserving federal rights that everyone values equally. It is over rights themselves and the scope assigned to rights.
>
> —Larry Yackle
> *Reclaiming the Federal Courts*

Organized interest groups participate in litigation on many issues of constitutional rights and liberties. Scholarly attention to group litigation naturally focuses on United States Supreme Court cases, given the Court's role at the pinnacle of the American judicial hierarchy. But in a federal judicial system, which consists of national (federal) courts and semiautonomous state courts, groups and other litigants have some choice in turning to the federal or state levels. This study examines the willingness and ability of organized interests to litigate on both sides of rights cases in state judiciaries.

This chapter sets the broader context in which we examine group litigation in state courts. It discusses the growing importance of state courts as judicial policy makers since the early 1970s. Since state judiciaries increasingly have had the final word on many issues of rights and liberties, interest groups that seek to influence judicial policy likely have more incentive to enter state litigation. But the importance of these trends in judicial federalism extends far beyond their effects on interest groups' litigation behavior. As Yackle's comment suggests, debate over the proper role of the federal and state courts on issues of rights may have important implications for the rights themselves. Thus, to understand more completely the context and consequences of interest group litigation in state courts, we must consider what the changes in judicial federalism may mean for judicial protection of rights.

STATE COURTS AND JUDICIAL FEDERALISM

While state courts are the "lower" tier of the American judiciary, any realistic portrayal of judicial federalism must acknowledge the critical role of state courts. They decide an overwhelming proportion of the cases initiated in American courts. In 1991, for instance, approximately 254,000 cases were filed in federal courts (Baum 1994, 31), compared to an estimated 94 million in state courts nationwide (Neubauer 1991, 183–184). Since only about 2 percent of state supreme court decisions ever get appealed to the U.S. Supreme Court (Glick 1991, 87), virtually all state supreme court decisions are final. Indeed, state supreme courts are "the final decision makers on most issues of commercial, property, family, inheritance, tort and criminal law, as well as state constitutional issues and local governmental powers and procedural issues" (Meeker 1986, 3).

State courts apply both federal and state law. On a daily basis, they interpret federal constitutional provisions. Formally, lower federal and state courts may not interpret the federal Constitution more narrowly or more broadly than does the Supreme Court. The Supreme Court provides a minimal level—a "floor"—of rights based on federal law, ensuring some uniformity in law nationwide.[1]

However, state courts have much more leeway when interpreting state law. So long as a federal right is not violated, state supreme courts are the final authority on the meaning of state constitutions and laws.[2] Thus, state courts are free as a matter of state law to impose greater restrictions on government activity than those the U.S. Supreme Court requires under federal constitutional standards. For that matter, they may interpret their constitutions to provide *less* protection, so long as they apply the level of protection federal law requires when interpreting the federal law.[3] State courts, then, have the power to determine the effective "ceiling" of individual rights through their interpretations of state constitutions.

State judiciaries have always played an important role in American judicial policy making. However, during some historical periods they have been more important policy actors than during others. For much of the twentieth century, state courts rarely relied on their constitutions to issue expansive protection for rights. As the Supreme Court incorporated rights into the Fourteenth Amendment, federal law became dominant in most state courts. Since the federal law standards were relatively protective, most state courts were unwilling to interpret their constitutions to provide broader protection. Many state court litigants, therefore, began to assert rights claims based exclusively on federal law. Law school training of lawyers and judges emphasized federal, not state, law. As a result, by the end of the 1960s, "the dominance of federal law was virtually complete" (Esler 1995, 5).

Not only did federal law come to dominate the resolution of cases in state courts, but also the Warren Court of the 1960s made state courts less important by liberalizing access to federal judicial forums. For instance, in *Fay v. Noia* (1963), the Supreme Court allowed state defendants to file habeas corpus petitions in federal district courts. If an individual was convicted, exhausted state appeals, and even unsuccessfully petitioned for certiorari to the Supreme Court, that defendant could seek a writ of habeas corpus to have the case retried in the federal courts. Expanded access to federal courts was not confined to criminal law. In *Monroe v. Pape* (1961), the Court allowed individuals whose rights were violated by state officials or under the color of state law to have their civil rights cases heard in federal courts.[4] Throughout the Warren Court era, then, battles over rights increasingly were fought in federal courts and decided on federal constitutional grounds.

It is important to recognize that the Warren Court's activism in protecting individual rights and the opening of the federal courts represented the exception, not the rule, to the Supreme Court's historic role in the American judicial system. Many are accustomed to thinking about the Supreme Court as the most active protector of rights, but often that has not been so. At times, state courts have taken the lead in protecting some rights. For instance, state supreme courts relied on their constitutions to recognize many economic rights before the U.S. Supreme Court protected them under the federal Constitution (Galie 1988).[5]

The Resurgence of State Courts

Since the early 1970s, state courts have come to occupy a more dominant position in the American judiciary. Richard Nixon's appointment of four justices to the Supreme Court marked the end of the liberal activism of the Warren Court and the rise of a more conservative Court led by Chief Justice Warren Burger.[6] Save for Jimmy Carter, who had no opportunity to appoint a justice to the Supreme Court, Republican presidents controlled the White House between 1968 and 1992, and in that time, appointed a majority of the justices. In addition, Presidents Reagan and Bush alone selected over half of the judges on federal district and appellate courts (Goldman 1993). Their appointments made the federal bench more conservative (Alumbaugh and Rowland 1990).

Under Chief Justices Burger and William Rehnquist, the Supreme Court has revitalized the policy-making role of state courts in two important ways. First, the Supreme Court has limited access to the federal courts, which increasingly leaves the final word in many individual rights disputes to state courts. The trend is most distinct in criminal law. In *Younger v. Harris* (1971) the Court held that federal courts must abstain from deciding cases brought to prohibit a state prosecution. The Court also prohibited federal courts from entertaining state prisoners' habeas corpus petitions that allege a Fourth Amendment violation if the state court provided a full and fair opportunity to litigate the issue (*Stone v. Powell* 1976). On other matters, such as the doctrines of standing, federal subject matter jurisdiction, and abstention, the Supreme Court has imposed stricter limits for raising claims in federal courts (see Yackle 1994).

Why has the Court restricted access to federal courts? There are a number of not necessarily competing explanations. The Court sought to promote state discretion and policy experimentation. Justice Lewis Powell argued that experimentation should be "unimpeded by unwarranted demands for national uniformity" (*Johnson v. Louisiana* 1972, 376).[7] Several justices—particularly Rehnquist and Sandra Day O'Connor—are noted for their strong support for the "principled" operation of federalism and dedication to limited national governmental authority. Restrictions on the oversight role of the federal courts help to carve out a more prominent role for state judiciaries and preserve the integrity of state court systems. Further motivating the justices was a desire to conserve scarce federal judicial resources. Concern over the growing federal judicial caseload led the Judicial Conference of the United States to commission a Long Range Plan for the Federal Courts. The Committee on Long Range Planning issued its initial report in March 1995, noting that "[if] the federal courts' civil and criminal jurisdiction continues to grow at the same rate it did over the past 53 years, the picture in 2020 can only be described as nightmarish. Federal law would be babel, with thousands of decisions issued weekly and no one judge capable of comprehending the entire corpus of federal law, or even the law of his or her circuit."[8] The much-criticized preliminary report called for many reforms, including the complete abolition of diversity jurisdiction and mechanisms to discourage the filing of civil rights cases in federal courts.

Others tie the restricted access to federal courts to case outcomes, suggesting that the Court's decisions "[provide] a pretext for funneling federal constitutional decisionmaking into state courts precisely because they are less likely to be receptive to vigorous enforcement of federal constitutional doctrine" (Neuborne 1977, 1105–1106).

In addition to the restricted access to federal forums, state courts have also become more important judicial policy makers for a second reason. The growing conservatism of the Supreme Court and lower federal bench has resulted in more restrictive doctrine in many areas of individual rights, and this in turn has given liberal interests incentive to turn to state judiciaries. The Court rejected further extensions of individual protections. For example, in *San Antonio v. Rodriguez* (1973) the justices refused to regard legislative classifications based on wealth as suspect, as are those based on race, ethnicity, and religion, and concluded that intrastate inequalities in public school financing do not violate the equal protection guarantee of the Fourteenth Amendment. On other issues, the Supreme Court scaled back on its previously broad protections. In areas such as abortion, criminal rights, and censorship, the Court overturned or restricted the precedents of the Warren and early Burger Courts.[9]

In response the federal courts' turn to the right, some rights advocates encouraged litigants to turn to state courts and to assert rights claims based on state constitutions. These advocates saw new opportunities to continue the rights revolution through the development of state law. Supreme Court Justice William Brennan (1986, 1977) urged state courts to "step into the breach" (1977, 503) left by the U.S. Supreme Court's unwillingness to protect many rights. A number of legal scholars and judges have examined the decisions of state supreme courts and advocated greater reliance on state constitutions (Kaye 1987; Abrahamson 1985; Collins 1985; Williams 1984; Linde 1980).[10]

The Supreme Court somewhat reluctantly provided the legal foundations for the new judicial federalism by refusing to review state court decisions that were clearly based on independent state grounds. In *Michigan v. Long* (1983, 1041), the justices held that to preclude Supreme Court review, state courts must make a "plain statement" that their judgment rests on adequate and independent state grounds. Where a decision rests on both federal and state law, and where the adequacy and independence of the state constitutional grounds are not established clearly by the state court, the Supreme Court will assume that the decision was based on federal grounds and, therefore, may review the decision. Abrahamson and Gutman (1987, 97) concluded that "the judicial presumption, therefore, is that a state court's decision does *not* rest on adequate and independent state grounds, and that a state court must clearly rebut that presumption if it wishes to insulate its decision from federal review."

By placing the burden clearly on the state court to ensure that its decision is based on state law, some suggest that the Supreme Court has made it difficult for state courts to develop an independent body of state constitutional law (for example, Friedelbaum 1987). Yet the fact remains that the Supreme Court carved out a category of state law cases that is not subject to federal review.[11] Consequently, state courts can issue more protective civil liberties decisions, and insulate them from Supreme Court review, by clearly basing their rulings on state constitutional guarantees. Justice O'Connor (1989, 9) noted that "state courts have substantial power to grant or withhold jurisdiction to the Supreme Court by the choice of grounds for the state court decisions."

To summarize, since the early 1970s, the Supreme Court increasingly has decentralized policy making in the American judiciary. Through more conservative interpretations of the federal Constitution, the Court has encouraged litigants to turn to state courts and assert state constitutional claims that seek broader protections than required under federal standards. The Court also has limited access to federal courts through its "procedural" decisions.[12] Thus, many battles over rights increasingly have been (and in the foreseeable future will be) fought in state courts, with state constitutions as an important weapon. Of course, these trends represent *tendencies* in American judicial policy making. In some areas of law, the Supreme Court has not decentralized policy responsibility as greatly as in other areas. And given its role at the apex of the judicial hierarchy, the U.S. Supreme Court seldom completely abdicates policy responsibility in any area of law. Nevertheless, the tendency is that policy responsibility on many issues of constitutional rights and liberties abides less in the federal courts and more in state court systems.

THE IMPLICATIONS OF DECENTRALIZED POLICY MAKING

The potential consequences of these trends in judicial federalism have not gone unnoticed. Many argue that the growing importance of state courts not only has altered the forum in which rights cases are adjudicated, but also has profound consequences for the protection of those rights. Indeed, debate over whether policy responsibility ought to be in the hands of state or national institutions is as old as the country. In *Federalist #10*, James Madison recognized important differences in policy making at the state vis-à-vis national levels. He argued that rights are in most jeopardy where government responds most immediately to the passions and interests of its constituents—in the democratic polities of the states rather than the extended republic of the national government. Majority factions seeking to oppress political minorities can more easily gain control of government in the smaller, less diverse states. In contrast, at the national level, less powerful interests can pool their resources and thus better organize and take part in policy making. The size of the nation and "diversity of factions" at the national level frustrate dominance by powerful majorities acting through their elected representatives (Hamilton, Madison, and Jay 1961).

Yet not all agree about whether the changes in judicial federalism are a bane or boon for individual rights. Are state courts willing and able to protect rights? Scholarly research provides some empirical insight into this normative dispute. State courts can protect rights through the application of either federal or state laws. In applying and interpreting federal law, legal scholars and practitioners debate the "parity" of the federal and state judicial systems. Neuborne (1977) examined the institutional settings of federal and state courts, concluding that the federal courts' superior judges and staff, greater resources, and insulation from popular pressures make them critical guardians of individual rights. In contrast, state judges, many of whom are subject to some form of electoral sanction, are tied too closely to the political milieu. Yackle (1994) charges that recent efforts to curtail access to federal courts have threatened the very ability of the judiciary to check the power of government in American society. He contends that state courts lack the institutional capacity to protect rights vigorously, and that—regardless of the preferences of judges—federal courts are more likely than their state counterparts to protect federal rights.

Others, however, view state and federal courts as essentially interchangeable. Justice O'Connor (1985, 248) argued that "there is no reason to assume that state court judges cannot and will not provide a 'hospitable forum' in litigating federal constitutional questions." According to Chief Justice Rehnquist: "State judges as well as federal judges swear allegiance to the Constitution of the United States, and there is no reason to think that because of their frequent differences of opinion as to how that document should be interpreted that all are not doing their mortal best to discharge their oath of office."[13]

There is little systematic evidence that directly addresses the parity debate.[14] But clearly many rights advocates believe that federal courts are the better guardians of federal constitutional rights. This view likely emanates from celebrated situations in which the federal courts protected unpopular movements and individuals. Perhaps most renowned is the legacy of federal judges in the South who, after *Brown v. Board of Education* (1954), faced a hostile local citizenry that resisted desegregation orders (see Peltason 1961). Strengthening rights advocates' preference for federal courts is the perception of state judiciaries as hostile to civil rights and civil liberties. An NAACP Legal Defense Fund attorney told Wasby (1984, 111) that "the general view, although perhaps changing now, has been that 'state courts are not hospitable to civil rights claims.'" Interestingly, the preference for federal courts is not limited to liberal interests, but appears to transcend ideological divides. In Chapter 4, I will show that conservative organizations active in takings cases preferred to litigate in federal courts. They viewed state courts as institutionally incapable of protecting property rights.

But even if state courts cannot or will not vigorously enforce federal rights, judges may recognize and apply rights through their interpretations of state constitutions. The new judicial federalism is motivated largely by the anticipation of state courts vindicating rights under state constitutions, thereby making federal constitutional analysis unnecessary (Abrahamson 1985; Linde 1980; Douglass 1978; Howard 1976; Wilkes 1974).

However, skeptics suggest that only very few activist state courts are willing to consistently interpret their constitutions to provide broader protections than required under federal standards. Studies of state supreme courts indicate that they only infrequently rely on state constitutions to resolve rights claims. For instance, examining self-incrimination cases, Esler (1994) reported that state supreme courts based nearly 80 percent of their decisions on federal law. He attributes the lack of reliance on state constitutions to the conservatism of most state political systems and to the potential political consequences, including electoral defeat of state judges and constitutional amendments, of the widespread development of state constitutional law. Even when state courts do interpret their constitutions, rarely do courts provide broader protection than that recognized under federal law. Latzer (1991a, 1991b) finds that only about a third of the criminal procedure decisions based on state law expanded rights beyond the level required by federal law. Only four state high courts consistently rejected the Supreme Court's doctrine in favor of more expansive protections, and in two of these states subsequent constitutional amendments compelled uniformity with federal law.

While much of the debate over the new judicial federalism involves concern over the nature and scope of rights, some favor the development of state law for reasons other than an orientation toward results. They call for a legally principled approach to the development of state law as a way to promote more robust federalism in the United States. These advocates want to revive the use of state constitutions as an active force in American constitutional law (Collins 1985, 1981; Linde 1985; Porter 1982).

To summarize, the growing importance of state courts as policy makers is an important trend in the American judiciary. However, it is not entirely clear what these trends have meant or, in the future, may mean for the judicial protection of rights. Decentralized policy making increasingly allows for diversity rather than uniformity in rights protection. Some activist state courts may be willing to protect federal rights vigorously, or even to expand protection through their state constitutions. Many state courts, however, appear more reluctant to do so. A more complete understanding of the impact of the trends in judicial federalism on rights requires continued analysis of policy making in federal and state courts.

The decentralization of policy responsibility likely has many implications for judicial policy making and for the protection of constitutional rights and liberties. This study examines one ramification—its effect on the litigation activities of organized interest groups. As state courts increasingly have the last word in many rights cases, interest group litigation strategies may respond accordingly. The growing importance of state judiciaries may make them more attractive venues for group participation. Indeed, Epstein (1994) provided some initial support for this hypothesis, documenting a general increase in amicus curiae ("friend of the court") filings in state supreme courts over the past four decades.

While groups may have incentive to litigate in state courts, it is important to recognize that no single state court decision has the nationwide policy impact of a similar decision by the United States Supreme Court. To achieve a comparable influence on public policy, then, groups have greater incentive to litigate across each of the fifty states, rather than in just one U.S. Supreme Court. The need to litigate numerous cases at the state level presents interest groups with several organizational obstacles. Groups must be able to track locally based litigation in each state. The earlier a group is aware of an emerging case, the more aspects of the case the group can affect. Organizations that are aware of important cases at the trial level can participate in the litigation at an early stage. Additionally, groups that aspire to be effective in state courts require access to attorneys familiar with state laws as well as the rules and procedures of state courts. Whereas federal courts have a single set of laws, rules, and procedures, there is no such uniformity across states, so groups must acquire the needed legal expertise in several court systems. In short, a decentralized litigation environment requires greater resources (such as time, money, and legal expertise) to litigate in more cases. While no group may choose to litigate in each and every state, the fact remains that the resources needed to mobilize the law and participate in the judicial process in a decentralized litigation environment are much greater than those necessary to engage in a more centralized strategy of participation in federal court cases.

Thus, a decentralized litigation environment presents interest groups with significant dilemmas. By requiring greater resource expenditures, a decentralized litigation environment makes it more difficult to mobilize the law and potentially shape judicial policies. Since interest groups have played a crucial role in financing and arguing rights cases in the U.S. Supreme Court, it is important to assess the impact of the trends in judicial federalism on the willingness and ability of groups to continue to participate in litigation at the state level.

If groups are unprepared to respond to changing trends in judicial federalism by litigating in a greater number of cases at the state level, then they may be unable to play an active and central role in the process of legal mobilization and legal change. This is particularly significant in rights litigation, where interest groups have been at the center of many legal developments because, in contrast to most individual litigants, groups often have the resources and incentives to bring cases and to pursue appeals. Since rights cases generally pit individual litigants against governmental institutions with much greater resources, it is here where interest groups can be particularly influential in the judicial process by helping to bridge the gap between the one-shooters and repeat players. But the strategic and organizational dilemmas associated with a decentralized litigation environment may provide powerful disincentives for interest groups to remain active in the litigation fray. Additionally, some organizations may be better able than others to respond to the decentralization of policy authority, which suggests that the configuration of group litigators may change as responsibility increasingly is relegated to state courts.

This book examines the conditions under which major litigating organizations participate regularly in state courts. It assesses the impact of the legal context, as well as the organizational and strategic hurdles associated with a decentralized litigation environment, on groups' willingness and ability to enter state judiciaries. Group participation is examined in eminent domain and obscenity law in the appellate courts of five states—Colorado, Indiana, Minnesota, New Jersey, and South Carolina. Before investigating groups' litigation behavior, however, previous scholarly studies of interest group litigation are briefly reviewed, and based on the lessons of those studies, the concepts and analytic framework that guide the analysis are developed. This is the purpose of the next chapter.

NOTES

1. Although formally bound to U.S. Supreme Court precedent when deciding questions of federal constitutional and statutory law, lower federal and state courts are important implementers of Supreme Court decisions (Johnson and Canon 1984). Studies suggest that under certain circumstances, the Supreme Court wields little influence over

lower courts (Kilwein and Brisbin 1997; Songer 1988; Baum 1977, 1976; Peltason 1961, 1955; Murphy 1959).

2. Federal courts also apply state law through their diversity jurisdiction (which allows federal courts to decide cases in which the parties come from different states or one party is a noncitizen of the United States, and the suit is for at least $50,000) and the doctrine of pendant jurisdiction (discretionary jurisdiction whereby federal courts may entertain state law claims, even without diversity jurisdiction, if they arise along with federal claims). Federal courts are bound to follow state court precedent when interpreting state constitutions and statutes.

3. State courts may have incentive to do this when they anticipate more restrictive Supreme Court precedent in the near future (Esler 1995).

4. These cases arose under 42 U.S.C. Section 1983. *Monroe v. Pape* was designed in large part to prevent blacks and civil rights workers from having to face hostile southern judges and juries (Schuck 1983, 47–51).

5. The Supreme Court relied on substantive due process, a concept developed first in state courts, to protect economic rights in the early years of the twentieth century (Galie 1988, 77).

6. The Supreme Court undoubtedly was more conservative on many rights issues under Chief Justice Burger than under Warren, but the difference often is overstated. Baum (1988) showed that changes in case content over time altered the average difficulty of reaching a pro–civil liberties decision. When adjusted to account for case content, the Warren Court during the 1950s was more conservative and the Burger Court more liberal than patterns of case outcomes suggest.

7. This view is consistent with the notion of the states as "laboratories of democracy." Justice Louis Brandeis noted that "it is one of the happy incidents of the federal system that a single courageous State may, if its citizens choose, serve as a laboratory; and try novel social and economic experiments without the risk to the rest of the country" (*New State Ice Co. v. Liebmann* 1932, 311).

8. Proposed Long Range Plan for the Federal Courts, pp. 18–19 (copy on file with author).

9. See *Webster v. Reproductive Health Services* (1989); *U.S. v. Leon* (1984); *Miller v. California* (1973).

10. For bibliographies of this literature, see Watts (1991) and Maltz, Williams, and Araten (1989).

11. Prior to *Michigan v. Long* (1983), the state of the law was somewhat less clear. Under *Fox Film Corp. v. Muller* (1935), when a state court decides both a state and federal constitutional question in favor of an individual, application of the "adequate state ground" doctrine should insulate the judgment from Supreme Court review. However, where it is unclear whether a state court has relied on federal or state grounds, the Supreme Court often has reviewed the federal constitutional issues involved in the case (see, for example, *California v. Krivda* 1972). Thus, even before *Michigan v. Long*, the only way for a state court to ensure that the Supreme Court does not review the decision is to base it solely on state grounds. For further discussion, see Neuborne (1985).

12. Distinguishing between substantive and procedural decisions is somewhat artificial, since procedural decisions are tied to substantive values (Tribe 1980). However, the distinction is useful for analytic purposes. The next chapter will argue that interest groups' responses to the Supreme Court's substantive and procedural decisions may affect the types of legal arguments groups offer in state litigation.

13. *Sumner v. Mata* (1981, 543). Quoted in O'Connor (1985, 248).

14. Solimine and Walker (1983) concluded that there was no state court hostility to federal claims, but have been criticized on methodological grounds (Chemerinsky 1988).

2

Understanding State Court Litigation in the Federal Context

The politicization of law and courts in America makes the judiciary a natural venue for interest group participation. Alexis de Tocqueville (1954, 290) noted more than 150 years ago that "scarcely any political question arises in the United States that is not resolved, sooner or later, into a judicial question." Over the past half century, conflicts over racial and gender discrimination, abortion, free speech and expression, religion, the right to die, and numerous other social issues—as well as economic and other regulations—have been addressed by American courts. Organized interest groups have attempted to shape the law in these and other areas. Given the importance of the courts to interest groups, a substantial scholarly literature has developed in recent decades. Studies examine the strategies and tactics of interest groups in the United States Supreme Court and other federal courts.

However, much less is known about organizational participation at the state level. While recent scholarship has examined the role and influence of interest groups in state legislative and executive institutions (Rosenthal 1993; Thomas and Hrebenar 1990), there has been little attention to interest groups' use of state courts. This chapter develops a framework to orient analysis of interest group litigation in state courts. State litigation, like all political action, does not occur in a void. The framework accounts for the legal context in which interest groups make litigation decisions. Of particular interest are the ways in which U.S. Supreme Court decisions provide incentives or disincentives for organizational action in state judiciaries. This chapter briefly examines previous studies of interest groups and courts and, based on the insights of those studies, identifies the concepts and factors used to assess group litigation in state courts. Finally, alternative explanations for group litigation are considered and the study's design is discussed in greater detail. This chapter provides the scholarly foundations for the analysis that follows.

INTEREST GROUPS' USE OF THE COURTS

Interest groups participated in takings and obscenity cases in both state and federal courts during the years examined in this study. But before exploring interest groups' use of state courts, it is important to assess the lessons of previous studies of group litigation. A brief review of the existing scholarly literature provides insight as to why groups enter the courts and what strategies and tactics they rely on in litigation. Scholars have focused their attention almost exclusively on group participation in the federal courts, particularly the United States Supreme Court. The role of groups in state courts remains largely unexplored, although recently there have been initial studies of group litigation at the state level (for example, Songer and Kuersten 1995; Epstein 1994; Jennings 1994). Nevertheless, the literature provides insights that can guide an analysis of the conditions under which interest groups are willing and able to litigate in state courts.

The earliest studies of interest groups recognized that they use the courts to pursue their goals. Bentley (1908) and Truman (1951) introduced a pluralist perspective on American politics, which placed groups at the heart of the policy-making process. According to the pluralist perspective, politics is the resolution of group conflict. Groups form around common interests, and in a complex political system with multiple points of access, groups help to coordinate and provide stability to policy making. As a consequence of competition among various groups, policies emerge that are responsive at least roughly to public needs, and no single interest dominates.

But it was Clement Vose (1959), in *Caucasians Only*, who conducted the first major study of group tactics in the judiciary. He examined attempts by the National Association for the Advancement of Colored People (NAACP) to eliminate enforcement of racially restrictive housing covenants. While Hakman (1966) criticized the early studies of group litigation as "scholarly folklore"—arguing that group pressure was minimal and generally unimportant to the development of legal policy in the Supreme Court between 1928 and 1966—other studies by Vose (1972, 1966, 1958, 1957, 1955) continued to demonstrate that groups played an important role in the judicial process. Kluger (1976) investigated the NAACP and Cowan (1976) the American Civil Liberties Union (ACLU), showing that these groups played an important role in Supreme Court litigation. Examinations of First Amendment establishment clause cases (Sorauf 1976) and gender discrimination litigation (O'Connor 1980) revealed groups competing on both sides of these issues. And a more systematic study showed that amicus participation by interest groups was increasing even in the period that Hakman studied (O'Connor and Epstein 1982). In light of these findings, scholarly interest in group litigation has grown considerably in recent years.

Strategies and Tactics of Organizational Litigants

Why do interest groups turn to the courts? Initially, many believed that it was primarily groups powerless in the "political" branches of government that turned to the judiciary (Cortner 1968). This "disadvantage thesis" asserts that courts are an alternate forum for the advancement of politically disadvantaged groups. Several studies support the view that the politically powerless turn to the courts (Wenner 1984; O'Connor 1980; Vose 1959). For instance, Sorauf (1976) argued that groups supporting the separation of church and state turned to the courts in the 1940s after several state legislatures passed "accommodationist" legislation. However, systematic empirical evidence does not support the disadvantage thesis. Studies show that advantaged groups—those favoring the status quo—litigate more often in the judiciary than disadvantaged interests (Walker 1991; Schlozman and Tierney 1986).

Alternate explanations offer a broader, more complex picture of group litigation. Groups litigate to consolidate policy victories won in other branches of government (Olson 1990; L. Epstein 1985), because they view the judiciary as having the final word on matters of public policy (Rubin 1987), and to provide balance against opposition interests already active in the courts (L. Epstein 1985). For many groups litigation is one component of broader, multi-institution lobbying efforts. Thus, a wide variety of interests turns to courts for many different reasons.

Whatever their motivation, groups turn to courts, as to other political institutions, primarily to advance their policy goals. Epstein and Kobylka (1992, 26) noted that "the most widely accepted reason [that interest groups turn to courts] is that they seek to etch their policy objectives into law—a goal most readily accomplished when the Court rules in their favor."

Some group litigants attempt to bring about broad ranging legal and constitutional change. Studies of the NAACP Legal Defense Fund (Kluger 1976; Vose 1959) and civil liberties organizations (for example, Neier 1979) demonstrate use of this strategy. The NAACP, for instance, used the legal system to chip away at the "separate but equal" doctrine in *Plessy v. Ferguson* (1896), and in the process helped to integrate school systems and end restrictive covenants. Groups may also pursue immediate victories for litigants involved in a specific problem. Olson (1984, 1981) examined efforts to secure access for handicapped citizens in public transportation through case-by-case, client-oriented litigation. This strategy contrasts with the apparently centralized, coherent strategy of the NAACP in civil rights litigation.

In addition to pursuing policy goals, another important reason that groups go to court is to further organizational maintenance and development. For group leaders, the need to appease existing members and attract new ones may lead groups to litigate. Under some circumstances, then, the outcome of a case may not be as important to leaders as the publicity and image of the group the case produces (Casper 1976; Cowan 1972). Nevertheless, the bottom line is that interest groups want to achieve legal victories. In pursuit of that goal, groups choose among different litigation strategies. They can participate directly in litigation as parties or sponsors, file amicus curiae ("friend of the court") briefs, or provide general support to other litigants. Each of these strategies has particular costs and benefits for groups (Wasby 1983, 256).

First, groups may become involved directly in litigation. Since rules of standing require that litigants have a direct stake in a case, ordinarily interest groups cannot bring suits in their own names. More often, they sponsor cases by finding aggravated parties, providing counsel, and directing the resulting litigation. Sponsorship may entail initiating cases in trial courts or taking cases at the appellate level. Often, sponsorship is associated with pursuit of the "test case" strategy (Wasby 1988; Sorauf 1976; Vose 1959), in which groups sponsor cases designed to test specific legal arguments and attempt through a series of decisions to incrementally eliminate adverse precedent and develop new legal rules for future cases. This strategy appears appropriate given the Court's inclination to avoid radical policy change. The NAACP, for instance, did not immediately ask judges to overturn the "separate but equal" doctrine of *Plessy*. Rather, it brought a series of cases, each designed to chip away incrementally at *Plessy*. The test case strategy often is seen as the ideal litigation mechanism, largely reflecting the success of the NAACP Legal Defense Fund in sequencing cases in civil rights litigation (Kluger 1976; Vose 1959).

Yet some doubt whether organized litigants truly can implement the ideal test case strategy. Wasby (1984) interviewed NAACP Legal Defense Fund attorneys and found that they did not select cases deductively on the basis of previously developed criteria but instead developed litigation more haphazardly from cases that came to the organization. Limited resources, the presence of other litigating organizations in race relations law, and additional pressures required that the NAACP deviate from its blueprint. Since "organizational litigators definitely do not dominate the domain in which they seek to operate" (Wasby 1984, 138), groups must be responsive and flexible to circumstances beyond their control (see also Tushnet 1987).

While interest groups cannot completely control their "planned" litigation, the fact remains that, compared to other means of organizational involvement, sponsorship gives groups a degree of control over the case. Groups generally make all major decisions, including what legal arguments to advance and whether to appeal the case to a higher court. Further, they can structure the factual context, determine the appropriate jurisdiction, and make other decisions that they believe best allow them to realize their goals. Along with these benefits, however, direct sponsorship entails costs. Sponsorship requires significant resources (money, staff, time, attorneys, fund-raising efforts) to pursue a case through trial and appellate courts. Since these resources are sunk into one case, a single loss can drain scarce resources.

A second means by which groups participate in courts is by filing amicus curiae briefs. Amicus curiae briefs are intended to supplement material provided by direct parties to the case.[1] They allow groups to make arguments in support of one of the parties in a case and provide a means for groups to make their views known to the court without the costs associated with being an immediate party to a suit. The briefs can serve an important role for courts, allowing judges to become aware of broader political and legal concerns. Groups typically must seek the permission of the court and/or the parties to submit a brief.[2] Parties also may submit amici at the request of others. For example, the Supreme Court regularly seeks the views of the U.S. government through the solicitor general.

Amicus briefs are less expensive than sponsorship and avoid the logistical difficulties associated with bringing suits. Through the briefs, groups may endorse the arguments of litigants or supplement them with other arguments not put forth by an immediate party. Groups that present new or novel legal arguments may induce a court to address issues beyond those presented by the immediate parties. However, participation through amicus briefs substantially reduces the control that pressure groups have over the development of judicial policy. Amicus briefs are filed generally at the appellate level, so groups have no influence on the factual settings of a case, its jurisdiction, or the arguments made by litigants.

A third way groups participate in the judicial process is through generalized support to other groups or individual litigants. Research shows that groups intervene in cases involving litigants with similar policy concerns (Sorauf 1976), provide expert information to support litigants as well as their own organizational goals (Vose 1972, 1959), help fund the litigation of others (Vose 1981), give legal advice (Kluger 1976), write law review articles to support legal arguments (Greenberg 1977), and arrange publicity supportive of group concerns (Sorauf 1976; Scheingold 1974; Vose 1959). While these are low-cost means of participation, interest groups do not often pursue these strategies because they provide very little control over a case. Generalized support most often supplements the more direct and formal means of participation.

In sum, interest groups rely on various avenues of influence in attempts to shape judicial policy. If groups are to affect judicial policies, they must be able to enter the courts and succeed in litigation. But it is important to recognize that money and other resources condition their ability to achieve their goals. Litigation is expensive. Even an amicus curiae brief can cost tens of thousands of dollars to prepare (Scheppele and Walker 1991; Caldeira and Wright 1990). Past studies have identified several resources critical to interest groups' ability to use the courts successfully.[3] The amount of money allocated to litigation can affect the type of strategy a group can use, the number and kinds of issues it can litigate, and its success (Cortner 1968; Vose 1959). During its early years, the NAACP focused on fund-raising, since it could not afford long and complex litigation campaigns.

Further, staff are a critical organizational resource. Organizational success in the courts is contingent upon having attorneys with the necessary expertise and commitment to the group's goals (Sorauf 1976; Manwaring 1962; Vose

1958). Time is also important. There is only so much time that groups can devote to litigation efforts, and this is a particular concern for organizations with a broad range of interests (Kobylka 1991). The ACLU, for instance, paid less attention to some issues once abortion emerged as a critical civil liberties issue in the wake of *Roe v. Wade* (1973) and the subsequent mobilization by the pro-life movement (Epstein, Kobylka, and Stewart 1995).

Related to time is a group's longevity. Only groups with a long time horizon can use the courts continuously and pursue test case strategies, as the NAACP did in racial desegregation litigation (Greenberg 1977; Kluger 1976). Longevity is crucial to attaining the benefits associated with the repeat player status in the courts (see Galanter 1974). Other resources important to the success of interest groups in courts include having extralegal publicity (Sorauf 1976; Vose 1959), cooperating with like-minded groups (Sorauf 1976), and having the support of the federal government (Cortner 1968; Krislov 1963; Vose 1959).

Although analytically distinct, organizational resources interact with one another (Epstein, Kobylka, and Stewart 1995). For instance, money can buy time and staff. Cooperation with like-minded groups can save time and money. The various organizational resources condition the ability of groups to engage and succeed in all political ventures, including litigation.

Thus far, the strategies and tactics available to organizational litigants have been discussed. Interest groups attempt to shape judicial policies, and their ability to do so is contingent at least in part on their resources. But does interest group litigation matter? What effect does group litigation have on judicial policies? Clearly, interest groups affect judicial agendas—who gets into courts, and who gets there repeatedly. As repeat players, many groups can bring cases to the courts on a regular basis (Galanter 1974). They can facilitate litigation that otherwise might not occur, since individuals lack the resources or incentives to carry forward such cases on their own. Thus, groups can make a difference by just getting cases to court and by pursuing appeals.

Groups have brought numerous issues to the Supreme Court's attention, including capital punishment (Epstein and Kobylka 1992; Meltsner 1973), abortion (Rubin 1987), gender-based discrimination (O'Connor 1980; Cowan 1976), racial discrimination (Kluger 1976; Vose 1959), and free speech (Cortner 1975). Caldeira and Wright (1988) have shown that amicus briefs filed by interest groups help the Court in setting its agenda, possibly by cueing the justices to important issues. Interest groups can also manipulate the Supreme Court's review process by generating circuit court conflicts and can attempt to attract the Court's attention by bringing numerous cases in lower federal and state courts (Epstein and Kobylka 1992, 30).

While groups play an important role in setting judicial agendas, the evidence is less conclusive as to what effect they have on case outcomes and judicial policies. Early case studies (Manwaring 1962; Vose 1959) appeared to indicate that group litigation efforts did matter. At least in the U.S. Supreme Court, groups win a great proportion of their cases (Epstein 1991, 360–361). For example, Lawrence (1989, 270) found that the Legal Services Program won 62 percent of its Supreme Court cases. Yet this evidence does not account for other factors, such as judicial attitudes, that may affect case outcomes. When proper controls are included, Epstein and Rowland (1991) showed that group litigants may fare no better than nongroup litigants in U.S. District Courts.[4] Further, Songer and Sheehan (1993) found that litigants supported by an amicus brief did not have a substantially greater chance of winning in the U.S. Supreme Court than comparable litigants in similar cases who received no amicus support.[5]

In addition to their direct impact on judicial policy making, interest groups play an important, albeit indirect, role by serving as catalysts of legal change. Courts cannot change or develop law unless they address legal doctrine. Groups facilitate legal change by initiating cases that might not otherwise be brought, raising issues, and seeking to place them on courts' agendas. When groups sponsor litigation, they select the issues, cases, and legal arguments that provide courts with the stimuli that can prompt legal change (Epstein and Kobylka 1992, 28–30).

To summarize, scholarly research has provided important insights into interest group litigation. First, groups turn to the courts, as they do to other political institutions, primarily to pursue their policy goals. To that end, they choose among a variety of litigation tactics and strategies. Second, in pursuit of their goals, groups rely on and are constrained by various resources. Finally, by seeking their goals through the courts, interest groups can have an important impact on the judicial policy process. Although not always successful, they help to determine the types of issues that courts address and how they decide cases.

GROUP LITIGATION IN STATE JUDICIARIES

While scholarly studies provide insight into various aspects of interest group litigation, most examine organizational participation in the Supreme Court and other federal courts. Much less attention has been given to groups' use of state courts. A complete understanding of group litigation in state judiciaries must account for the federal judicial context. In a dual court system, litigants have some choice as to whether to litigate in state or federal courts. Concern with the federal judicial context assumes that there are features of this context that govern the willingness and ability of groups to litigate in state courts.

The lessons and insights of previous studies can be relied upon to explore interest group litigation in state courts.[6] Scholars suggest that interest groups become involved in the governmental process primarily to pursue policy goals and influence the policy-making process (Epstein and Kobylka 1992). While groups have other objectives, including organizational maintenance (Kobylka 1991; Moe 1980; Wilson 1973), setting institutional agendas (Cobb and Elder

1983), and influencing public opinion (Key 1961), the ultimate goal of influencing policy subsumes other goals (L. Epstein 1992; Petracca 1992).

To best influence the process and policies of government, groups must locate policy conflicts where they can maximize their goals, and then attempt to affect those institutions involved in the conflict. Schlozman and Tierney (1986, 160) noted that "an organization is likely to try to locate a controversy in the institutional setting most likely to produce favorable results." Groups do this by going "where the action is," moving toward government institutions that they perceive are relevant for the policies of concern or will produce favorable policies. Of course, things can be more complicated than this. Sometimes groups may litigate in arenas not hospitable to their cause. This is most likely to occur because their opponents move a policy conflict to a more favorable arena. By doing so, the opponents change the location of the policy conflict, altering "where the action is." This may expand the scope of conflict, and groups may follow their opponents' lead (Schattschneider 1960).

This perspective informs our understanding of interest group litigation in a federal judicial system. All else being equal, interest groups typically prefer to locate policy conflicts in national rather than state courts. Given limited resources, groups must pursue their goals where they most effectively can influence policy. Only federal court (especially U.S. Supreme Court) decisions have a potentially broad nationwide policy impact. Supreme Court interpretations of federal law apply to the entire nation. In contrast, state court judgments are binding only in that state. Thus, it is generally more efficient for groups to litigate in federal courts, since the ratio of external benefits (benefits for those other than the immediate parties) to total benefits—external benefits and internal benefits (benefits for the immediate parties)—is greater in federal than in state courts (Lee and Weisbrod 1978, 321).

Groups asserting rights claims have another reason to prefer the federal courts. They often are viewed as the essential guardians of constitutional rights. Because of the federal courts' perceived superior judges and staff, greater resources, and insulation from popular pressures, many believe that they are better institutionally situated to protect individual rights (Yackle 1994; Neuborne 1977). In contrast, state courts lack the institutional capability to protect rights vigorously. Many state judges are electorally accountable and tied too closely to the political milieu.

Evidence from previous studies supports the general preference for federal court litigation. For example, Wasby (1984, 137–138) reported that "civil rights lawyers have a clear preference for the federal courts when the choice of forum is theirs to make." And I will show that both ideologically liberal and conservative groups asserting rights claims in obscenity and takings cases revealed a general preference for federal litigation. Marsha Wenk (1995), a staff attorney for the American Civil Liberties Union of New Jersey, noted that the group prefers federal courts "because they are quicker, easier, and more efficient. [Y]ou can avoid the local political disadvantages [found in state courts]." Paul Seby (1995), of the

Mountain States Legal Foundation, argues that federal courts better protect property rights because they are "more distant from the actor [government] and therefore less subject to political pressure." According to another group official, "instinctively we go to federal courts. It's a federal right we are trying to vindicate, so that's where we feel we should be. [Federal courts] are where you get the biggest impact."[7]

Legal Incentives

This preference for the federal courts, however, does not preclude the use of state venues. Under what conditions are groups likely to turn to state courts? They are most likely to do so when legal precedent makes state judiciaries important policy makers on an issue relevant to the group. Supreme Court decisions may give interest groups incentive to litigate in state courts. Legal precedent defines opportunities for litigation and structures the conflicts litigants bring to courts. Since litigants must confront and respond to existing precedent, it affects the efficacy of different litigation and argumentative strategies. In short, the law matters because it establishes the rules of the game.

The last chapter showed that the growing importance of state courts as policy makers is tied to changes in the legal context since the early 1970s. By discouraging or prohibiting federal court litigation, the Burger and Rehnquist Courts have given litigants incentives to turn to the states. For analytic purposes, two specific *legal incentives* can be identified. The first reason groups may turn to state courts is to seek broader protection for rights under state constitutions than the Supreme Court recognizes under parallel federal standards. I call this the *new judicial federalism incentive*, since it is associated most often with proponents of state constitutional activism. When the Supreme Court, interpreting the federal Constitution, issues doctrine restrictive of individual rights, groups may have incentive to turn to the state courts. Sorauf (1976, 112) noted that the "go-to-the-federal-court strategy holds only so long as the Supreme Court is a hospitable forum for cases." When it is not, state courts are a potentially viable alternative. The new judicial federalism incentive has parallels to the disadvantage thesis (Cortner 1968), in that interests disadvantaged under federal law turn to state courts and state law to vindicate their rights.

The second incentive to turn to state courts is the *federal restriction incentive*. In addition to mobilizing state constitutions, groups may turn to state courts as a consequence of the Supreme Court's decisions that restricted access to federal courts and decentralized policy responsibility increasingly to the state level. As the Court decentralized policy making in many areas of law, state courts more often have had the final word on important legal issues. Groups seeking to affect judicial policy have to go where the action is—to state courts.

Although analytically distinct, can be difficult to determine empirically whether an organization litigating in state courts is motivated by the new judicial federalism or federal restriction incentive. But examination of the arguments offered in litigation does shed some light on what motivates groups. In state litigation, interest groups and other litigants may assert rights claims based on federal law, state law, or both. One case is clear: if an interest group does *not* mobilize state constitutional law when asserting a rights claim, then the group was not motivated by the new judicial federalism incentive. After all, a state court potentially may be more protective of rights than the federal judiciary, but only if the court issues decisions based on the state constitution. Thus, when only federal rights claims are advanced, it appears that the federal restriction incentive impelled the group into state litigation. However, in many cases, litigants assert claims based on both federal *and* state constitutional grounds, in hopes that the state court accepts at least one of the claims. Under these circumstances, we cannot distinguish between groups motivated by the new judicial federalism or federal restriction incentive based solely on analysis of the arguments offered in litigation. Likewise, when organizations assert rights claims based solely on state constitutional grounds, we cannot determine conclusively—based on analysis of the legal arguments—why they entered state litigation.

The analysis of legal incentives provides insight into the ways in which the Supreme Court may affect the politicization of state judiciaries. By issuing decisions that alter legal precedent, the Court may give interest groups incentive to litigate in state courts. The presence of a legal incentive appears to be an important, perhaps a necessary, condition for major litigating groups to participate regularly in state courts. Investigation of the legal context also provides insight as to *why* plaintiffs' groups turn to state courts and the role that these groups may play in the mobilization of state constitutional law. When they enter state courts in response to the Supreme Court's restrictive interpretations of federal law (new judicial federalism incentive), groups are more likely to seek broader protection on state law grounds than when groups are in state courts because federal court jurisdiction is unavailable. Thus, for proponents of state constitutional activism, the growth in rights litigation in state courts is not necessarily a boon. To understand the role of interest groups in the new judicial federalism, we must examine why groups enter state courts and what legal arguments they advance in litigation.

Organizational Threshold

The analysis thus far has suggested that legal context shapes interest groups' willingness to enter state judiciaries, and two specific incentives have been identified that may impel groups into state litigation. However, while the legal context is important, certainly it does not completely drive litigation decisions. Other factors influence groups. In particular, factors internal to a group orient it to its environment and influence its political activities, including litigation (Ivers 1995; Kobylka 1991; Moe 1981, 1980; Wilson 1973). There is an *organizational threshold* needed for groups to litigate consistently in state courts.

There are two primary components of the organizational threshold. First, and most important, are *organizational resources*. Limited resources may prevent groups from litigating as often and on as many issues as they might like. It may seem odd that even major litigating groups such as the NAACP or ACLU face limited resources. But while "the organizational names carry an impressive ring . . . the truth of the matter is vastly less impressive" (Sorauf 1976, 42). Resources constrain or expand interest groups' range of choices and their opportunities to achieve goals through litigation (Epstein, Kobylka, and Stewart 1995).

While many resources are relevant for understanding interest groups' use of the courts, we can pinpoint those that are particularly essential for litigation at the state level. The resources needed to participate in state courts are not identical to those needed to litigate in the U.S. Supreme Court. Groups with state or local affiliates are better able to track locally based litigation and to develop legal expertise at the appropriate level (Wasby 1983; O'Connor 1980). Keeping abreast of emerging litigation is important for organized litigants. Particularly if they wish to act in any role other than amicus, they must have information about an emerging case as early as possible (Sorauf 1976, 73). The earlier a group enters a case, the more aspects of the case it can influence. State and local affiliates allow organizations to track and develop local litigation. Affiliates of the ACLU, for instance, receive thousands of complaints annually about civil liberties violations, and some of these complaints develop into ACLU lawsuits.

Through state and local affiliates, groups can cultivate legal expertise in state courts. Attorneys representing state chapters of interest groups generally are members of the state bar and, therefore, are familiar with the laws of the state as well as the rules and procedures of state courts. While federal courts typically apply federal law and have one procedural framework, there is no such uniformity across the fifty state court systems. Wasby (1984, 112) noted that, among other reasons, NAACP Legal Defense Fund attorneys preferred federal to state litigation because "the complexities of the wide variety of state procedural and substantive provisions, which force a group's national staff attorneys to devote scarce time to their mastery, can thus be avoided."

In addition to state and local affiliates, access to attorneys is particularly important for state litigation. Groups that have state affiliates but no attorneys may have little opportunity to pursue their goals in court. Given the sheer number of cases required to participate in a decentralized litigation environment, groups must rely on a number of attorneys in many states.

Interest groups have access to attorneys from several sources. They may have staff or in-house attorneys to represent the organization on a continuing basis. In many instances, organizations retain outside private counsel when they need to litigate. But litigation resources are made much greater through the use of cooperating attorneys.[8] Cooperating attorneys are private practice lawyers who handle cases for groups either as pro bono (for free) or for a fee much less than regular hourly rates. The interest groups often assist with expenses. Cooperating attorneys often serve a supplemental role to full-time staff attorneys, and can increase greatly groups' ability to handle a large number of cases. Through cooperating attorneys, organizations can enter the litigation fray with little or no resource expenditure.

Local cooperating attorneys are especially useful for state litigation. According to Wasby's (1984, 123) interviews with NAACP Legal Defense Fund attorneys, cooperating attorneys "'tend to know local people and problems better' [than national staff], being local leaders with 'knowledge that is indispensable.'" They also are familiar with the rules and procedures of state courts. Often groups rely on cooperating attorneys for state court cases, while the national staff are used for federal and Supreme Court litigation. This can lead to a sequential relationship, where the local attorneys begin cases in state courts and national staff handle appeals.

Of course, there are disadvantages to organizational reliance on local cooperating attorneys. They are not always of the highest quality; they "cover the 'whole gamut of skill and efficiency'" (Wasby 1984, 122). Further, the attorneys may lack expertise in the specific legal area required for a case. Since cooperating attorneys also have private practices, they often cannot take on a case when the group needs the time, and generally cannot handle long and complex litigation. Finally, the delegation of responsibility to cooperating attorneys often leads to organizational decentralization. Sorauf (1976, 44) suggested that the ACLU's decentralization of litigation decision making from the national office to state chapters during the 1960s "springs naturally" from the group's dependence on local cooperating attorneys.

Nevertheless, cooperating attorneys are a considerable asset to interest groups, particularly those that seek to litigate repeatedly. Though cooperating attorneys are by no means a panacea for groups faced with scarce resources, they are a significant advantage, especially in decentralized litigation, where groups have incentive to handle a large volume of cases in a variety of state courts.

While the presence of state and local affiliates and access to attorneys provide the opportunity to enter state cases and to litigate successfully, all groups face resource scarcity and therefore must conserve litigation resources. One way a group can do this is by "free riding" on other litigants. If other groups or expert attorneys are involved in litigation and present legal arguments substantially similar to those an interest group would offer, the group can avoid litigating when it otherwise might. For instance, Kobylka (1991) argues that after organizations representing commercial interests became active in U.S. Supreme Court obscenity litigation, the ACLU, which previously had been the most active group litigator, was able to downplay obscenity litigation in the Court and focus instead on other issues. Such free riding may occur because the number and diversity of legal *arguments*, rather than actors, is central to the lobbying of courts (Epstein and Kobylka 1992; Kobylka 1991).[9]

Litigation resources are an important component of the organizational threshold. Lacking sufficient resources, groups cannot enter the courts as often as they might like. Resources, however, are not the only element of the organizational threshold. A second component, *organizational goals*, is also examined. Understanding the nature, range, and scope of groups' goals aids our ability to explain their litigation behavior. Many groups have a wide array of policy interests and also participate in a variety of both political and nonpolitical activities besides litigation. Given limited resources, they must set priorities among their issues and activities. For instance, the ACLU exists primarily to litigate and has a broad agenda that includes myriad civil rights and civil liberties issues. In contrast, the National Association of Home Builders is involved in substantially less litigation; legal action is not its primary purpose. The diversity of organizational settings requires consideration of the priority of the issue and the priority of litigation for interest groups.

Informing our understanding of organizational goals is how interest groups orient themselves to the political system. Kobylka (1991) identified two primary types of organizations, and showed that organizational type affects the kinds of interests on which groups litigate and their range of interests. *Purposive* organizations exist for distinctly political or ideological purposes; through their political activities, they seek to benefit society as a whole (Moe 1980; Wilson 1973; Clark and Wilson 1961). In contrast, *material* groups exist primarily to promote the exclusive economic or commercial interests of their members (Salisbury 1969; Olson 1965). Material groups are most likely to enter the political fray—including litigation—only when those interests are at stake.

This distinction is useful for explaining the willingness of groups to enter litigation on a consistent basis. For example, in Chapter 4, I show that the Pacific Legal Foundation (a purposive group) participated in takings cases arising in a variety of fact situations. This organization seeks to protect property rights against what it believes are excessive and unwarranted government infringements. Given its primarily political orientation, almost any claim that government violated property rights is of interest to the group and may impel it into litigation. In contrast, the American Farm Bureau Federation generally litigated only when a takings case directly implicated the interests of farmers. As a material organization, its primary goal is to protect and advance the interests of farmers. While this naturally leads the Farm Bureau to oppose what it views as excessive government regulations, takings cases that do not involve farmers or agricultural interests are clearly a lower priority.

To summarize, an explanation of interest groups' use of state courts must account for factors specific to the organization. Prior scholarly studies and my interviews with group officials suggest that group goals and priorities, as well as their resources, influence organizations' willingness and ability to litigate on a regular basis. These factors may account for the fact that some organizations enter the litigation fray more often than others.

It is important to acknowledge the close relationship between an organization's goals and its resources. Groups for which political lobbying, and litigation in particular, is an organizational priority are likely to allocate more of their available resources to litigation efforts. For instance, the ACLU commits 44 percent of its budget to legal activities (O'Connor and Epstein 1989, 12). In contrast, the National Wildlife Federation (NWF) is involved in numerous political and nonpolitical activities. The NWF operates public education and conservation projects such as the Ranger Rick program for children. Given its many nonpolitical ventures, the group devotes only 1 percent of its outlays to lobbying efforts.[10] Consequently, resources devoted to litigation in part reflect groups' goals and priorities.

An examination of the impact of the organizational threshold on the litigation behavior of interest groups allows for an assessment of the extent to which they are equipped to respond to changing trends in judicial federalism and to litigate in state courts. Decentralized judicial policy making divides responsibility among the fifty states. Factors specific to interest groups may inhibit them from mobilizing the law and potentially shaping judicial policy across the many states. Consequently, it may be increasingly difficult for many groups to participate in a policy making process that affects their interests. And since different resources are needed to litigate in state courts than in the U.S. Supreme Court, some groups may be better able than others to respond to the decentralization of judicial policy making. If this is the case, then the configuration of group litigators in a policy area may be distinctly different as policy responsibility is relegated to state courts. The consequences of decentralizing policy to state courts may be more than simply changing the venue of policy making. Such decentralizing potentially alters the range and types of interests that participate in the judicial process.

In sum, studies of interest group litigation and judicial federalism provide insights into the conditions under which groups are most likely to litigate in state judiciaries and, when asserting rights claims, the legal arguments they offer. Figure 2.1 illustrates the primary hypothesis. Groups are most likely to litigate when the legal context provides incentive to do so and when the groups have sufficient resources. Further, groups are most inclined to seek broader protection under state constitutional law than that required by the Supreme Court's interpretations of the federal Constitution when groups enter state courts in response to Supreme Court decisions restricting the scope of federal rights.

ALTERNATIVE PERSPECTIVES ON STATE COURT LITIGATION

This study examines how the legal context influences the willingness of major litigating groups to participate in state courts and how factors specific to groups condition their use of state courts. It does not directly control for all factors that possibly affect the willingness and ability of interest groups to litigate in state courts.

Figure 2.1
Conditions under which Interest Groups are Most Likely to Litigate in State Courts

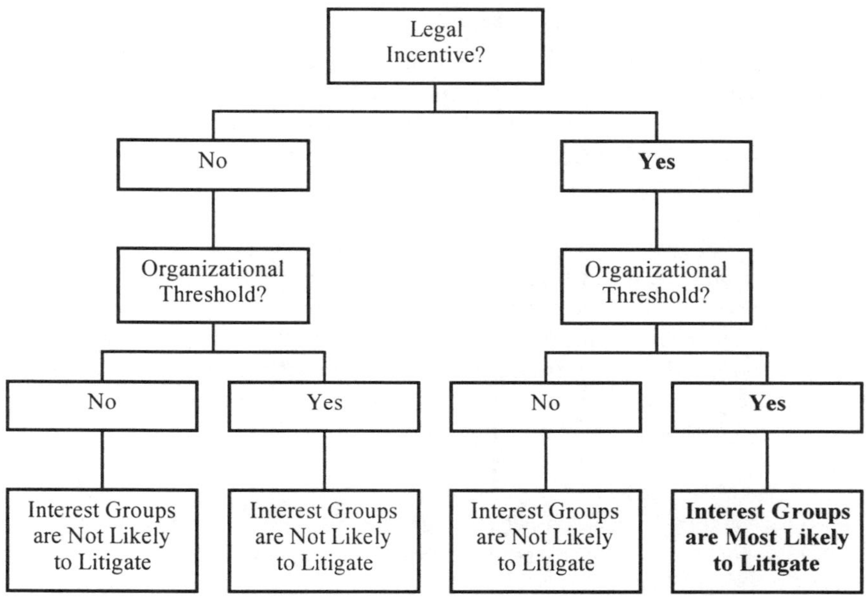

Some might object that I do not directly control for the policy preference of state court judges. Certainly, it matters who sits on the bench. Liberal interests may be less likely to litigate in state courts dominated by conservative judges. But I find that the judges' policy preferences are not the principal or most proximate influence on the groups. Instead, interviews reveal that groups' appraisals of the receptivity of state courts are issue specific and related to legal precedent.[11] For instance, a staff attorney for the ACLU of New Jersey asserted that "on cutting edge issues, New Jersey courts offer broader protections than federal courts. This makes state courts more attractive and we turn there" (Wenk 1995). However, Wenk emphasized that despite being generally more progressive than their federal counterparts, New Jersey courts have not provided greater protection in obscenity law—a fact that matters to Wenk.[12] ACLU of South Carolina Executive Director Steven Bates (1995) noted that the choice of forum (between federal and state courts) is "governed more by the nature of the issues to be resolved than by the [general] desire to be in one venue or another." My interviews suggest that group officials take care to distinguish among issues and that litigation decisions rest not on a general sense of the liberalism or conservatism of the courts, but rather on legal precedent in the issue area in question.[13]

In addition to the ideological composition of state supreme courts, other factors not formally controlled in this analysis include traditions of state court activism (Emmert 1988; Collins, Galie, and Kincaid 1986; Caldeira 1983; Porter and Tarr 1982; Wold 1974; Beiser 1973; Glick 1971), or political (Elazar 1984) or legal culture (Porter and Tarr 1982; Richardson and Vines 1970). These factors, too, may influence interstate variations in the willingness of groups to turn to state courts. Indeed, rates of amicus curiae participation in state supreme courts tend to be highest in traditionally activist courts (Epstein 1994).

There is, unfortunately, little agreement on the appropriate way to conceptualize and operationalize state high court activism. Caldeira (1983) focused on the influence of state high courts among their sister courts. Using data from 1975, he developed a state supreme court reputation scale, in which courts whose decisions are cited most often are considered the leaders among state high courts.[14] The most activist high courts, including those in California, New York, and New Jersey, typically produce liberal, innovative policies.[15] Yet some supreme courts, while not influencing fellow high courts, still play an active and important role in their own state policy-making process. Emmert (1988) examined judicial review by state supreme courts between 1981 and 1985 and developed a rank ordering that indicates which courts invalidated laws in the highest percentage of their cases.

There is little correlation between the two measures of state court activism. State high courts generally regarded as policy leaders and active in the new judicial federalism do not rank high on Emmert's measures. But regardless of the measure employed, there is no consistent, direct relationship between activism and interest group participation in either area of law. For example, based on Caldeira's (1983) reputation score, the New Jersey Supreme Court is the most active of the five in this study. Yet it does not have the highest rates of group participation in takings or obscenity cases. Likewise, South Carolina ranks first in the nation on Emmert's (1988) score, but the state by no means has the most group participation in takings or obscenity cases. While this does not necessarily mean that state court activism is unimportant, it suggests that other factors mediate its influence on groups' litigation decisions.

Further, even when a relationship between activism and levels of group participation does emerge, other factors have a more proximate influence. For instance, based on Caldeira's measure, the South Carolina and Indiana high courts are the least active of the five in this study. Chapter 6 will show that rates of group participation in obscenity cases were lowest in these two states. While this evidence seemingly reveals a relationship between activism and group litigation, a closer examination shows that the organizations, particularly ACLU affiliates, that were not active in state obscenity cases were similarly inactive in the *federal* courts. This suggests, and the interview evidence corroborates, that other factors (namely, resources) are more important in accounting for the lack of participation. State court activism cannot explain why these groups seldom participated in federal court litigation.

Contrary to some expectations, then, judicial attitudes and state court activism are not the principal factors influencing groups' decisions to participate in state takings and obscenity cases. Others might object that this analysis does not directly account for differences in the formal methods of selection and retention of state court judges. There is a great variety, both nationwide and in the sample of states, of methods to select state court judges. They include gubernatorial appointment (New Jersey), legislative election (South Carolina), partisan election (Indiana), nonpartisan election (Minnesota), and the Missouri Plan (Colorado and Indiana).[16] These methods may potentially affect groups' views toward state court venues. For instance, perhaps groups are less willing to litigate in states whose judges are chosen through partisan elections, since the judges are tied closely to the political milieu and consequently may be less inclined to protect individual rights against majoritarian impulses.

However, scholarly research is, at best, inconclusive as to the effects of formal selection methods on judicial behavior and policy. While there is some evidence that selection methods influence voting behavior on state supreme courts (Brace and Hall 1995, 1990; Hall and Brace 1992) and perhaps courts' policies (Pinello 1995), there is little to show more than a marginal impact. Additionally, my interviews provided no indication that the selection method affected group litigation decisions.

Finally, this study's emphasis on legal and organizational influences is not necessarily inconsistent with an explanation based on political or legal culture. I do not wish to imply that these factors are unimportant to the process of state judicial policy making. Obscenity, for example, may generate more vigorous debate in a moralistic political culture, where issues of moral precepts find their way into the political fray, than in a traditionalistic culture. As a result, more intense group activity may be expected in states with moralistic cultures. But it is also plausible that, given the nature of political and social debate on obscenity, interest groups in moralistic states have greater resources (perhaps from more donors) and view obscenity as a higher priority than do groups in traditionalistic states. Thus, while political culture may be an important underlying cause of differences in levels of group activity across states, it may manifest itself in the organizational posture of interest groups.[17]

In sum, based on my interviews and analysis, I am confident that this study examines the principal and most proximate factors influencing the willingness and ability of major litigating organizations to participate in state judiciaries. No study can examine all factors affecting group litigation. But in order to understand state court litigation in the federal judicial context, I believe that this study addresses the most theoretically and empirically important factors.

THE DESIGN OF THIS STUDY

I have identified two conditions that may be particularly important in influencing the willingness and ability of interest groups to participate consistently in state judiciaries. First, groups are more likely to turn to state courts in response to Supreme Court decisions that provide a legal incentive to do so. Second, groups must have the necessary organizational threshold, particularly sufficient resources, to litigate in numerous state cases. The analytic framework allows us to explore the context in which interest groups make decisions to litigate in state courts.

This study evaluates the importance of legal incentives and organizational thresholds through a comparative analysis of interest group participation in the intermediate appellate and supreme courts of five states between 1960 and 1994 in two areas of law, eminent domain (takings) and obscenity. I identify the groups most active in U.S. Supreme Court litigation and then explore the extent to which some of these organizations also litigated at the state level. The scope is limited for several reasons. Since there is little knowledge about interest group participation in state litigation, interviews with group officials and detailed analysis of a relatively limited number of cases allowed for the clarification and development of hypotheses about group litigation in state courts. Further, as a practical matter, the evidence needed made more extensive research efforts prohibitive. While published court reporters generally identify amici, determining other forms of group participation is more demanding, since opinions often do not report the group affiliations of attorneys. To guarantee the validity of the data required on-site examinations of group and court files. While this limited the scope of the research, such a sacrifice is well justified, since amicus filings constitute only a fraction of groups' litigation activities (Scheppele and Walker 1991).

The analysis relies principally on qualitative methods. Design issues in qualitative analysis recently have received considerable attention from political scientists (see especially King, Keohane, and Verba 1994). To alleviate problems associated with a "small-n" study, particularly the danger of generalizing from dramatic but often unrepresentative cases, the qualitative analysis is framed within the context of a broader quantitative database (see Tarrow 1995, 472–473). I began by identifying the population of cases with interest group participation in the five states. Within this quantitative profile, I relied on evidence from interviews and other sources to explain the observed patterns of group participation by national organizations and their affiliates. (Appendix C discusses in more detail how the population of cases was chosen as well as how interviews were conducted.) The national organizations examined appear to have the characteristics of repeat players, which makes them most capable of using courts to bring about legal change. They are very likely the most influential groups involved in takings and obscenity litigation.

The two issue areas—takings and obscenity—vary considerably on the extent to which the Supreme Court provides incentive to turn to state litigation. Obscenity law is among the most decentralized of all areas of individual rights. After Supreme Court decisions in the 1960s that generally were receptive to litigants' free speech and expression claims, the Court altered dramatically the legal context of obscenity. In *Miller v. California* (1973), the Supreme Court issued a more expansive definition of "obscenity" and indicated a willingness to defer increasingly to the judgments of the states on this issue.

In contrast, the Supreme Court has provided litigants in takings cases little incentive to participate consistently at the state level.[18] Takings is peculiar among rights issues in that the Supreme Court has, in recent years, become arguably more receptive to rights claims. Decisions such as *Nollan v. California Coastal Commission* (1987) and *Dolan v. City of Tigard* (1994) reveal that the Court has become more hospitable to claims that government regulations unconstitutionally infringe on property rights.[19] Thus, through comparative examination of takings and obscenity cases, we can evaluate the importance of legal incentives on group litigation decisions. The analysis also assesses the importance of legal incentives by examining the impact of *Miller v. California* on group participation in state obscenity litigation. Variations across interest groups and affiliates of the same organization are explored to assess the importance of the organizational threshold. Table 2.1 illustrates the basic research design and shows how variations in issues and groups allow us to explain observed patterns of group litigation.

Table 2.1
Variations on Legal Incentive and Organizational Threshold by Issue Area

	Takings	Obscenity
Legal Incentive?	No	Yes
Organizational Threshold?	Varies by Group	Varies by Group

The states examined in this study are Colorado, Indiana, Minnesota, New Jersey, and South Carolina. Certainly, no five court systems are representative of those in all fifty states. However, an analysis that requires interviews with group officials and examinations of group and court files makes a larger sample of states prohibitively expensive. While the states do vary by political culture and by two measures of state supreme court activism (see Table 2.2), these factors are not controlled for and no formal attempt is made to generalize the findings to all states.

Table 2.2
Variations by Region and State Supreme Court Activism in Five States

State	Political Culture	Activism I: State Court Reputation	Activism II: Judicial Review
Colorado	Moralistic	II	IV
Indiana	Individualistic	III	III
Minnesota	Moralistic	II	III
New Jersey	Individualistic	I	II
South Carolina	Traditionalistic	IV	I

Sources: Political culture from Elazar (1984, 135). Activism I based on Caldeira's (1983) rank ordering of state supreme court reputation, divided into quartiles. Activism II based on Emmert's (1988) rank ordering of state supreme courts' tendency to strike down laws in judicial review cases, divided into quartiles.

Instead, the choice of states helps to provide variation on the explanatory variables of interest. For example, the National Wildlife Federation has an affiliate in each of the five states except New Jersey. In obscenity law, the Colorado Supreme Court provided clear incentive to assert rights claims in state courts by holding that its constitution protects speech and expression more broadly than does the First Amendment. The goal of this study is analytic rather than statistical generalization (Yin 1989, 21, 44–45). The findings generalize to broader theoretical propositions rather than to a particular statistical population.[20]

Throughout the analysis, I identify and attempt to explain patterns of group litigation. Litigation rates are compared across interest groups, across states, and over time. As often as possible, a triangulation strategy is employed, which brings multiple independent measures to bear on empirical questions (Tarrow 1995; Kritzer 1994; Miles and Huberman 1984, 234–35). I will show that a preponderance of the evidence supports, or at least does not contradict, my conclusions. Previous studies of legal mobilization (McCann 1994) have profited greatly from the use of triangulation techniques.[21]

To assess a group's litigation capacity, interview evidence is supplemented with a variety of indicators of resources. The first indicator is whether the group has state or local affiliates, which aid its efforts to track and develop local litigation and to cultivate legal expertise in state courts. Second, since access to attorneys is crucial, evidence is presented on the number of staff and cooperating attorneys associated with the organization. Finally, the groups are examined to determine whether they have participated in cases raising legal questions other than those of principal concern (that is, takings or obscenity). If so, this serves as a valuable piece of evidence that the group had at least minimal capacity to litigate.

I also examine whether groups asserting rights claims mobilized state constitutional law to seek broader protection than that recognized under federal law. Determining whether rights litigants make such independent state law claims is problematic, so specifying an indicator requires some discussion. In many state cases, litigants often invoke and courts consider both federal and state constitutional claims. For instance, Esler (1994, 27) finds that state supreme courts considered both federal and state law in 64 percent of their self-incrimination decisions. Often this leads to ambiguity between federal and state law grounds for decisions, reflecting a lack of clarity by both litigants and courts. The Supreme Court attempted to rectify this problem in *Michigan v. Long* (1983), where the Court ruled that it would assume ambiguously worded decisions were based on federal law unless state courts explicitly declared that their decisions rested on independent and adequate state grounds.

Investigating state court reliance on state law, scholars have used similar criteria to code decisions (Esler 1994; Latzer 1991a; Fino 1987a, 1987b). For example, Fino (1987a) coded a decision as based on state law only if it referred exclusively to state law, unless the reference to federal law was purely for rhetorical purposes or when the federal approach was discussed only to reject it. While the status of litigants' arguments differs somewhat from court decisions, the lessons of this research were followed in evaluating the arguments of interest groups in state courts. If a group offered only federal constitutional arguments, then obviously it did not mobilize state law. Conversely, if it offered only state constitutional arguments, I proceeded as follows. If the group either (1) argued that the state standards should provide greater protection than federal standards or (2) invoked state court precedent that claims broader protection than that under the federal Constitution, I concluded that the group sought to mobilize state law to seek more expansive protection.

If the group offered both federal *and* state law arguments, the following criteria were applied. When the group did not engage in any independent analysis of state law claims, the state law citations were deemed merely "filler" to the primary federal arguments. Remember that under *Michigan v. Long*, it is exactly in this situation—when state law is not examined independently of federal law—that the Supreme Court assumes the decision is based on federal grounds. However, where the group did engage in independent state law analysis, the arguments were evaluated using the same criteria that were used for groups who offered only state constitutional arguments.[22]

CONCLUSION

Throughout this century, organized interest groups have been an important mechanism for legal mobilization and change. They have played a crucial role in battles over constitutional rights in the U.S. Supreme Court. But under what conditions do major litigating groups make concerted efforts to shape state judicial agendas and policy by participating in state courts?

This chapter outlined a framework in which to address that question. The analysis suggested that groups are most likely to turn to the states when the legal context prohibits or discourages federal litigation. Indeed, in many areas of law, rights battles increasingly have been fought at the state level. Following the liberal activism of the Warren Court of the 1950s and 1960s, the Supreme Court issued numerous decisions that were less protective of rights and that relegated policy responsibility to state courts. The Court altered the balance of policy responsibility between the national and state courts, and the latter have emerged as more important policy makers.

While the legal context may provide incentive to turn to the states, interest groups' organizational settings condition responses to changes in the political and legal environment. Previous studies suggest that the range and scope of groups' interests, as well as their resources, shape their willingness and ability to enter the litigation fray. To understand group litigation in state courts, we must examine both legal incentives and the organizational threshold. Furthermore, groups may be more inclined to assert rights claims based on state constitutional law when they turn to state courts in response to Supreme Court decisions that restrict the scope of protection under the federal Constitution. It appears that groups typically are not inclined to litigate in state courts, and even less often will they assert rights claims on independent state law grounds.

The rest of this book is devoted to evaluating the propositions developed in this chapter. The comparative case study provides variations on legal incentives and organizational thresholds, thereby allowing for an assessment of these concepts' capacity to explain patterns of group litigation in state courts. Chapters 5 through 7 examine obscenity law, an area in which the Supreme Court has provided groups with clear incentives to turn to the states. Before this, however, group litigation on takings is explored. Unlike obscenity, in recent years the Supreme Court has become more receptive to rights claims in takings law. The next chapter examines takings jurisprudence and evaluates the extent to which it gives major litigating organizations motivation to turn to the states.

NOTES

1. For a history of the amicus curiae brief, see Krislov (1963).

2. In the U.S. Supreme Court, groups may file an amicus brief with the permission of the parties, although governments need not seek such leave. If the parties refuse, then the groups may file a motion with the Court to submit a brief (Caldeira and Wright 1988, 1113). In state supreme courts, there are a variety of procedures. Some states allow filing by permission of the court only. Others allow filings by consent of the parties, and then by leave of the court. In a few states, there are no formal application procedures to file amicus briefs (Epstein 1989a).

3. The discussion of resources relies heavily on L. Epstein (1985, 12-13) and Wasby (1995, 76-98).

4. Another line of research does not directly examine group litigants but is informative nonetheless. Scholars have explored the success rates of different types of litigants. The general conclusion is that "upperdogs" (which include many interest groups) are more successful in court than "underdogs" (see Songer and Sheehan 1992; Wheeler et al. 1987). But Sheehan, Mishler, and Songer (1992) found that in U.S. Supreme Court litigation, party type is not a strong predictor of success on the merit. They suggest that this may reflect the fact that justices' preferences have a strong impact on case outcomes.

5. This does not necessarily mean that amicus briefs have no influence. Through legal arguments, groups that file briefs may affect the content of opinions or the long-term policy direction of the Court without affecting the overall probability of winning a case.

6. This perspective on group litigation relies in part on L. Epstein (1992).

7. This official requested anonymity.

8. The discussion of cooperating attorneys relies heavily on Wasby (1995, 252–62, 1984, 112–13).

9. Illustrating the importance of legal arguments is the U.S. Supreme Court's antipathy toward "me-too" amicus curiae briefs, which simply restate arguments offered by the parties to the case. Instead, the Court prefers that an amicus brief "brings relevant matter to the attention of the court that has not already been brought to its attention by the parties." See Tony Mauro, "Court Gets a Tad Less Friendly to Amici," *Legal Times*, 19 February 1990, 10–11.

10. Source: 1995 budget of NWF (copy on file with author). Certainly, one can make a convincing argument that many of the ostensibly nonpolitical activities of material organizations are tied to their broader political objectives. For example, the NWF's public education programs can be understood as part of an effort to advance its environmental agenda by influencing public opinion. Nevertheless, it is useful to distinguish direct lobbying of political institutions, including the courts, from the many other organizational activities.

11. A potential objection might be that the influence of judges' preferences is so obvious that group officials would not even think to mention it in the interviews. To avoid this complication and ensure the validity of my data, I specifically raised the issue during interviews, inquiring as to (1) the extent to which state court judges were receptive to the group's policy position, and (2) whether and how this affected the decision to become involved in litigation.

12. Chapter 6 examines in more detail the influence of the New Jersey Supreme Court's obscenity doctrine on the ACLU of New Jersey's litigation behavior.

13. This does not necessarily mean that judicial attitudes have no effect on the decision to litigate in state courts. To the extent that judges' policy preferences influence the legal doctrine that courts promulgate, they may provide incentive to turn to the states. At the most general level, state courts have two options in rights cases: to apply the same level of protection that the Supreme Court recognizes under the federal Constitution or to accord broader protection based on the state constitution. If state courts opt for the latter course of action, they provide increased incentive for rights litigants to bring cases in state courts.

Scholars interested in the influence of judicial attitudes on group litigation indeed may uncover a significant (though likely not strong) effect. But in the context of this study, which is concerned with the broader question of what accounts for groups' decisions to enter state litigation, I find that the ideological composition of state courts is not a principal influence on groups. Groups appraise the receptivity of state courts primarily in terms of their rulings in the discrete policy area.

14. Caldeira (1983) argues that citation almost always means approval and indicates influence or deference to a sister court.

15. Caution is needed in exploring the influence of state supreme courts on sister courts. Policy leadership varies greatly across policy areas. For instance, Canon and Baum (1981) examined tort law innovations and found that no state court consistently was innovative in all areas of tort law.

16. Indiana judges are chosen by different methods at different levels of courts. Under the Missouri Plan, a commission (which usually includes lawyers selected by the state bar association and nonlawyers selected by the governor) nominates candidates for judgeships. When a position becomes vacant, the commission produces a short list (usually three) of nominees and the governor makes the appointment from the list. After the judge has served for a short time, and periodically after that, the judge is subject to a retention election, where there is no opposing candidate.

17. More generally, throughout this analysis, interest group resources and priorities are treated primarily as independent variables. The principal objective is to explore the capacity of organizational factors and legal incentives to explain litigation behavior, rather than to account for variations in the these factors.

18. There is one exception concerning the Court's procedural decisions, which will be addressed in more detail in Chapters 3 and 4.

19. Analysis of group participation in takings cases helps to fill a gap in the scholarly study of conservative organizations, since most studies of group litigation investigate the activities of liberal groups seeking social reform (but see L. Epstein 1985). This study also explores the willingness of property rights organizations to mobilize state constitutional law. While the new judicial federalism generally is associated with ideologically liberal policy outcomes, takings cases allow property rights groups to use state constitutions to pursue conservative policy goals.

20. To the extent that the states help to provide variations on the explanatory variables of interest, there is no reason to believe that they are in any way an unrepresentative sample.

21. King, Keohane, and Verba (1995) note that triangulation is consistent with their appeal to bring more information to bear on research questions.

22. This coding scheme rests on the assumption that litigants' legal arguments structure the issues that appellate courts address in their decisions. Certainly this is not always the case. In the Supreme Court, there is evidence of issue fluidity, where the justices examine legal issues not raised by the parties or (more often) ignore issues that were

raised (McGuire and Palmer 1995; Ulmer 1982). Nevertheless, state court litigants have little choice but to follow the strictures of *Michigan v. Long*. It is safe to assume that those seeking to compel a court to address an independent state law claim are aware of the precedent and tailor their arguments accordingly.

3

Legal Incentives in Takings Law

> The urgent environmental revolution of the late 1960s and the 1970s changed, and did not change, the way we view the legitimacy and use of local land use controls—planning, zoning, development codes, environmental requirements and growth management regulations. The movement toward heightened environmental awareness . . . coupled with the parallel intensification of government regulation, has led unavoidably to legal clashes. And so, inevitably, the fundamental, most vexing issue of American land use law—the "taking" issue—has rapidly gained new prominence.
>
> —Gus Bauman
> Counsel, National Association of Home Builders

The last chapter developed a framework with which to examine interest group litigation in state courts. The framework suggests that major litigating groups are most likely to litigate regularly when they have the legal incentives and organizational resources to do so. An evaluation of these hypotheses begins with examination of interest group litigation in eminent domain, or takings, law. A great number of organized groups, both large and small, participate on both sides of the takings debate. Their interest in this area of law is easily explained.

Eminent domain litigation generally pits private property owners against government and those who wish to use the power of the state for public benefits. These disputes arise when the state's public actions affect individual ownership or use of property. The Fifth Amendment, which provides that "private property [shall not] be taken for public use, without just compensation," attempts to balance individual property rights with the need of the people through government to undertake projects in the public interest. Federal and state constitutional takings provisions determine the relative burdens that members of the community bear in relation to public projects. For instance, although government has the authority to build a public highway through an individual's property, it cannot force the property owner to bear the costs of the public good. Instead, government must internalize those costs. The requirement of just compensation is based on the notion that government should not "forc[e] some people alone to bear public burdens which, in all fairness and justice, should be borne by the public as a whole" (*Armstrong v. U.S.* 1960, 49). To many, these issues of fundamental fairness and justice are at the heart of the takings debate (Marzulla and Marzulla 1991; R. Epstein 1985; Comment 1981; Siegan 1980; Ackerman 1977; Michaelman 1967).

The Fifth Amendment does not apply solely to the direct government acquisition of property, but also may pertain to situations where regulations substantially diminish property values. These so-called "regulatory takings" potentially arise from many activities undertaken by state and local governments. Litigants challenging laws dealing with environmental protection, zoning, rent control, coastal management, and historic preservation contend that they impair or destroy the ability of citizens to use and enjoy private property.

While takings claims are considered most often in the context of land use regulations, the impact of the Fifth Amendment is much broader. "Property" includes not only land but also anything that an individual or corporation can own, such as money, goods, interests in land, bonds, patents, and trademarks. Indeed, litigants have claimed that numerous policies take their property and require just compensation. These policies include retirement health plans,[1] social security controls on health care costs,[2] provisions governing access to public accommodations for disabled individuals,[3] Medicare limits on costs to patients,[4] sobriety roadblocks,[5] regulations designed to protect minors from obscene speech,[6] local "open container" laws,[7] pollution controls,[8] and civil rights legislation.[9] Because of the numerous contexts in which takings disputes arise, and thus the variety of interests implicated, many diverse organized groups attempt to shape takings law.

Beyond their constitutional dimensions, then, eminent domain disputes involve enormous public and personal stakes. Government decisions concerning public projects directly affect individuals' ability to use and enjoy their property. In particular, the potential impact of holding governments liable for compensation when they engage in regulatory activities is profound. Such liability affects the government treasury and can have the practical effect of nullifying numerous regulations. Recognizing the larger stakes involved, Chief Judge Loren Smith of the United States Court of Claims suggested that the court's decisions "may have profound effects on the ability of the government to operate" (Smith 1991, 512). In short, debate over property use is emotionally charged and has important implications for both property owners and the ability of government to manage resources for this and future generations.

This chapter examines the context in which interest groups have participated in takings litigation. The purpose of this chapter is twofold. First, it provides a general overview of eminent domain law, discussing constitutional challenges that arise under federal and state takings provisions, their implications, and the development of federal takings law in recent years. Since it is the most contentious area of eminent domain law in recent decades, the analysis focuses on regulatory takings claims, in which property owners assert that government regulations are so intrusive that they take private property and require compensation. The discussion provides a framework to understand the legal and political context in which most group litigation occurred.

Second, this chapter demonstrates that the Supreme Court's regulatory takings decisions have *not* provided interest groups with a strong incentive to litigate in state courts. While state courts have become more important actors in many policy domains in recent years, state judiciaries have not become decidedly more important in takings law. Despite the requirement to raise some takings claims in state courts, since the late 1970s the Supreme Court has shown a renewed interest in regulatory takings cases and has expanded protection for individuals whose property is subject to government regulations. An understanding of the Supreme Court's takings jurisprudence provides a foundation upon which to examine group participation in state takings cases.

EMINENT DOMAIN AND PROPERTY RIGHTS IN AMERICAN HISTORY

The right to own and use private property holds a cherished place in the Anglo-American legal tradition. The basic property right was derived from seventeenth- and eighteenth-century English legal tradition that prohibited the king from taking a subject's property except by a duly enacted law of the land and with full restitution (Note 1985; Horowitz 1977; Stoebuck 1972). The Magna Carta provided that property could not be taken without the consent of either the owner or the legislature. Indeed, as early as the statutes of sewers of 1427, Parliament authorized compensation for government takings of property (Stoebuck 1972).

Despite a strong tradition of recognizing property rights, equally strong was the tradition—originating in feudal notions of the inherent power of the sovereign—that government could take individual property. According to this perspective, property was held by the state so it could limit ownership claims. Appeals to the inherent power of the sovereign provided justification for takings of property in colonial America. Even at the time of the American Revolution, an individual right to compensation when government took private property was by no means universally accepted. Indeed, in the years immediately following Independence, only three state constitutions had any type of takings clause, and none required that just compensation be paid when the state took property (Note 1985, 697-98).

The movement for just compensation requirements at the state and local levels began by the early 1780s. It was part of a broader ideological emphasis on liberalism, which stressed the protection of individual rights against undue government interference (Note 1985, 694). The importance of property rights during this era is reflected in the number of provisions in the United States Constitution that explicitly or implicitly protect individual ownership and use of property. For example, Article 1 limits congressional regulation to interstate commerce and prohibits tax on exports. The Third Amendment prohibits housing troops in private homes. But perhaps the most significant protection is the Fifth Amendment's "Takings Clause," which expressly limits the manner in which government can take private property.

The Fifth Amendment provides that "private property [shall not] be taken for public use, without just compensation."[10] The eminent domain authority allows government to take private property subject to two limitations. First, the private property must be taken for a "public use," not solely for private benefit. Second, when government takes private property for public use, it must provide the owner with "just compensation." Nearly every state constitution has a similar takings clause.[11] In addition, the Fifth Amendment's just compensation clause was made applicable to the states through the Fourteenth Amendment in *Chicago, B. & Q.R.R. v. City of Chicago* (1897). The federal Constitution's takings clause was "meant to have broad moral implications as a statement of national commitment to the preservation of property rights" (Note 1985, 708).

Thus, the American legal tradition acknowledges limits to eminent domain authority, and the importance of property rights more generally. Nevertheless, because property use "invariably affects neighbors and the community health and welfare, *absolute* use has never been considered a protected property right" (Duerksen and Roddewig 1994, 2). Property rights are limited in two primary ways. First, an individual may not use property in ways that directly impair others' right to enjoy their property. Common and tort law rules such as nuisance and trespass address these circumstances.[12] Second, through its eminent domain authority, the state has the authority to take private property when public needs demand its use.

TAKINGS LAW

The following discussion details the Supreme Court's renewed interest in and receptivity to rights claims in regulatory takings cases, the area of eminent domain law in which most interest group litigation occurred since 1960.[13] But before turning to regulatory takings jurisprudence, it is necessary to set the broader context by discussing the basic constitutional aspects of eminent domain law. There are two general phases of an eminent domain action. The first phase deals with whether a taking has occurred. If the property is taken, the second phase concerns how much compensation is due the property owner. Figure 3.1

displays these phases. Not surprisingly, there is significant debate over precisely when property is taken, and thus when an individual is entitled to just compensation.

Figure 3.1
Phases of a Condemnation Action

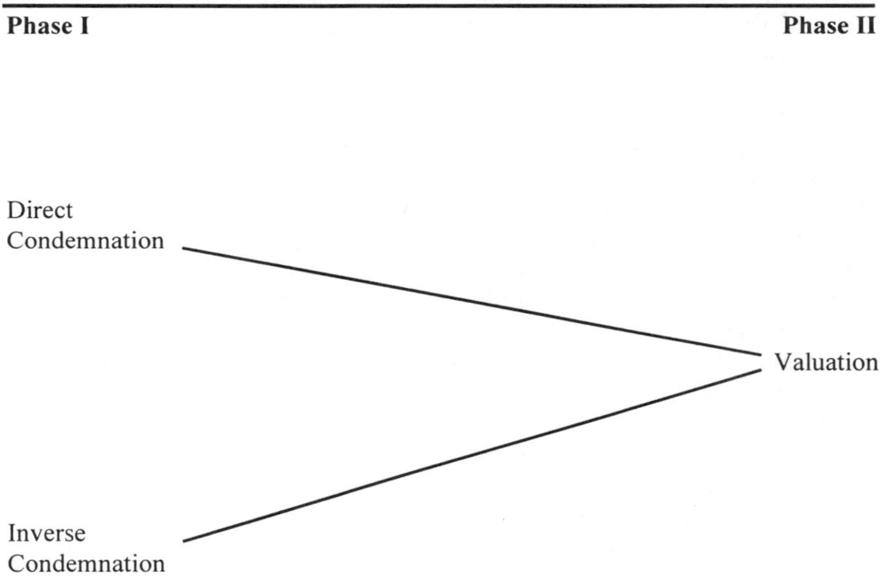

Direct Condemnation

The most fundamental distinction among takings is that they may occur either directly or inversely. Direct condemnation is the formal exercise of eminent domain authority, where the condemning authority (usually government) recognizes that it is taking private property. In direct condemnation suits, there is no question as to whether the property is "taken"; the government concedes this by filing the action. A typical example of direct condemnation is the purchase of private property through which a public road is to be built.

Until the late nineteenth century, federal and state takings clauses were connected only with direct condemnation. And for at least the past several decades, the constitutionality of most direct condemnation actions generally is accepted, so that the only question becomes how much compensation is due to the property owner. Yet some recent challenges to the direct condemnation of property have arisen under the Fifth Amendment's "public use" requirement. The

Supreme Court grants legislatures significant leeway in determining what is a public use (R. Epstein 1985; Note 1949). Throughout this century, the Court upheld a variety of land use controls against challenges that they violate the public use requirement. In the landmark case of *Berman v. Parker* (1954), the Court upheld an urban renewal program and enunciated the modern understanding of the public use requirement: any legislative purpose that would be considered constitutional is sufficiently "public" to survive a takings challenge. It appears that the public use requirement only limits government from taking property solely to make money for itself or for a private enterprise. But government may use its eminent domain authority to acquire property and then resell it to private companies for purposes such as urban renewal and the development of industrial parks or shopping centers (O'Brien 1995, 287).

That the public use requirement places few limits on government authority to condemn private property is illustrated nicely by *Hawaii Housing Authority v. Midkiff* (1984). A unanimous Court approved a state land reform act that, in an effort to eliminate the last vestiges of Hawaiian feudalism, authorized the use of eminent domain authority to condemn residential lots and sell ownership to existing tenants of the land. The justices rejected the claim that the program constituted a taking of property for private, not public, purposes.

Once a taking is established, the second phase of a condemnation action concerns the amount of compensation due.[14] The general rule is that the fair market value of the property provides just compensation. Underlying the rule is the notion that the owner of condemned property should be placed "in as good a position pecuniarily as if his property had not been taken. He must be made whole but is not entitled to more" (*Olson v. U.S.* 1934, 255). While litigants have raised various issues pertaining to the valuation of property, the Supreme Court has not addressed them regularly for many years.

Inverse Condemnation

In addition to direct condemnation, takings may occur without explicit government recognition of the condemnation of property. For instance, zoning regulations that allow only residential uses can affect greatly the value of farmland. Environmental regulations designed to protect wetlands or endangered species may prohibit individuals from building on privately owned land. Coastal management ordinances that prohibit rebuilding on a shoreline may render valueless (or nearly so) privately owned beaches.

When a government agency, through its regulatory authority,[15] nevertheless acts in a manner that takes someone's property or interest in property, it results in an inverse condemnation, or regulatory taking. Regulatory takings, a concept developed entirely through judicial interpretation, recognizes de facto takings of property. Unlike direct condemnation, the property owner brings an inverse condemnation action. The most fundamental issue in regulatory takings law concerns the extent to which the Fifth Amendment constrains the government's exercise of legitimate regulatory powers. In other words, at what point is a regulation so intrusive on the use and enjoyment of private property that it effectively "takes" the property, requiring just compensation? Central to the notion of regulatory takings is that government cannot, through its regulatory powers, circumvent the just compensation requirements of federal and state takings clauses.

In regulatory takings jurisprudence, the distinction between regulations that trigger just compensation requirements and those that do not is critical. Numerous governmental regulations may infringe on property rights to some degree, but the Constitution generally furnishes no right to compensation. Compensation is required only when a regulation amounts to a taking of property in the Fifth Amendment sense.

Throughout the nineteenth century, the Supreme Court maintained that takings occur only by government appropriation or physical possession. In *Mugler v. Kansas* (1887), Justice John Marshall Harlan established a clear distinction between police power regulations and eminent domain actions. He argued that the former affect the use of property and do not constitute a taking, while the latter involve a "physical invasion" of property and result in "a practical ouster" of possession of the property. A valid police power regulation is one that has a "real or substantial relation to the public health, public morals, or the public safety" (*Mugler* 1887, 661). Indeed, as late as 1915 in *Hadacheck v. Sebastian*, the Court held that an ordinance that banned brick making from certain areas of a city and resulted in the diminution in the value of a factory owner's property from $800,00 to $60,000 did not constitute a taking. The Court noted that the ordinance promoted a legitimate public need and that the property owner could still use the parcel of land for a different purpose.

However, in *Pennsylvania Coal Company v. Mahon* (1922), the Supreme Court for the first time recognized that regulations could cause takings even if there is no actual physical invasion of the property. In striking down a Pennsylvania law forbidding coal mining that would cause buildings or streets on the surface to collapse into mine shafts, the Court found that, even though the law pursues a valid public purpose, the only acceptable way to accomplish the goal was for the government to buy the property interest held by the coal company. Justice Oliver Wendell Holmes declared that "the general rule at least is, that while the property may be regulated to a certain extent, if the regulation goes too far it will be recognized as a taking" (*Pennsylvania Coal Company* 1922, 415).

Holmes offered a new, modern understanding of the relationship between the police powers and eminent domain authority. Whereas Harlan in *Mugler* distinguished clearly the two powers, Holmes developed the idea that the regulatory and eminent domain powers form a continuum. As a result, the constitutional requirement that government pay for the private impact of regulations is a matter of degree. No general proposition can determine when a regulation goes too far and becomes a taking; courts must make determinations on a case-by-case basis.

The "general rule" laid down in *Mahon* was vague. While the Court asserted that most residential zoning does not constitute a taking (*Village of Euclid v. Ambler Realty* 1926), it held that certain zoning regulations may go too far and require compensation to property owners (*Nectow v. City of Cambridge* 1928). After this, the Supreme Court did not regularly address the takings issue for nearly fifty years. For instance, the Court decided no zoning cases between 1928 and 1974 (Bauman 1983), leaving it to the lower federal and state courts to work out rules on a case-by-case basis. By the 1970s, the majority of American courts did not consider most regulatory actions to be inverse condemnations, but rather legitimate uses of regulatory powers, which do not require compensation (Hagman 1975).

Regulatory Takings Revisited. However, beginning in the 1970s a new wave of challenges to governments' regulatory authority emerged. Most observers attribute the rising number of disputes to the increased scope of regulations by governments at all levels in the 1960s and 1970s (Jacobs 1995; Sugameli 1993; Bauman 1983). Undoubtedly, as Bauman's comment at the beginning of this chapter suggests, an important catalyst was the proliferation of environmental regulations. The expanded use of governments' regulatory powers once again placed the takings issue on judicial agendas. In response, the U.S. Supreme Court has developed its jurisprudence in this area of law (Meltz 1993), and organized interest groups have become active in regulatory takings litigation.

The Supreme Court reentered the regulatory takings arena in *Penn Central Transportation Co. v. New York City* (1978). *Penn Central* involved a takings challenge to a New York landmark preservation law. Justice William Brennan recognized that "[t]he question of what constitutes a 'taking' has proved to be a problem of considerable difficulty" (*Penn Central* 1978, 123). The Court discussed the need to conduct factual inquiries to identify whether the regulation balances public needs with the rights of property owners and does not place an undue burden on the latter. While acknowledging that there is no "set formula" for determining when a taking occurs, Brennan identified several factors that are especially important. These factors include: (1) "the character of the governmental action," (2) the "economic impact of the regulation on the claimant," and (3) the "extent to which the regulation has interfered with distinct investment-backed expectations" (*Penn Central* 1978, 124).

The balancing test reaffirmed the Court's position that takings determinations remain an ad hoc, case-by-case matter. However, since the decision, the Court has begun to modify and qualify the ad hoc approach in three different areas of regulatory takings jurisprudence.[16] While the Court has had difficulty fashioning rules to determine whether government regulations go too far and take property, each of the doctrinal changes, to varying degrees, has expanded the rights of private property owners.

The first doctrinal modification since *Penn Central* deals with the appropriate remedy for a regulatory taking, which has been among the most controversial questions in takings law. Arguably, on this issue property rights advocates have won their greatest victory in the U.S. Supreme Court. They argued that when government regulations are found to have taken private property, compensation must be paid. Opponents, however, asserted that it is sufficient for the Court to invalidate the offending statute. The compensation issue rose to prominence with Justice Brennan's strong endorsement of damage remedies in his dissenting opinion in *San Diego Gas & Electric Co. v. San Diego* (1981, 658-59):

> The constitutional rule I propose requires that, once a court finds that a police power regulation has effected a "taking," the government entity must pay just compensation for the period commencing on the date the regulation first effected the "taking," and ending on the date the government entity chooses to rescind or otherwise amend the regulation. Ordinary principles determining the proper measure of just compensation . . . should provide guidance to the courts in the award of compensation for a regulatory "taking."[17]

Ultimately, the Court adopted this position in *First English Evangelical Lutheran Church v. County of Los Angeles* (1987). It held that when a regulation takes property, the Fifth Amendment requires compensation for the time during which the regulation was in effect (until the date that the regulation either is repealed or invalidated in court). Even if the regulation subsequently is repealed, restitution is required for temporary losses. As a result of *First English*, states that did not pay damages for temporary takings were required to develop procedures to do so.

A second modification to the law of regulatory takings has been the articulation of a substantive due process line of reasoning to protect property owners from arbitrary or unreasonable government actions. The justices addressed the growing practice by local governments of requiring land or other contributions from developers to offset the costs of public facilities created by their projects. In *Nollan v. California Coastal Commission* (1987), the Court held that when these development conditions, known as exactions, do not "substantially advance" a "legitimate state interest," they result in a taking. In that case, the state required that Nollan allow public access to his private beach in return for a building permit for a vacation home.

Justice Antonin Scalia's majority opinion struck down the property regulation, declaring that it lacked a requisite "essential nexus" between the "end advanced" and the "condition imposed by [the] application of the regulation to a specific piece of property" (*Nollan* 1987, 837). Lacking such a nexus, governments cannot pursue policies in the public interest through regulations, but instead must rely on their eminent domain authority and compensate property owners. Subsequently, the Court elaborated further on its *Nollan* analysis. In *Dolan v. City of Tigard* (1994), the Court struck down as unconstitutional a condition attached to a business expansion permit that required Dolan to dedicate bike path as well as greenway and floodplain easements to the city, which would allow public access to parts of Dolan's property. The Court adopted a three-prong test to determine the conditions necessary for government to pass the costs of public facilities to landowners (Callies 1994). The first two questions were developed in *Nollan*: (1) Does the permit condition seek to promote a legitimate state interest? (2) Is there an essential nexus between the legitimate state interest and the permit condition? The *Dolan* Court then added a third prong to the test: (3) Is there a required degree of connection between the exactions and the projected impact of the development?

In *Dolan*, the Court held that the city failed the third prong of the test by not demonstrating that the impact of Dolan's expanded business was reasonably related in "rough proportion" to the requirement for public access. *Dolan* did not alter fundamentally the Court's analysis as developed in *Nollan*, but did place a greater burden on governments to justify land dedication requirements. Regulations cannot require property owners to bear costs out of proportion to the impact that their property use will have on the community. The Court's decisions in *Nollan* and *Dolan* have placed the burden increasingly on governments to justify the legitimacy of the interests at stake and to prove the effective connection between those interests and the government actions that property owners challenge.

The third modification to *Penn Central*'s ad hoc rule is the Court's increasing emphasis on "per se" categories of impacts caused by regulations. In the context of regulatory takings, a per se rule states that certain government regulations are so intrusive on private property owners that, no matter how important the legislative interest in the regulation, compensation is always required.

The Court has acknowledged two categories of regulatory actions that effect per se takings. The first is when the regulation eliminates all economically viable use of private property. While the Court did not explicitly hold that the denial of all economically viable use is a per se taking until *Lucas v. South Carolina Coastal Council* (1992), previous decisions hinted at such a rule. For instance, in *Hodel v. Irving* (1987), the Court struck down a federal statute concerning Indian land because it abolished completely, rather than merely regulated, the right to pass property to one's heirs, a right basic to the concept of property rights. In other cases, the Court emphasized that the mere diminution in value does not in itself effect a taking. Instead, all economic value must be lost (see *Keystone Bituminous Coal Association v. DeBenedictis* 1987; *Penn Central* 1978).

Lucas involved a challenge to a coastal zoning restriction that prohibited the rebuilding of houses along the shoreline in order to preserve the beach and sand dunes as a storm barrier. David Lucas argued that the restriction denied him the use of his property without just compensation. The Supreme Court held that the restriction of all economically viable use may constitute grounds for a takings claim, but (since individuals have no right to use property in a nuisancelike manner) any regulation that bars property owners from engaging in nuisancelike activities can never result in a taking, even if that regulation causes the loss of all economic value of the property. The Court then remanded the case to the state court to determine whether Lucas in fact had been deprived of all economically viable use and whether the state's regulation could be justified as preventing a public harm or nuisance.[18]

In *Lucas*, the Court recognized a taking in one of those rare situations in which regulations deprive owners of all economically viable use of the property. As Justice Stevens noted in his dissenting opinion, "[a] land-owner whose property is diminished in value 95 percent recovers nothing, while an owner whose property is diminished 100 percent recovers the land's full value" (*Lucas* 1992, 1064). Many commentators on both sides of the takings debate argue that the practical effect of the decision is to incur liability on only very few regulatory actions (Lazarus 1993; Rubenfeld 1993; Ayer 1992). A lawyer for the National Wildlife Federation labeled *Lucas* a decision "full of sound and fury, signifying nothing" (Sugameli 1993). Richard Epstein (1992, 4) disapprovingly notes the limited importance of *Lucas* because "the Court appears to have adopted a powerful 'hands off' attitude to all forms of partial restrictions on land use—a subject that dwarfs the importance of the peculiar circumstances of Lucas, the total wipeout of all land uses." Nevertheless, *Lucas* does suggest that the Court may be reevaluating its regulatory takings jurisprudence (Berger 1992; Gallagher 1992; Fischman 1991), moving away from balancing interests to increased use of per se rules (Sugameli 1993).

In addition to the elimination of all economically viable use of property, a second situation in which a per se taking occurs is when the government regulation involves a permanent physical invasion of property. The leading modern decision is *Loretto v. Teleprompter Manhattan CATV Corporation* (1982), in which the Court struck down a New York statute that required landlords to physically install cable television wires to each tenant's apartment. The Court held that the law effected a permanent physical invasion of Loretto's property, interfering with the owner's right to exclude others from the property. Thus, a regulation that causes a *physical* invasion of private property, no matter how small, is a taking and requires compensation.

The Court has interpreted this per se rule narrowly, holding that temporary physical invasions are not per se takings and must submit to a balancing of factors under *Penn Central*. Further, in *F.C.C. v. Florida Power Corp.* (1987), the Court restricted the per se rule to apply only where the permanent physical occupation is coerced, and not entered into voluntarily. Nevertheless, the importance of the physical invasion factor deserves note. Since 1962, save for one case,[19] the Supreme Court has required compensation only when the government action affected an owner's right of exclusive occupancy (Lunney 1992).

To summarize, since the late 1970s the Supreme Court has given increased attention to regulatory takings cases. And not surprisingly, this increased attention coincided with doctrinal modification. Recent decisions have expanded the rights of private property owners affected by government regulations. The Court has carved out categories of regulations that always require compensation, has mandated monetary awards for all regulatory takings (even temporary ones), and has made it more difficult for governments at all levels to justify regulatory schemes that impose conditions on the use of private property. O'Brien (1995, 287) identifies takings as "one area of constitutional law in which the Rehnquist Court moved toward giving somewhat greater protection for property rights."

Particularly when compared to other areas of law, the Supreme Court has not become more hostile to rights claims in regulatory takings jurisprudence. In fact, the analysis suggests that the Court has become more receptive to property rights claims. The changing legal context has not been lost on interest groups. The following comments illustrate their perspectives:

> The Court successes, especially in *First English*, *Nollan*, *Lucas*, and *Dolan*, gave vitality to the [property rights] movement. (Roger Marzulla [1995], Former President, Mountain States Legal Foundation)

> Because of the decisions, they [the property rights movement] are on the offensive right now. (Brett Smith [1995], Conservation Coordinator, Sierra Club of Minnesota)

> The tide is rolling in their direction right now. (Trish Jerman [1995], Former Executive Director, South Carolina Wildlife Federation)

Group officials acknowledge that the Supreme Court's takings decisions have helped to increase the power of the property rights movement. Their perspectives are consistent with the conclusions that emerge from the doctrinal analysis. In regulatory takings cases, the Supreme Court has endorsed many of the legal arguments proposed by property rights advocates. Consequently, it appears unlikely that property rights supporters would have reason, under the new judicial federalism incentive, to turn to state courts and seek broader protections under state constitutions. Legal precedent gives property rights groups incentive to litigate in federal courts and on federal constitutional grounds.

This does not mean that the U.S. Supreme Court has sided completely with property owners in takings disputes. On the contrary, governments at all levels retain broad discretion to use their regulatory powers to pursue public projects. The Court has been reluctant to expand too far the rights of property owners. Nevertheless, trends in takings law, as well as my interviews with group officials, suggest that property rights proponents likely have little reason to turn to the states to avoid federal court decisions.

It is also important to acknowledge that in regulatory taking law, state courts have been loathe to provide broader protection for property rights under their state constitutions. Given that the U.S. Supreme Court has not enunciated clear standards for distinguishing between valid regulatory activities and takings that require compensation, it is difficult to determine precisely whether state constitutional doctrine offers more expansive protection. Yet in virtually all instances, state courts have adopted principles to interpret their takings clauses that are similar to the federal standards.[20] Thus, despite the emergence in recent years of state constitutional takings jurisprudence (Caira 1992; Sullivan 1988), state law rarely provides more expansive protection for property rights than does federal constitutional law.

However, while the Supreme Court's precedent provides interest groups, particularly property rights organizations, with little reason to turn to the states under the new judicial federalism incentive, groups do appear to have some motivation under the federal restriction incentive. The Supreme Court has made it difficult to obtain judicial consideration of regulatory takings claims and, more important, the Court has made it difficult for property owners to obtain a federal court forum for compensation claims brought against state or local governments.

The Court erected these barriers in decisions about whether takings claims are ripe for review. Courts typically refuse to decide cases in which the legal issues are not clear enough and sufficiently evolved so that a clear decision can come from the case. Specifically, ripeness requires that an actual controversy has developed between the parties. Courts refrain from deciding hypothetical or speculative cases.

In regulatory takings law, the U.S. Supreme Court, in a series of decisions,[21] asserted that an actual development plan must be filed before a landowner can bring a takings claim. Since most regulatory takings challenges involve ad hoc determinations of the extent to which a regulation interferes with the property owner's investment-backed expectations, courts must have the final word on what development will be permitted before conducting their examinations. If a development proposal is rejected, the landowner must pursue all avenues of administrative relief available under state law before filing suit. Save for exceptional situations, then, theoretical challenges are not allowed.[22] Ripeness requirements present substantial obstacles to judicial consideration of inverse condemnation suits and effectively bar many potential litigants from the courtroom. The decisions frustrated property rights proponents, who contended that the Supreme Court erected an "exaggerated procedural threshold which enabled it to avoid deciding cases on the merits" (Marzulla and Marzulla 1991, 533).

Just as it is difficult to obtain judicial consideration of takings claims, many property owners lack access to *federal* courts in inverse condemnation suits. State and local governments conduct most regulatory activity, particularly land use regulations. In *Williamson County Regional Planning Commission v. Hamilton Bank* (1985), the Court asserted that a Fifth Amendment claim is not ripe until the state refuses to pay compensation. Since the Constitution does not prohibit takings, only takings without just compensation, there is no federal cause of action until a state court denies compensation to the property owner. Thus, property owners must bringing regulatory takings claims against state and local governments in state courts. This requirement, coupled with the principle of res judicata, which bars relitigation of the same claim, arguably denies property owners a federal forum (save for a direct appeal to the United States Supreme Court) for these takings claims (Roberts 1995, 1992).

Consequently, under most circumstances, litigants have no choice as to which forum (federal or state court) in which to initiate compensation claims for regulatory takings. Claims against state or local governments generally must be brought in state courts. Compensation claims (in excess of $10,000) against the actions of the federal government go to the United States Claims Court. This court has jurisdiction to hear only suits for damages. In contrast, federal district courts typically decide takings cases that challenge the constitutionality of federal laws, as well suits for damages of less than $10,000.

A note of caution is in order. In regulatory takings jurisprudence, ripeness and forum selection issues are complex and controversial (see Roberts 1995, 1992; Blaesser 1988). For instance, there is some disagreement over when a claim is ripe for federal court review. The Ninth Circuit Court of Appeals held that litigants bringing a facial takings claim (asserting that a regulation takes property in all instances, rather than just as applied in the case at hand) must first seek compensation from the state under the *Hamilton Bank* precedent (*Pacific Transportation Co. v. City of Los Angeles* 1990). But in *Crow-New Jersey 32 Limited Partnership v. Township of Clinton* (1989), a federal district court held a facial taking claim ripe for review even though the property owner did not first seek compensation.[23]

Nevertheless, the discussion serves to highlight the difficulty of bringing inverse condemnation claims against state or local governments in federal courts. Since the claims typically must be brought in state judiciaries before receiving federal court consideration, organized interests—particularly those initiating regulatory takings claims—appear to have some motivation, under the federal restriction incentive, to litigate at the state level. In the next chapter, I examine more thoroughly the effects of the Court's ripeness decisions on group litigation strategies.

To summarize, despite the Court's ripeness decisions, a vast preponderance of the evidence suggests that legal precedent provides interest groups little reason to turn consistently to state judiciaries. The Supreme Court, interpreting the federal Constitution, increasingly has supported legal arguments offered by property rights advocates. While some cases must be initiated in state courts, the Supreme Court by no means has abdicated policy responsibility on takings issues. In fact, since *Penn Central* (1978), the Court has been increasingly active in developing regulatory takings jurisprudence (Meltz 1993). Given these trends in takings law, the incentive for groups to turn to state judiciaries appears relatively weak.

TAKINGS IN LEGISLATURES AND EXECUTIVES

Spurred on by successes in the courts, property rights advocates not only have brought more judicial actions but also have asserted themselves more vigorously in other political forums. Regulatory takings has changed from a matter of prime interest solely to courts to one of concern to other political actors as well. In 1988 President Ronald Reagan signed Executive Order No. 12360, which required federal agencies to conduct a takings impact analysis, in which the agency would examine a regulation's potential effects on property rights, before approving the regulation. The stated purpose of the executive order was to consolidate takings doctrine enunciated in the Court's 1987 decisions, especially *Nollan* and *First English.* Critics suggested that Reagan's primary goal was to advance an antiregulatory agenda, aimed specifically at the federal wetlands program (Sugameli 1993; Engel 1989; Jackson and Albaugh 1988).

In recent years, numerous takings bills have been introduced in the U.S. Congress and state legislatures. Through the legislative process, property rights advocates have attempted to codify and expand the logic of the recent Supreme Court decisions. Congress considered, and the House in March 1995 passed, a federal takings bill. In addition, between 1991 and 1996, over 300 property rights bills have been introduced across the 50 state legislatures. Fifty-two measures have been adopted in 26 states (Emerson 1996). Undoubtedly there will be legal challenges to this legislation; state and federal courts will have further occasion to consider their regulatory takings jurisprudence.

CONCLUSION

This chapter has provided an overview of the politics of eminent domain disputes and the development of regulatory takings law in the United States. The U.S. Supreme Court provides little incentive for organized interest groups to turn consistently to state judiciaries to litigate takings cases. Since the late 1970s, the Court has shown renewed interest in regulatory takings jurisprudence and has expanded rights under the federal Constitution for individuals whose private property is affected by government regulations. While litigants must initiate certain compensation claims in state courts, and therefore do have some reason to enter these tribunals, the overall conclusion emerging from the analysis is that there is no strong legal incentive to turn to state courts on a regular basis.

This assessment of takings law allows us to address the following question. Lacking strong legal incentives to turn to state judiciaries, to what extent have interest groups participated in state takings litigation? The next chapter considers this question and explores how the absence of such legal incentives affected groups' propensity to engage in litigation at the state level.

NOTES

1. *Barrick Gold Exploration, Inc. v. Hudson* (1993).
2. *Metrolina Family Practice v. Sullivan* (1989).
3. *Pinnock v. International House of Pancakes Franchisee* (1993).
4. *Whitney v. Heckler* (1986).
5. *Get Away Club, Inc. v. Coleman* (1992).
6. *Carlin Communications, Inc. v. F.C.C.* (1988).
7. *Glasheen v. City of Austin* (1993).
8. *Triple G Landfills v. Board of Commissioners* (1992).
9. *Heart of Atlanta Motel, Inc. v. U.S.* (1964).
10. U.S. Constitution, amend. 5.
11. Each state constitution includes a compensation clause except North Carolina's, whose courts have added such a protection by interpretation. Twenty-six state constitutions provide compensation not only for property "taken" but also for property "damaged," but their courts generally interpreted the words to mean the same (Stoebuck 1972).
12. Many legislative regulations codify and supplement these common law principles. Other legislative actions, such as aesthetic regulations, expand on those principles. The latter category is the subject of much of the regulatory takings controversy (see Morrison 1996, 270-91).
13. Volumes have been written on the law of eminent domain (for example, Randolph 1991; Sackman 1964). My discussion focuses on those areas that were the subject of most group litigation during the time of this study. This means paying much greater attention to regulatory takings than to other areas of eminent domain law.
14. As Figure 3.1 reveals, almost any taking (whether in the direct or inverse condemnation context) triggers the compensation phase.
15. At the most general level, the constitutional source of regulatory authority for states is the "police power" reserved to the states under the Tenth Amendment and for the federal government are the powers enumerated in Article 1 of the Constitution.
16. Discussion of the three modifications relies heavily on Emerson and Wise (1995).
17. The case, however, was decided on other grounds.
18. On remand, the South Carolina Supreme Court held that the Coastal Council had not demonstrated any common law nuisance or state property law basis by which it could restrain Lucas's use of his land. The court further held that Lucas had suffered a temporary taking of property. On April 5, 1993, the Coastal Council issued David Lucas a permit to build on his beach property (Sugameli 1993, 496-97).
19. The exception is *Hodel v. Irving* (1987).
20. Arguably, in some instances, some state courts have read their takings clauses to give property owners added protection against state regulation (Caira 1992).
21. The most important decisions are *San Diego Gas & Electric Co. v. San Diego* (1981), *Williamson County Regional Planning Commission v. Hamilton Bank* (1985), *U.S. v. Riverside Bayview Homes, Inc.* (1985), and *MacDonald, Sommer & Frates v. County of Yolo* (1986).
22. In some situations, the final decision rule does not restrict landowners. When a landowner brings a physical takings claim, it is the physical invasion of property that establishes what has been taken, and no final decision is necessary. Likewise, a facial challenge to a statute or regulation is not subject to the final decision rule since the prop-

erty owner asserts that the enactment of the law, rather than its application in a specific situation, takes the property. See Roberts (1995, 42-43).

23. Examples taken from Roberts (1992, 488-91).

4

Interest Group Litigation in State Takings Cases

> Today farmers and ranchers, timber workers, fishermen and women, energy developers, and property owners feel besieged by environmental laws and regulations that have lost all touch with reason and reality. For example, "wetlands" and endangered species policies are damaging to the economy while threatening liberties guaranteed under our Constitution.
>
> —Representative W.J. (Billy) Tauzin (D-LA)

> We see our ox being gored; takings decisions and legislation can damage habitats . . . planning and zoning are necessary for environmental regulation.
>
> —Trish Jerman, Former Executive Director, South Carolina Wildlife Federation

Whether Supreme Court decisions provide incentive for interest groups to litigate in state courts may be important in explaining the willingness of major litigating organizations to turn to the states. In eminent domain (takings) law, the Court did not provide strong legal incentives to litigate in state courts. The Supreme Court has been active in developing takings jurisprudence since the late 1970s, and has expanded protections for individuals whose property is subject to government regulations. The Court has identified categories of regulations that always require compensation, has required that individuals whose property is taken (even for a temporary period) receive monetary awards, and has made it more difficult for governments to justify regulations that impose conditions on the use of private property. Thus, despite the fact that litigants must initiate certain takings claims in state courts, interest groups lack strong legal incentives to turn to the states. Under these circumstances, to what extent have interest groups participated in state takings litigation?

This chapter will show that the groups most active in U.S. Supreme Court takings cases rarely litigated at the state level. While many groups filed amicus curiae briefs in the Supreme Court, major litigating organizations active in this policy domain rarely ventured into state judiciaries. Further, property rights groups were reluctant to assert takings claims based on independent state constitutional grounds, instead relying on the Fifth Amendment. Property rights groups typically viewed state courts as less independent than federal courts and therefore less able to protect property rights. This perspective, coupled with the expansion of federal rights, provided little incentive for these organizations to seek greater protection through state constitutions.

The primary goal of this chapter is to explain why interest groups on both sides of the takings debate chose to litigate in state courts on an infrequent basis. The impact of legal incentives and organizational factors is explored to account for the lack of litigation. The principal reason that groups did not litigate regularly is the lack of a legal incentive to do so. The organizational threshold is important as well; some groups lacked the resources or organizational incentives to litigate at the state level. But groups operating in various organizational contexts all were reluctant to turn to state judiciaries. It appears that when the U.S. Supreme Court provides little incentive to turn to state courts and state constitutions, major litigating organizations may be unlikely to do so.

INTEREST GROUPS IN STATE TAKINGS CASES

Table 4.1 presents a comparison of interest group litigation in eminent domain cases in the United States Supreme Court and five state court systems. Groups participated in nearly 65 percent of the U.S. Supreme Court's cases. Virtually all of this participation was as amicus curiae, although occasionally groups sponsored litigation or were direct parties. For instance, attorneys from the Pacific Legal Foundation represented the plaintiffs in *Nollan v. California Coastal Commission* (1987). In the state judiciaries, groups litigated in only 7 percent of the eminent domain cases. When we examine only state supreme courts, that figure increases, but not considerably. Interest groups participated in less than one out of ten state supreme court cases.

Further examination presents a clearer picture of group involvement in takings litigation. Table 4.2 reveals interesting trends in interest group litigation. In the U.S. Supreme Court, the 1980s emerges as the decade in which takings litigation became most clearly politicized. This finding should not be surprising, since the Court reentered the regulatory takings arena in *Penn Central Transportation Co. v. New York City* (1978), addressing inverse condemnation seriously for the first time since the 1920s. The trend of heightened group litigation has continued into the 1990s. Another indicator of the increased politicization of takings litigation in the Court is the average number of organizations on each amicus curiae brief, which broken down by decade is: 1.14 in the 1960s, 1.71 in the 1970s, 3.41 in the 1980s, and 3.28 in the 1990s. These data reveal an increasingly dense group litigation environment in the past two decades.

Table 4.1
A Comparison of Interest Group Participation in Takings Litigation in the U.S. Supreme Court and Five State Courts, 1960–1994

	U.S. Supreme Court	State Court Systems	State Supreme Court Only
Percent of Cases with Group Participation	64.7%	7%	9.6%
Number of Cases with Group Participation	46	86	59
Total Number of Cases	71	1,236	616

Note: Figures refer to cases in the U.S. Supreme Court and the intermediate appellate and supreme courts of the five states in which an interest group participated as a party, counsel, or amicus curiae.

Table 4.2
Percentage of U.S. Supreme Court and State Court Takings Cases with Interest Group Participation by Decade, 1960–1994

	1960s	1970s	1980s	1990–1994
U.S. Supreme Court	15.3% (2 of 13)	43.8% (7 of 16)	85% (29 of 34)	100% (8 of 8)
State Courts	5.3% (16 of 302)	5.3% (21 of 429)	7.5% (26 of 346)	13.2% (21 of 159)

Note: Figures refer to cases in the U.S. Supreme Court and the intermediate appellate and supreme courts of the five states in which an interest group participated as a party, counsel, or amicus curiae.

In the state judiciaries, rates of group participation also increased, though the trend is more attenuated. As in the U.S. Supreme Court, interest group participation in state courts grew over the decades. Group involvement in state takings cases from 1990 to 1994 may indicate the start of a new, heightened level of activity, although it is difficult to draw firm conclusions from these data. The growing rates of group litigation provide one measure of an increasingly politicized policy area in both state and federal courts.

An examination of the types of parties that file amicus curiae briefs uncovers important differences between state and federal court litigation.[1] Following Epstein (1994), those filing amicus briefs are categorized as either groups, businesses/corporations, governments or groups representing governmental interests, or individuals/unidentified (Table 4.3 provides examples of each classification). Figure 4.1 reveals the identity of amicus participants in Supreme Court takings litigation. Groups and governmental interests dominate amicus filings, while businesses constitute only 6 percent of the amici.

Table 4.3
Classification Scheme for Amici Curiae

Classification	Examples
Business/Corporation	Rose Building Company South Carolina Gas & Electric, Inc. Chubb Insurance Company
Government	State of Colorado National League of Cities League of Minnesota Cities
Group	Pacific Legal Foundation Sierra Club American Planning Association of New Jersey
Unidentified	Amici reported without affiliation

The amicus participants in state courts differ markedly from those in the Supreme Court. Figure 4.2 shows these data. The most notable difference is that 31 percent of the amici in state takings cases are businesses or corporations, which is a much greater percentage than in U.S. Supreme Court cases. The relatively high rate of amicus participation by businesses in state courts is similar to Bowen's (1994) finding in sexual harassment litigation.

Figure 4.1
Identity of Amici in U.S. Supreme Court Takings Cases, 1960–1994

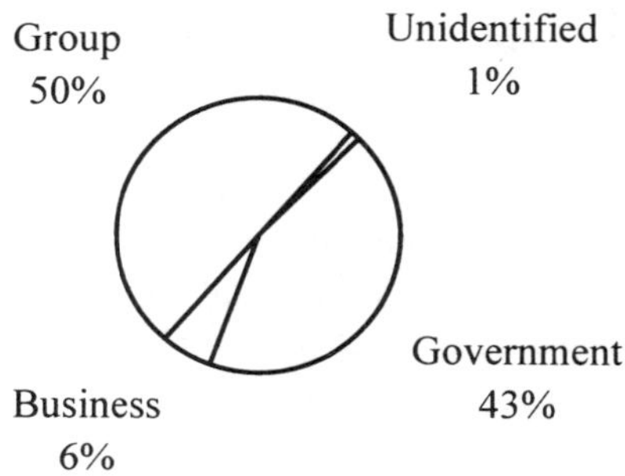

Note: N=1040.

Figure 4.2
Identity of Amici in State Court Takings Cases, 1960–1994

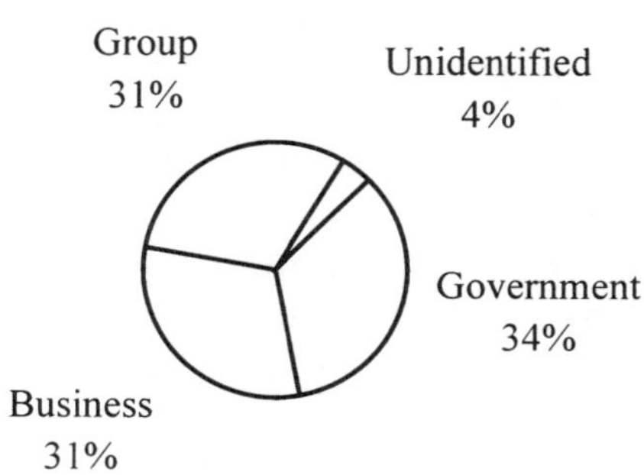

Note: N=167.

These data provide some insight into the characteristics of state court takings litigation. Most of the businesses, and some of the group litigants as well in state courts appear to be smaller businesses operating in that state.[2] In other words, the groups likely had a relatively direct stake in the outcome of a case and therefore filed the briefs.[3] Most groups only once entered state courts to face a specific, immediate threat. They did not participate in takings cases on a regular basis.

Furthermore, state takings cases typically do not present the novel and debated legal issues that the U.S. Supreme Court addressed regularly. Forty-eight percent of the state cases with group participation dealt with the direct condemnation of property, which are cases in which governments file eminent domain actions in court. Jurisprudence in this area of eminent domain law has not been strongly debated in recent decades. In contrast, virtually all of the cases in the U.S. Supreme Court dealt with claims of regulatory takings, in which property owners file suits challenging the validity of governmental regulations. Only two U.S. Supreme Court cases (4 percent) with group participation arose outside of the regulatory takings context.[4]

To summarize, compared to their federal court counterparts, many state appellate cases appear relatively routine. There are much lower rates of group participation in state takings cases. Even the observed rates of group litigation at the state level may overstate its importance. Much of the activity occurred in direct condemnation cases, not in the more controversial regulatory takings context. Furthermore, business organizations that only infrequently enter the litigation fray make up a much greater proportion of amici in state courts than in the U.S. Supreme Court. Of course, these data are suggestive and meant only to illustrate the context of federal and state takings litigation. But they do imply that the litigation environment in state takings cases is distinctly different from that in the federal courts.

These data provide a framework within which to examine the specific national organizations most active in takings litigation. Table 4.4 lists the groups that participated most often in takings litigation in the U.S. Supreme Court and the five states since 1960. In the Supreme Court, the Pacific Legal Foundation (PLF) has been more active than any other organized litigant, participating in seventeen cases. A variety of environmental organizations, including the Sierra Club and National Wildlife Federation, also participated in takings cases. In addition to litigating on the merits, some organizations also participate at the certiorari stage. The PLF, for example, regularly files amicus briefs asking the Court to accept and decide takings cases.

To what extent have these organizations also litigated in state courts? Table 4.4 shows that, save for a few instances, national organizations and their state or regional affiliates are notably absent from state judiciaries. The most frequent litigators before the U.S. Supreme Court either have never or only rarely participated in takings cases in the five states. In less than 1 percent of the cases, a total of twelve, did the major litigating organizations participate in state cases (see Appendix A). Given so few cases, there is little meaningful variation across states or across groups. But while there are few instances of national organizational participation in state takings cases, it is important to note that when these groups did enter the courts, they appear to have done so to address debated issues of law. Seventy-five percent (9 of 12) of the cases involved regulatory takings claims. More often than all group litigants, then, national organizations entered state courts to participate in regulatory takings litigation.

Table 4.4
Interest Groups Most Active in Takings Litigation, 1960–1994

Group	Number of Cases	
	U.S. Supreme Court	State Courts
Property Rights Groups		
Pacific Legal Foundation	17	1
National Association of Home Builders	7	2
National Realtors Association	7	0
Mountain States Legal Foundation	5	0
American Farm Bureau Federation	3	3
Pro-Regulation Groups		
National Audubon Society	9	0
Sierra Club	8	6
National Wildlife Federation	8	2
American Planning Association	8	2

Note: Figures refer to cases in the U.S. Supreme Court and the five states in which the interest groups participated as a party, counsel, or amicus curiae.

These data raise several important questions. First, why have the major litigating organizations seldom turned to state judiciaries? The analytic framework suggests that the paucity of litigation may be a function of either a lack of legal incentive to litigate at the state level or insufficient resources. Second, when the organizations did litigate, why did they do so? Low rates of participation may mask involvement in doctrinally important cases. In particular, have property rights groups turned to state courts to advance rights claims based on state constitutions that seek broader protection than that provided by the Fifth Amendment? Or are their forays into state courts a consequence instead of the federal restriction incentive, which suggests that groups litigate at the state level because they lack access to a federal court forum? Scholars and commentators have noted the emergence of distinct state constitutional decision making on takings issues (Caira 1992; Sullivan 1988). To what extent have organized interests been involved in these legal developments?

The remainder of this chapter examines the litigation activities of interest groups in a variety of organizational contexts. In addition to investigating the frequency of group litigation, this chapter examines why groups entered state courts and what arguments property rights organizations offered in litigation.

PROPERTY RIGHTS GROUPS

Purposive Organizations: Pacific Legal Foundation and Mountain States Legal Foundation

The Pacific Legal Foundation and Mountain States Legal Foundation (MSLF) are purposive organizations that support property rights and other conservative legal causes. They engage in litigation primarily for ideological reasons, rather than to represent the exclusive commercial or economic interests of a particular group. Since the PLF and MSLF are property rights groups, they have initiated takings suits, and therefore, their perspectives on state court litigation are particularly helpful for understanding patterns of participation in federal and state cases.

Both the PLF and MSLF are nonprofit law firms organized under I.R.C. 501(c)(3). Groups organized under 501(c)(3) carry a tax-exempt status, so contributions to the groups are tax deductible. However, Section 501(c)(3) includes a specific prohibition against lobbying Congress. Although groups may litigate and approach administrative agencies, there are strings attached. Litigation must be "'in representation of a broad public interest rather than a private interest' and the organization must not receive either fees for its services or court-awarded judgements that exceed half the organization's operating costs in the preceding five years" (Scheppele and Walker 1991, 163). Since they are barred from engaging in most other forms of traditional political lobbying, litigation generally is the sole formal lobbying tactic for 501(c)(3) groups, including the PLF and MSLF.

The PLF, founded in 1973, was the first conservative public interest law group formed in response to the growth and success of liberal groups in the previous decade (L. Epstein 1985). Ronald Zumbrun and Raymond Momboisse, founders of the organization, were members of then–California Governor Ronald Reagan's administration. The group was created to present to courts a different view of the public interest, one that opposes the perspectives of liberal public interest groups. The PLF has a particular interest in environmental litigation, an issue tied closely to the regulatory takings and property rights debates. It encourages courts to take a balanced approach to environmental and land use regulations, one that considers not only the public interest but also the rights of individual property owners.

The PLF is not a membership organization per se, though it claims the support of 20,000 individual and corporate donors. In 1994, it employed fifty staff members and had a budget of $4,000,000 (*Encyclopedia of Associations* 1994, 624), making it by far the largest of the regional public interest law firms. The PLF maintains litigation offices in Anchorage and Seattle, along with its Sacramento headquarters. Because the organization was the first conservative public interest legal foundation, it helped to create other purposive groups, including the Mountain States Legal Foundation (L. Epstein 1985).

The MSLF is a Colorado nonprofit organization devoted to initiating court cases dealing with issues "vital to the defense and preservation of individual liberties, the right to own and use property, limited government, and the free enterprise system" (MSLF amicus brief in *Lucas v. South Carolina Coastal Council* 1992, ii). MSLF was created in 1978 as a regional affiliate of the National Legal Center for the Public Interest (NLCPI). The PLF commissioned Leonard Theberge to investigate the need for other regional legal foundations. In 1975, he created NLCPI for the sole purpose of developing regional legal foundations throughout the country (Singer 1979).

Like many foundations established by NLCPI, MSLF no longer considers itself dependent on its parent organization (L. Epstein 1985). MSLF is most concerned with issues that affect its region of the country, focusing on land use and other environmental issues. Its president and chief legal officer, William Perry Pendley, documented the work of individuals and groups engaged in the "grassroots battle against environmental oppression" (Pendley 1994).

Both the PLF and MSLF view takings as an important issue.

> Pacific Legal Foundation . . . has litigated numerous cases from local courts to the United States Supreme Court in order to fight for the continuing vitality of the rights of property owners as found in the United States Constitution. [PLF] also has participated in numerous cases involving the takings implications of wetlands and other environmental regulations. [We have a] long-held interest in the protection of property rights. (Burling 1995, 1-2)

> PLF's concern . . . is that . . . government not interfere with constitutionally guaranteed private property rights and . . . when the federal government does take property, it pays just compensation as required by the Constitution. (PLF amicus brief in *Hodel v. Vir-*

ginia Surface Mining and Reclamation Association [1981, i])

MSLF is . . . greatly concerned with the erosion of private property rights taking place in the name of "environmental protection." (MSLF et al. amicus brief in *Lucas* [1992, i-iii])

Both groups, which rely on litigation as the sole formal political lobbying strategy, view takings as an organizational priority. Each organization has participated, primarily as amicus, in U.S. Supreme Court takings litigation. However, in the five states, the PLF was active in only one takings case, filing an amicus brief in the South Carolina Supreme Court in *Lucas v. South Carolina Coastal Council* (1991). The MSLF participated in no cases in these five states. What explains the lack of state litigation by the conservative legal foundations?

Since the PLF and MSLF both are concerned with the takings issue, it is necessary to examine organizational resources. Perhaps the lack of state court litigation reflects resource scarcity. The PLF was created in 1973, MSLF in 1978. For much of the time period under study, the organizations did not exist and thus could not have litigated. Yet the Supreme Court did not reinvigorate debate over regulatory takings until *Penn Central* (1978), so both groups have existed during virtually the entire time in which federal courts have addressed seriously regulatory takings issues.

Neither organization has an extensive network of affiliates, although the PLF does have litigation offices in Seattle and Anchorage. Both the MSLF and (to a lesser extent) the PLF tend to litigate primarily in distinct regions of the country. Computer searches and group files reveal that the majority of MSLF cases arise in federal or state courts in Colorado, Arizona, and New Mexico. Most PLF cases arise in California. Nevertheless, each group has entered state and lower federal court litigation nationwide,[5] in addition to arguing cases in the U.S. Supreme Court. Despite concentrating on regional disputes, then, the PLF and MSLF by no means are confined to those regions.

Both the PLF and the MSLF have a minimal litigation capacity, having entered state courts on a variety of legal questions other than takings.[6] Currently, the PLF has eleven staff attorneys; MSLF has four.[7] While this certainly allows them to enter the litigation fray, they are by no means abundant resources. PLF staff attorney James Burling complained that he is "increasingly frustrated of working in an office with attorneys who spend hours on the phone each week turning down cases from desperate property owners who have run out of everything except hope. After we tell them that we can only accept a small fraction of the cases of government abuse that comes across our desks, many run out of hope too" (Burling 1995, 14).

Even discounting for rhetorical excess, the evidence suggests that resource limitations do restrict the ability of the groups to litigate. It is also important to note that the PLF and MSLF seldom participate in the same case. Lee Epstein's (1985, 124) interviews with PLF officials reveal that "the PLF has 'seldom gone into litigation that other public interest law firms are doing because there's only a limited amount of manpower . . . when the same view is being presented.' . . . [T]he PLF follows the deliberate noncooperation tactic to avoid needless duplication of effort." To conserve scarce resources, the PLF and MSLF typically avoid entry into litigation when other actors present similar arguments to a court. This point, however, is most relevant for understanding federal, not state court litigation, because neither the PLF nor MSLF participated often at the state level, particularly in states examined here.

While resources certainly prevent the PLF and MSLF from entering litigation as often as they might like, resources do not provide the primary explanation for the fact that the foundations' forays into state courts are only occasional. Instead, my interviews and other evidence indicate that the paucity of group litigation is due principally to the lack of legal incentives to litigate at the state level. A staff attorney for the PLF noted that "we litigate in both federal and state courts. . . . Generally, federal courts are more independent and better protectors of property rights. If we could we'd bring all takings cases there. But we can't so we have to go to the state courts as well."[8] Paul Seby (1995) of the MSLF observed that most of the group's takings litigation has been in federal courts. He argued that federal courts are a better forum for the protection of property rights because "they are more distant from the actor [government] and therefore less subject to political pressure." According to Roger Marzulla (1995), former president of MSLF, "there has been abject failure in some state [courts]."

These statements provide important insights into the perspectives of the conservative legal foundations. The groups view federal courts as more protective of property rights than state judiciaries, and therefore they prefer to litigate takings cases at the federal level. Moreover, in my interviews, the group officials appeared to view all states as uniform in this regard. The officials did not distinguish among states, which is understandable since, as noted in the last chapter, state courts generally have not provided more expansive protection under their constitutions' takings clauses than is available under federal standards. The context of state (vis-à-vis federal) judicial policy making appears to have provided the conservative legal foundations little incentive to focus their litigation activities on state judiciaries.

Examination of the PLF's patterns of litigation on takings generally supports the preference for federal court litigation. In addition to participation in seventeen U.S. Supreme Court cases, the PLF has been involved in numerous lower federal court cases.[9] To be sure, PLF has litigated in state courts as well,[10] although it is important to note that more than half (10 of 19) of these cases were in California and Washington, two states in which the PLF has litigation offices. Given that PLF occasionally has to litigate in state courts (an issue to which I return to shortly), it overcomes the organizational obstacles associated with state litigation by participating where it has the relevant resources, namely a formal organizational presence and access to attorneys. Resources do help to explain the PLF's litigation patterns.

The MSLF's preference for federal court litigation is even more apparent in its behavior. The group litigated only two takings cases nationwide in state appellate courts,[11] compared to many more in lower federal courts.[12] In sum, my interviews suggest that the groups preferred to litigate takings claims in federal rather than state courts, and the out-of-sample evidence reveals behavior consistent with this preference.

In addition to preferring federal to state courts, the property rights groups distinguished among federal tribunals, noting a preference for the Claims Court over other federal courts. Seby (1995) viewed the Claims Court's jurisprudence as better developed than that of the U.S. Supreme Court. According to Roger Marzulla (1995), "federal court is not a monolith. We anticipate greater success in Claims Court than from district courts." He has written that "the Claims Court, almost alone among judicial tribunals in this country, has intuitively understood the importance of the *ad hoc* factual inquiry prescribed by the Supreme Court for regulatory takings cases" (Marzulla and Marzulla (1991, 550).[13]

Because the Claims Court hears only cases for monetary damages against the federal government, the MSLF and PLF seldom litigate in this tribunal. Still, occasionally they have participated in the Claims Court and the U.S. Court of Appeals for the Federal Circuit, which typically hears appeals from the Court of Claims.[14]

To summarize, my interviews suggest that the lack of a legal incentive is important in explaining why the PLF and MSLF litigated infrequently in state courts. The organizations viewed federal courts and federal law as more protective of property rights. Staff attorneys also believed that state courts typically are too close to state governments and insufficiently independent to protect the rights of property owners against what they believe are governmental infringements. Thus, for property rights organizations, federal courts have a double advantage. Not only do their precedents apply more broadly than those of state judiciaries, but also they are a more receptive forum for property rights claims.

This is not to suggest that the Supreme Court's takings jurisprudence completely pleases these organizations. On the contrary, Seby (1995) views the decisions as undeveloped and incoherent. Nevertheless, the PLF and MSLF prefer federal to state court forums to assert takings claims.

If the PLF and MSLF prefer to press takings claims in federal courts, then why do they enter state courts even occasionally? The Supreme Court's procedural rules appear to explain the groups' forays into state judiciaries. Seby (1995) noted that the MSLF prefers to litigate in federal court on all issues, but takings is unique because "when a state regulates property, cases aren't ripe for federal court until you get the last word from the state supreme court. To make the cases ripe … we have to go through state courts … it's frustrating." According to a PLF staff attorney: "if we could we'd bring all takings cases there [federal courts]. But we can't, so we have to go to the state courts as well."[15] These comments suggest that the groups were motivated primarily by the federal restriction incentive. The groups turned to state courts because the Supreme

Court's ripeness requirements demand that state procedures be exhausted before federal jurisdiction is granted. When a takings dispute arises in the context of state or local regulations, the groups have no choice but to bring the case at the state level.

The arguments that the PLF and MSLF offered in state takings litigation further support the conclusion that the federal restriction incentive, rather than the new judicial federalism incentive, motivated their entry into state courts. In *Lucas* (1991), the PLF filed an amicus brief in the South Carolina Supreme Court, arguing only on federal constitutional (Fifth and Fourteenth Amendment) grounds that the state's regulation of Lucas's property resulted in a taking and therefore required just compensation. As authority, the PLF cited only federal court cases. The PLF sought to shape federal—not state—constitutional law. It was motivated by the federal restriction incentive.

An examination of the PLF and MSLF's participation in takings cases in other states provides further evidence to support this conclusion. When in state courts, the property rights groups argued primarily on federal constitutional grounds.[16] The only state takings case nationwide in which PLF attorneys based a taking claim solely on state constitutional grounds is *Dodd v. Hood River County* (1993, 1992). They did not assert federal constitution arguments because the plaintiffs represented by the PLF reserved their federal takings claim for a related action pending in federal court.

To summarize, the conservative legal foundations preferred to litigate in federal courts because of the receptivity of federal courts and the federal constitution to takings claims and the view that state courts are institutionally incapable of protecting property rights. Without a clear legal incentive to litigate in state courts, the MSLF and PLF have seldom done so, save for the latter's participation in California and Washington. In most instances, the groups waited until cases originated in state courts were appealed to the U.S. Supreme Court, though both the MSLF and the PLF also turned occasionally to state courts to pursue their policy goals and to make cases ripe for Supreme Court review. These forays in state judiciaries are a result of the federal restriction incentive, since property owners must initiate compensation claims against state and local governments in state court.

Material Group: American Farm Bureau Federation

Not all of the property rights organizations are purposive groups. Unlike the PLF and MSLF, the American Farm Bureau Federation (AFBF) is a material organization. It enters the political arena primarily to represent the exclusive economic and commercial interests of its members. The AFBF was formed in 1919 as a nonprofit voluntary organization whose stated purpose is to "preserve, protect, promote, and represent the business, economic, social, and educational interests of American farmers and ranchers" (AFBF amicus brief in *Lucas* 1992,

1-2). The organization claims to represent almost four million member families.

Due to the farming industry's close ties to land, the AFBF retains a particular interest in property rights issues, including eminent domain law. The group asserts that its members "own or lease significant amounts of property, and depend on their land for their livelihoods." As a result, they are "vitally interested in the property interpretation of the Just Compensation Clause of the United States Constitution" (AFBF amicus brief in *Lucas* 1992, 2).

Officials in state affiliates suggest that takings is among the most important issues for the group in recent years.

> This is one of the most important issues for farmers in South Carolina. (Peter Gustafson [1995], South Carolina Farm Bureau Federation)

> There is more at stake in the takings debate for farmers than for most others. . . . The single most important issue is to get the highest and best use of the land. (Ray Christianson [1995], Colorado Farm Bureau Federation)

The AFBF has been active particularly in the legislative debate over takings; it is a leading proponent of takings bills at both the state and national levels. The South Carolina Farm Bureau, for example, helped to write a property rights bill that was introduced in the state legislature in 1995. The bill required, among other things, that state regulatory agencies formally consider the property rights implications of their activities. Affiliates in Indiana and Colorado have helped to write similar bills that have been introduced in their state legislatures.

Yet despite the importance of the takings issue for AFBF and its affiliates, the group litigates only occasionally. It has filed amicus briefs in three U.S. Supreme Court cases and participated in only two takings cases in lower federal courts.[17] In the five states, the organization participated in three cases—two regulatory takings cases in New Jersey and one direct condemnation case in Colorado. Given its concern with property rights and takings, why has the Farm Bureau not litigated more often, particularly at the state level? The primary explanation appears to focus on organizational goals and resources.

The AFBF has affiliates in all fifty states. The formal organizational presence makes the group well situated to track local litigation. Indeed, on a variety of legal issues, there is some evidence of litigation by the group in each of the five states, except Minnesota.[18] But closer examination of the organization reveals that state affiliates lack the specific resource most important for litigation—attorneys. Most of the affiliates do not have litigation departments or staff attorneys. The sole exception in these five states is the Indiana Farm Bureau, which since the mid-1980s has had a full-time general counsel. Notice that since that time, the Indiana affiliate litigated more often than the others.

My interviews suggest that the organization's limited litigation resources are related closely to the relatively low priority the Farm Bureau affiliates assign to litigation as a political tactic.

We don't have a litigation department. In fact, we almost never get involved in litigation. Occasionally, we retain counsel on a case-by-case basis when the need arises. Most litigation concerns national issues, and the American Farm Bureau takes care of that. (Ray Christianson [1995], Colorado Farm Bureau Federation)

We don't litigate often. We go to court only when we have to. (Peter Gustafson [1995], South Carolina Farm Bureau)

We don't litigate very much. Sometimes we will file a friend of the court brief, but that's all. We leave it [litigation] to the national [office]. (Group Official, New Jersey Farm Bureau Federation)[19]

Group officials at the AFBF affiliates do not view litigation as a principal organizational activity. This analysis illustrates the relationship between organizational goals and resources. Because litigation is not a priority for affiliates of the Farm Bureau, they do not have the resources (namely, a litigation office and staff or cooperating attorneys) needed for consistent litigation. Most litigation is conducted by the national office.

In contrast to the PLF and MSLF, the AFBF is a material organization that engages in a variety of political and nonpolitical activities. It does not focus solely on political lobbying, nor does it exist primarily to litigate. Because it represents the commercial and economic interests of its member farmers, it generally enters litigation only when those interests are directly at stake. The group's justification for filing amicus briefs in the U.S. Supreme Court illustrates this:

The American Farm Bureau Federation and the South Carolina Farm Bureau Federation [SCFBF] have a direct interest in the outcome of this case. The members of AFBF and SCFBF own or lease significant amounts of property, and depend on their land for their livelihoods. They are, therefore, vitally interested in the proper interpretation of the Just Compensation Clause of the United States Constitution. The South Carolina Supreme Court's expansion of the circumstances in which a state may effectively dispossess an owner of his or her property without paying compensation is contrary to the interests of AFBF, SCFBF, and their members. (AFBF, SCFBF amicus brief in *Lucas* [1992, 2])

Many of those who are directly affected by Rails-to-Trails, both in Vermont and throughout the country, are farmers. (AFBF, Vermont Farm Bureau Federation amicus brief in *Preseault v. I.C.C.* [1990, 2])

The group's entry into state takings cases shows that the organization mobilized when a case had a relatively direct impact on the Farm Bureau's members. In *Grand Land Company v. Township of Bethlehem* (1984), the New Jersey Farm Bureau filed an amicus brief in a state supreme court case challenging the validity of a zoning ordinance that conditioned subdivision approval on an involuntary reservation of land within the subdivision for agricultural use.[20] *New Jersey Builders Association v. Dept. of Environmental Protection* (1979) challenged state regulations that established certain water quality standards. The

Farm Bureau argued that the water quality standards affected farmers' ability to use and dispose of nitrate and phosphates from fertilizers. Finally, in *City of Thorton v. Farmers Reservoir & Irrigation Co.* (1978), the Colorado Farm Bureau challenged the authority of a city to condemn certain water and ditch rights that affected the distribution of water to area farmers. The decisions in each of these cases would have clear and direct impact on the agricultural interests represented by the Farm Bureau.

To summarize, litigation is not a priority for the AFBF, as it is for the PLF or MSLF. As a material organization, the AFBF and its affiliates enter the courts only when their members' interests are affected directly. This occasionally leads the group into court, but by and large the organization has not been active in state takings litigation.

PRO-REGULATION GROUPS

Purposive Groups: Sierra Club and National Wildlife Federation

Examination of the litigation activities of pro-regulation organizations focuses on the two environmental groups most active in the state judiciaries, the Sierra Club and National Wildlife Federation (NWF). Since these groups generally support governmental interests in eminent domain disputes, they do not initiate takings claims and typically (although not always) participate as amicus curiae in takings litigation. Both organizations view the expanded protection for property rights as a threat to a variety of governmental regulations dealing with environmental protection, conservation, and natural resource management.

The Sierra Club litigated in state takings cases more often than any other national organization, yet this still amounts to only six cases in the five states. Furthermore, the group participated in only two states: four cases in Minnesota and two in South Carolina (see Appendix A). Two of the cases in Minnesota involved the direct condemnation of property; the remaining cases dealt with regulatory takings claims. The NWF has been less active in state takings litigation. Only in South Carolina, in *Lucas* (1991) and *Beard v. South Carolina Coastal Council* (1991), has the Wildlife Federation joined in takings cases. I examine the legal and organizational contexts to explain why these organizations have been relatively inactive in state takings litigation.

The Sierra Club is a nonprofit conservation organization of approximately 650,000 members. It was formed in 1892 for purposes that include "the exploration, enjoyments, and preservation of scenic and natural resources and to enlist public interest and cooperation in the protection of such resources" (Sierra Club amicus brief in *Lucas* 1992, 1). The Sierra Club engages in a wide array of political actions; the group attempts to "influence public policy at all governmental levels through legislative, administrative, legal, and electoral means" (*Encyclopedia of Associations* 1994, 466). The organization has affiliates in all states as well as numerous regional and local groups.

Although not technically part of the organization, the Sierra Club Legal Defense Fund, Inc. (LDF) was founded in 1971 to provide legal representation for public interest groups and individuals involved primarily in environmental litigation. The LDF is a 501(c)(3) organization that spends three-fourths of its budget on litigation (O'Connor and Epstein 1989, 186). Its principal client—not surprisingly—is its parent organization, the Sierra Club, but the LDF does bring litigation on behalf of other environmental organizations as well.

The Sierra Club is a purposive organization that typically opposes takings litigation and legislation because they affect the ability of governments at all levels to regulate for a variety of reasons, including environmental protection.

> The Sierra Club nationwide is concerned with the takings issue because we see this as an effort to elevate the property rights of one individual over the property rights of the community at large. And we see this as a threat to regulations, specifically environmental regulations, or any regulations for the public health and safety. (Sandra Eid [1995], Legislative Coordinator, Sierra Club, Rocky Mountain Chapter)

> Takings is an attempt to eviscerate environmental laws. (Brett Smith [1995], Conservation Coordinator, Sierra Club of Minnesota)

At least in recent years, takings has become a critical issue for the Sierra Club. The group's interest is illustrated not only by its participation in U.S. Supreme Court litigation but also by the activity of state groups opposing takings legislation. Sandra Eid (1995) of the Rocky Mountain (Colorado) Chapter of the Sierra Club asserted that "takings has been the single most important issue for the Sierra Club in the last three years." Indeed, a 1995 poll of Sierra Club affiliates indicated that one of the top three priorities of the state organizations was to counter the property rights movement, which relies heavily on takings litigation and legislation to achieve its goals (Smith 1995).[21] Not only in these five state, then, but also nationwide, takings issues and countering the property rights movement more generally are important to the Sierra Club.

The National Wildlife Federation (NWF) was founded in 1936 as a federation of state and territorial conservation organizations. Its purpose is to encourage "the intelligent management of the life-sustaining resources of the earth and [promote] greater appreciation of these resources, their community relationship, and wise use" (*Encyclopedia of Associations* 1994, 457). To that end, the NWF engages in a variety of activities ranging from lobbying the federal government to educational programs such as Ranger Rick Wildlife Camps for children. The group focuses on education and related projects; litigation is only a small (but important) part of its work (O'Connor and Epstein 1989, 157). It also monitors federal agencies that implement environmental legislation and regulations. The NWF claims over 6,000,000 members and has regional affiliates and chapters in most, although not all, states.

Like Sierra Club, the NWF is a purposive group that opposes the expanded use of regulatory takings because of its potential impact on environmental regulations. Given its concern for environmental and conservation issues, the National Wildlife Federation has been among the most frequently active pro-regulation organizations involved in takings litigation. According to one staff member, "Takings is a very important issue . . . one of the most important" (Jerman 1995). Indeed, group literature includes among a list of six issue priorities, "defeating cynical 'Takings' proposals which threaten citizens' ability to protect their health, their safety and the value of their property." Similarly, according to officials in the Mid-Atlantic Office (which includes both New Jersey and South Carolina), "[our] primary issues are water quality and wetlands, takings, and land use planning."[22] The NWF views takings as a priority issue, one that implicates many of the group's specific policy concerns.

To summarize, both the Sierra Club and NWF believe that the property rights movement poses a threat to the continued vitality of environmental and other regulations. The Supreme Court's expanded protection for property rights claims in regulatory takings cases has helped to mobilize these organizations in opposition to the property rights movement. The groups view takings as a critical issue. They have entered U.S. Supreme Court litigation, although their forays into state judiciaries have been much rarer. Given the importance of the takings issue to the Sierra Club and NWF, why have they seldom entered state courts?

One possible explanation is that the groups lack the resources to enter state courts more often. However, an examination of organizational resources shows that the Sierra Club has greater resources relevant to state court litigation than any other organization active in takings cases. The group has affiliates in each state as well as fifteen regional affiliates. The state affiliates tend to state and local issues, while the regional groups work closely with the national organization on national issues.

While most state affiliates (and all in the five states examined here) have no permanent staff attorneys, the affiliates do have volunteer legal committees that advise the organization on legal matters, including entry into litigation. The Sierra Club also has access to attorneys from numerous sources. The national organization itself has only two litigating staff attorneys. However, the Sierra Club Legal Defense Fund (LDF), with approximately thirty attorneys, provides counsel for roughly a quarter of the Sierra Club's cases. In addition to the LDF, other public interest environmental organizations, such as the Western Environmental Law Center and the Natural Resources Defense Council, provide attorneys for Sierra Club litigation. Finally, "at least 50" volunteer attorneys nationwide provide pro bono services for the organization, accounting for "35 to 40 percent" of the group's work.[23] Minnesota's chapter, for instance, has local attorneys who occasionally volunteer time and other resources to litigation. Volunteer attorneys represented the Sierra Club in *Central Baptist Theological Seminary v. City of New Brighton* (1992). In short, the Sierra Club has considerable access to attorneys when it is necessary to litigate.

Thus, the Sierra Club has a formal presence at all levels of government and, although it does not have permanent staff attorneys in each state, the group has access to numerous lawyers, particularly compared to other organizations active in takings litigation. Evidence of group participation on legal questions other than takings confirms the group's capacity to litigate in state courts. Save for Indiana, the Sierra Club has litigated often in each state.[24]

The NWF, too, has considerable litigation resources. NWF has state and regional affiliates, although it does not have a formal organizational presence in every state. Of the five examined here, it has an affiliate in each state except New Jersey. The state affiliates have neither permanent staff attorneys nor legal committees. Nationwide, however, the NWF has eighteen staff attorneys, including three general staff and fifteen in-house environmental specialists. About half of these attorneys are actually involved in litigation. The attorneys generally work in the national office and regional affiliates.[25] Like the Sierra Club, the NWF has links with attorneys from other environmental organizations. Indeed, the NWF and Sierra Club often join litigation together. For example, in South Carolina courts, the groups litigated together in *Lucas v. South Carolina Coastal Council* (1991) and *Beard v. South Carolina Coastal Council* (1991). James Chandler of the South Carolina Environmental Law Project represented the organizations. Major law firms provide pro bono assistance to the NWF, accounting for slightly less than a quarter of the group's work.[26]

While NWF's resources are substantial, they are not as great as those of the Sierra Club. Nevertheless, the NWF does enter both federal and state court litigation. Like Sierra Club, the NWF has litigated on other issues in each of the states except Indiana.[27] Although it does not litigate as often as the Sierra Club, the National Wildlife Federation does appear to have the capacity to participate in state litigation on a regular basis.

To summarize, given that the Sierra Club and NWF both view takings as a priority issue and appear to have the resources to litigate in state courts on a regular basis, the organizational threshold does not appear to provide the principal explanation for the lack of state court litigation on takings. Consequently, our attention turns to the legal context.

When asked why their organization does not litigate often in takings cases, the following responses are illustrative:

> Except for *Lucas*, we haven't litigated on takings because nothing is ripe [but] the National Wildlife Federation has been involved in many cases. (Trish Jerman [1995], South Carolina Wildlife Federation)[28]

> On takings, we lack good issues to litigate. Many cases don't clearly present a takings question. And the takings cases that affect us most are in the Supreme Court. (Brett Smith [1995], Sierra Club of Minnesota)

> There are a number of cases that we are involved in right now. There are usually a number of cases [but] we're not litigating in Colorado on takings . . . there aren't any high

profile cases on takings. In federal court, however, the national organization has litigated. (Sandra Eid [1995], Sierra Club Rocky Mountain [Colorado] Chapter)

The interviews suggest that affiliates of the Sierra Club and NWF did not typically become active in state cases because there were few important cases in which the takings issue was ripe and presented clearly. The groups recognized that the most important takings cases were conducted by the national organizations in the U.S. Supreme Court. There is no evidence that the environmental groups actively sought to avoid state litigation. Instead, the Sierra Club and NWF seldom entered takings cases because there was no pressing need to do so. Since the U.S. Supreme Court consistently has addressed regulatory takings issues in recent years, pro-regulation organizations appeared willing to wait for high-profile cases to be heard by the U.S. Supreme Court.

When the Sierra Club and NWF did enter state cases, it was because the cases directly involved policies important to the organizations. Trish Jerman noted that the South Carolina Wildlife Federation entered the *Lucas* case primarily to protect the Beachfront Management Act, the application of which Lucas claimed resulted in a taking of his property. The Sierra Club and South Carolina Wildlife Federation justified their amicus brief in the South Carolina Supreme Court by noting: "Both of these groups have been active in South Carolina's coastal management process, participating in the promulgation of Coastal Council regulations, commenting on permit applications, and exercising other opportunities for pubic input into the regulatory process" (Sierra Club and South Carolina Wildlife Federation amicus brief in *Lucas* [1991, 1]). Similarly, the Sierra Club filed an amicus brief in *Central Baptist* (1992), noting

The Environmental Groups believe this case raises important and far reaching issues of public interest involving environmental and wetland protection, management, preservation and conservation; [t]he importance to the State of Minnesota of the preservation of the environment in general, and the wetlands specifically, is well established. The public interests in preserving wetlands and the environment and preventing their impairment are of paramount concern. (Sierra Club et al. amicus brief in *Central Baptist* [1992, 1, 16-17])

This analysis is not meant to suggest that the organizational threshold is unimportant. Goals and resources also help to explain the groups' involvement in takings cases. Though both the Sierra Club and National Wildlife Federation are concerned with the takings issue generally, they assign greater importance to cases that affect environmental or conservation policies. For these organizations, takings cases that arise in fact situations unrelated to environmental policies are less important.[29]

Further, group officials acknowledged that limited resources did affect their organizations' ability to litigate.

There are things that could be resolved through litigation, but we simply don't have the money. (Trish Jerman [1995], South Carolina Wildlife Federation)

We lack legal resources and good issues to litigate. (Brett Smith [1995], Sierra Club of Minnesota)

Indeed, the groups have been involved in relatively few lower federal court takings cases.[30]

To summarize, while the evidence is mixed, the lack of a legal incentive appears to provide an important explanation as to why the Sierra Club and NWF have litigated infrequently in state takings cases. While both groups, particularly the Sierra Club, have been active in state judiciaries on a variety of issues, they seldom participated in takings cases. They had the organizational capacity to litigate but little incentive to participate regularly in state litigation.

DISCUSSION

The most convincing evidence for the importance of the lack of a legal incentive in explaining the paucity of interest group litigation emerges in a comparative analysis of the organizations examined in this chapter. Despite significant variations in the organizational setting, particularly resources (see Table 4.5), there is little variation in the frequency with which the groups participated in state takings cases. Each group litigated at nearly the same, low rate in the five states. Though the Sierra Club has much greater resources than the AFBF or the PLF, for example, it has not litigated significantly more often than these property rights organizations. The absence of a legal incentive, the only factor common to all the groups, explains why each seldom participated in state courts. No organization had an incentive to litigate consistently at the state level.

Obviously, organizational factors are also necessary to explain the observed patterns of litigation. The Sierra Club, which had greater litigation resources than the other groups examined in this chapter, did litigate most often. Goals and resources are important in explaining the AFBF's infrequent forays into both federal and state courts. Yet while the low priority assigned to litigation and lack of resources explain why the AFBF has been inactive in state courts, these factors do not explain why purposive groups with much greater resources have been equally inactive. The absence of a legal incentive to turn to state courts primarily accounts for the lack of variation in patterns of litigation across groups. Interview evidence, case analysis, and comparative analysis all support this conclusion.

CONCLUSION

Two general conclusions emerge from the analysis in this chapter. First, lacking a clear legal incentive, major litigating groups active in takings cases seldom entered state judiciaries. The U.S. Supreme Court in recent years has taken renewed interest in regulatory takings cases and has expanded the rights of property owners whose private property is affected by government regulations. Unlike other areas of law, the Supreme Court has not relegated many of the important legal questions to lower federal and state courts. Consequently, from the perspective of national organizations, most state cases are not especially vital.

Table 4.5
Resources of Interest Groups Active in Takings Litigation

Group	State Affiliates?	Staff Attorneys	Volunteer Attorneys
PLF	No	11	0
MSLF	No	4	0
AFBF	Yes	2	0
Sierra Club	Yes	32	50
NWF	Yes[a]	18	15

[a]NWF has affiliates in each of the give states except New Jersey.

Key:

PLF Pacific Legal Foundation
MSLF Mountain States Legal Foundation
AFBF American Farm Bureau Federation
NWF National Wildlife Federation

Sources: Interviews with interest group officials; group files; *Encyclopedia of Associations* (various years). Figures for cooperating attorneys represent approximate numbers.

The quantitative analysis presented at the beginning of this chapter lends some support to the groups' perspective that most takings cases in state appellate courts are not particularly important. Many of the cases with group participation arose in the less controversial context of the direct condemnation of property. While these cases, taken together, certainly had important consequences for public policy, they did not address debated questions of regulatory takings jurisprudence. Further, a large proportion of group activity in state courts consists of governmental or business interests that have a direct stake in the outcome of the case.

The second conclusion from this chapter is that when property rights organizations brought takings claims in state courts, they were motivated by the federal restriction incentive. They turned to these tribunals primarily because the Supreme Court requires that compensation claims against state or local governments be brought in state courts before they are ripe for federal review. The PLF and MSLF viewed federal courts and federal law as more protective of the interests of private property owners. They considered state judiciaries too closely tied to state governments and therefore unable to protect vigorously the rights of property owners.[31] The significance of these views is that in the few instances that the PLF and MSLF entered state courts, they asserted primarily federal, not state, constitutional arguments.

The implications of these findings are intriguing. Certainly, legal mobilization requires resources. Scholars have suggested that the "haves" are better able to mobilize the law to protect their interests (Galanter 1974). While my findings in no way dispute this proposition, they show that the reality of state court litigation is somewhat more complex. Interests that *do not* mobilize the law are not necessarily *unable* to do so. While it is often difficult to determine precisely why groups do or do not enter cases, there are other reasons why they may not participate consistently in state litigation.

In particular, legal precedent did not provide incentives for major litigating organizations to participate in state courts. My interviews suggest that the lack of legal mobilization by many interest groups resulted largely from a voluntary choice not to enter takings cases regularly. Interestingly, however, the Sierra Club and NWF had greater resources relevant to state litigation than did the property rights groups. When cases implicated their concerns, the environmental organizations appeared to possess the capacity to participate consistently in the judicial process.

My findings also have implications for the continued politicization of state courts and the development of state constitutional law. While state courts have become more important policy actors and rates of group litigation have increased, the willingness of interest groups to enter state judiciaries on a regular basis likely varies greatly across issues areas, and depends in large part on Supreme Court precedent. Where Supreme Court decisions do not provide sufficient incentives, as in takings law, forays by national organizations into state courts may remain sporadic.

Property rights groups have been loath to rely on state constitutions to assert regulatory takings claims against state and local governments. Given that the U.S. Supreme Court, interpreting the federal Constitution, has expanded the rights of citizens whose private property is affected by government regulations, groups have taken advantage of an emerging federal doctrine to push for greater protection under the Fifth Amendment's Takings Clause. With the emergence of broader federal protection, organized interests have not needed to rely on takings clauses in state constitutions as a basis for rights claims. The PLF and MSLF did invoke state constitutional law in some cases, but almost always they appended the state law claims to their primary federal constitutional claims. The groups never provided a state court with an invitation to interpret its takings clause as more protective than required by the Fifth Amendment.

The analysis of takings law has demonstrated that regardless of their resources, national organizations did not litigate frequently in state courts when they lacked a legal incentive. But do groups turn to the states when such incentives are present? We explore this question in the next part of the book by examining obscenity law. Unlike takings, obscenity law has provided groups asserting rights claims with considerable incentive to turn to the states. In the next chapter, I examine obscenity law and identify the emergence of those legal incentives as a consequence of the U.S. Supreme Court's landmark decision in *Miller v. California* (1973).

NOTES

1. Although amicus filings do not capture all types of group participation, the briefs are useful in lending insight into the differing litigation environments in state and federal appellate courts.

2. For example, amicus briefs were filed by the Chubb Insurance Company of New Jersey in *In re Plan for Orderly Withdrawal* (1991), the Belfer Development Corporation in *State v. Carroll* (1991), the NCNB Bank of South Carolina in *Lucas v. South Carolina Coastal Council* (1991), the Bessemer Irrigation Ditch Company in *Jacobucci v. District Court in and for Jefferson* (1975), and the Rose Building Corporation in *Hendrickson v. State* (1964).

3. In her study of group participation in sexual harassment litigation, Bowen (1994) provides a similar interpretation of comparable data.

4. The cases are *National Railroad Passenger Corp. v. Boston and Maine Corp.* (1992) and *Hawaii Housing Authority v. Midkiff* (1984).

5. See, for example, *Miller Brothers v. Department of Natural Resources* (1994); *Lucas v. South Carolina Coastal Council* (1991); *Graham v. Estuary Properties, Inc.* (1981); *Loveladies Harbor, Inc. v. U.S.* (1994); *Stupak-Thrall v. U.S.* (1994); *Noranda Explorations Inc. v. Ostrom* (1983).

6. The PLF's state court participation includes *Graham v. Estuary Properties, Inc.* (1981); *Batch v. Town of Chapel Hill* (1990); *Robinson v. City of Seattle* (1992); and *Miller Brothers v. Department of Natural Resources* (1994). For the MSLF, see *Mountain States Legal Foundation v. Apache County* (1985); *In re City of Aurora* (1990); *Miller Brothers v. Department of Natural Resources* (1994); and *Noranda Explorations Inc. v. Ostrom* (1983).

7. Source: Interest group files; interviews with group officials. For at least some of the period under study, the MSLF had more than four staff attorneys. Lee Epstein (1985, 126) notes that in the early 1980s, MSLF had "more than five" attorneys.

8. Telephone conversation with author. The staff attorney requested anonymity.

9. *Golden Gate Hotel Association v. City and County of San Francisco* (1994); *Florida Rock Industries v. U.S.* (1994, 1986); *Dodd v. Hood River County* (1995); *Loveladies Harbor, Inc. v. U.S.* (1994); *Lockary v. Kayfetz* (1990, 1984); *Azul Pacifico, Inc. v. City of Los Angeles* (1991); *Shelter Creek Development Corp. v. City of Oxnard* (1988); *Associated Builders & Contractors v. Baca* (1991); *M.J. Brock & Sons v. City of Davis* (1975).

10. *Morehart v. County of Santa Barbara* (1994); *Littoral Development Co. v. San Francisco Bay Conservation Commission* (1995); *Antoine v. California Coastal Com.* (1992); *Sparks v. Douglas County* (1995); *Buechel v. State Dept. of Ecology* (1994); *Guimont v. Clarke* (1993); *Margola Associates v. City of Seattle* (1993); *Sintra, Inc. v. City of Seattle* (1992); *Robinson v. City of Seattle* (1992); *Tampa-Hillsborough City Expressway Auth. v. A.G.W.S. Corp.* (1994); *Miller Brothers v. Dept. of Natural Resources* (1994); *Manocherian v. Lenox Hospital* (1994); *Rent Stabilization Assn. v. Higgins* (1993, 1990); *Seawall Associates v. City of New York* (1989); *520 East 81st St. Assoc. v. Lenox Hill Hospital* (1990); *Dodd v. Hood River County* (1993, 1992); *Dolan v. City of Tigard* (1993); *Lucas v. South Carolina Coastal Council* (1991).

11. *Miller Brothers v. Dept. of Natural Resources* (1994); *Suess Builders Co. v. City of Beaverton* (1982).

12. *Mountain States Legal Foundation v. Hodel* (1986); *Stupak-Thrall v. U.S.* (1995, 1994); *U.S. v. Jenks* (1994); *Mountain States Legal Foundation v. Clark* (1984); *Wyoming Trucking Association Inc. v. Bentsen* (1995); *Mountain States Legal Foundation v. Espy* (1993); *Sierra Club v. Watt* (1985); *Ptasynski v. U.S.* (1982); *City and County of Denver v. Bergland* (1981); *Utah v. Andrus* (1979). In addition, the MSLF filed amicus briefs in five U.S. Supreme Court cases.

13. Nancie G. Marzulla, former staff attorney for the MSLF, now heads Defenders of Property Rights, an organization formed in 1991, which claims to be the only nationwide legal foundation devoted solely to the protection of property rights.

14. For example, the PLF filed amicus briefs in *Florida Rock* (1994, 1986) and *Whitney Benefits v. U.S.* (1991).

15. The staff attorney requested anonymity.

16. See *Miller Brothers* (1994); *Suess Builders Co. v. City of Beaverton* (1982), *Rent Stabilization Assn. v. Higgins* (1993); *Dolan v. City of Tigard* (1993); *Robinson v. City of Seattle* (1992); *Antoine v. California Coastal Commission* (1992).

17. The AFBF and Missouri Farm Bureau Federation filed an amicus brief in *Glosemeyer v. Missouri-Kansas-Texas Railroad* (1989), as did the California Farm Bureau Federation in *Rank v. Krug* (1956).

18. In Colorado: *People v. Emmert* (1979); *In re City of Aurora* (1990). In Indiana: *State ex rel. Firestone v. Parke Circuit Court* (1993); *Welsh v. Sells* (1963); *CSX Transp., Inc. v. Clark* (1995); *Laux v. Chopin Land Associates* (1990, 1989); *Shatto v. McNulty* (1987). In New Jersey: *Switz v. Kingsley* (1962); *South Harrison v. Board of Chosen Freeholders of Gloucester* (1986); *Township of Bass River v. Hogwallow Inc.* (1982); *Vasquez v. Glassboro Service Association* (1978). In South Carolina: *State Dairy Commission of South Carolina v. Pet, Inc.* (1984); *South Carolina Farm Bureau v. Scott* (1980); *Clemson University v. First Provident Corp.* (1973).

19. This official requested anonymity.

20. The Farm Bureau also sought to participate in oral argument, but was denied leave.

21. The other two priority issues are to protect wetlands and to protect endangered species. Regulatory takings suits have challenged statutes and regulations designed to protect wetlands and endangered species.

22. Source: Group literature (on file with author).

23. Source: Telephone conversation with Joanne Spalding, legal assistant, Sierra Club, January 17, 1996.

24. In Colorado: *Aspen Wilderness Workshop v. Colorado Water Conservation Board* (1995); *Submission of Interrogatories on Senate Bill 93-74* (1993); *U.S. v. City*

and County of Denver (1982); *Green v. Castle Concrete Co.* (1973); *City of Colorado Springs v. Board of City Commrs. of Eagle* (1994). In Minnesota: *State v. Minnesota Dept. of Natural Resources* (1994); *Central Baptist Theological Seminary v. City of New Brighton* (1992); *Berggren v. Town of Duluth* (1981); *Urban Council on Mobility v. Minnesota Dept. of Natural Resources* (1980); *Floodwood-Fine Lakes Citizens Group v. Minnesota Envtl. Quality Council* (1979); *Minnesota Public Interest Research Group v. White* (1977); *Reserve Mining Company v. Herbst* (1977); *Minnesota Public Interest Research Group v. Minnesota Envtl. Quality Council* (1975); *Reserve Mining Co. v. Minnesota Pollution Control Agency* (1972). In New Jersey: *Crema v. New Jersey Dept. of Envtl. Protection* (1984, 1983, 1982); *Oakwood at Madison, Inc. v. Township of Madison* (1977); *Humane Society of the U.S. v. State Fish and Game Council* (1976, 1974); *API v. New Jersey Dept. of Envtl. Protection* (1989); *In re Township of Berkeley* (1986). In South Carolina: *Sierra Club v. Kiawah Resort Associates* (1995, 1994); *Stono River Environmental Protection Assn. v. South Carolina Dept. of Health and Environmental Control* (1991); *South Carolina Wildlife Federation v. South Carolina Coastal Council* (1988); *Energy Research Foundation v. Waddell* (1988).

25. For instance, the Rocky Mountains Natural Resources Center (a regional affiliate) has three attorneys on staff.

26. Source: Group literature (on file with the author).

27. In Colorado: *Clajon Production Corporation v. Petera* (1995); *In the Matter of the Application for Water Rights* (1995); *Submission of Interrogatories on Senate Bill 93-74* (1993); *National Wildlife Federation v. Cotter Corp.* (1983, 1981); *U.S. v. City and County of Denver* (1982); *Colorado River Water Conservation District v. Colorado Water Conservation Board* (1979). In Minnesota: *Reserve Mining Co. v. Minnesota Pollution Control Agency* (1972). In New Jersey: *Humane Society of the U.S. v. State Fish and Game Council* (1974). In South Carolina: *South Carolina Wildlife Federation. v. South Carolina Coastal Council* (1988); *Energy Research Foundation v. Waddell* (1988).

28. Jerman's memory here is somewhat inaccurate. Along with the Sierra Club and Charleston Natural Historical Society, the South Carolina Wildlife Federation filed an amicus brief in *Beard v. South Carolina Coastal Council* (1991).

29. For example, although they involved regulatory takings claims, neither organization participated in the U.S. Supreme Court in *Yee v. City of Escondido* (1992) (mobile home rent control law), *Hodel v. Irving* (1987) (statute concerning ownership of Indian lands), or *Williamson County Regional Planning Commn. v. Hamilton Bank* (1985) (nonenvironmental zoning ordinance). The PLF filed an amicus brief in each case.

30. *Clajon Production Corp. v. Petera* (1995, 1994); *Fallini v. Hodel* (1992); *Glosemeyer v. Missouri-Kansas-Texas Railroad* (1989); *National Assn. of Property Owners v. U.S.* (1980); *Ely-Moose Lake Wilderness Canoe Trips and Outfitters, Inc. v. U.S.* (1981); *Florida Rock Industries v. U.S.* (1994).

31. Whether this assessment is valid, of course, is another matter. See Roberts (1995, 71–72) for an alternative perspective.

5

Legal Incentives in Obscenity Law

> There is no reason to believe that the majority of the Court which decided *Miller v. California* . . . is any less adamant than the minority. Accordingly, regardless of how I might vote on the merits after full argument, it would be pointless to grant certiorari in case after case of this character only to have *Miller* reaffirmed time after time.
>
> —Justice Stevens, concurring opinion to denial of writ of certiorari, *Liles v. Oregon* (1976)

This part of the book examines interest group litigation in obscenity cases. Obscenity presents a fundamental conflict between constitutional guarantees of free expression and the collective goal that society represent some type of moral order (Daynes 1988). To achieve such order, virtually every society restricts the display of sex and enforces standards of sexual morality. The confiscation of hard-core pornography, requirements for opaque covers over "girlie" magazines sold at newsstands, restrictions on totally nude and topless barroom dancing, and (most recently) the attempted prohibition of obscene, lewd, or indecent material on the Internet represent just a few of the numerous efforts to restrict access to obscene and pornographic material.[1]

The anti-obscenity movement often is associated with the "religious right," whose members are disturbed by the perceived decline of Judeo-Christian morality and ethics in American society (Canavan 1984; Neuhaus 1984). Yet anti-obscenity efforts are not confined to the religious right. There are numerous bases, both religious and secular, for opposition to obscene and pornographic material. The recent emergence of a feminist critique of pornography, for instance, provides a radically different justification for the restriction of sexual materials. The common thread that holds together the disparate views is that they reflect what Downs (1989) calls a "conservative theory" of sexuality, one that suggests a cautious approach to sexual interest and desire. From this perspective, sexual intimacy is legitimate only in a committed relationship. Recreational, irresponsible sex is bad and degrading; obscenity and pornography encourage impersonal desires and recreational sex.[2]

Opponents of restrictions on obscene or pornographic expressions emphasize the values of free speech and expression embedded in the First Amendment to the United States Constitution as well as similar provisions in state constitutions. Free speech doctrine rests on a liberal theory of the state that promotes state neutrality toward ideas and values citizens hold and express. While society may attempt to control sexual expressions, free speech values suggest some degree of tolerance toward alternative forms of expression. The best way to achieve political and social justice is though an open marketplace of ideas in which all views are expressed freely. Speech should be protected unless it is unlawful or directly tied to unlawful actions, as are libel or incitement.

Tied to moral and political debate surrounding the politics of obscenity are commercial and professional interests. Beginning in the nineteenth century, the growth of realism in literature has meant that (sometimes graphic) depictions of sex are available through books, films, and other communication mediums. As a result, anti-obscenity laws may directly affect authors, publishers, film producers, and others with professional and financial stakes in materials containing arguably obscene or indecent sexual expressions.

Debate over the control of sexual materials and expressions has moral, constitutional, vocational, and financial elements. Not surprisingly, then, a wide variety of interests have been involved in political disputes in many forums, including the courts. This chapter examines the political and legal context in which interest groups have participated in obscenity litigation. The chapter serves two primary purposes. First, it provides a general overview of the politics of debate over obscenity. I discuss legal challenges to anti-obscenity laws that arise under federal and state constitutions, their implications, and the development of obscenity law in recent decades.

Second, this chapter shows that the Supreme Court's landmark obscenity decision in *Miller v. California* (1973) provided interest groups with clear incentives to litigate in state judiciaries. *Miller* gave groups reason to turn to state courts under both the new judicial federalism and the federal restriction incentives. Substantively, the Supreme Court issued a broader definition of obscenity, one that narrowed rights protection for sexual speech and expression. The Court also indicated its unwillingness to continually review obscenity convictions, instead leaving to lower federal and (most often) state courts the final say on what is and is not obscene. Clearly, state courts became more important policy makers in obscenity law because of *Miller*. With an understanding of *Miller*'s impact, we can then examine how interest groups responded to a decision that provided legal incentives to turn to the states.

OBSCENITY IN AMERICAN HISTORY

Debate over obscenity has a long history in American politics. As early as 1815, a Pennsylvania court held it illegal to exhibit pictures of nude bodies for profit. The first state anti-obscenity law was passed in Vermont in 1821 (Daynes 1988, 41). The first action by the U.S. Congress was the Tariff Act of 1842, which prohibited obscene prints and depictions. State anti-obscenity statutes proliferated in the post–Civil War period (Schauer 1976), when social reformers urged legislatures to pass obscenity statutes and courts to convict offenders under these statutes (Pivar 1973; Boyer 1968).

The post–Civil War fight against obscenity was part of a broader campaign by progressive forces, to build a more perfect society marked by moral prosperity. Numerous organizations, including the Woman's Christian Temperance Union and the American Association for the Prevention of Licentiousness and Promotion of Morality, were part of this fight. The leader of the anti-obscenity movement at this time was Anthony Comstock, who in 1873 formed the New York Society for the Suppression of Vice. Comstock was instrumental in bringing about the first significant federal anti-obscenity statute. Dubbed the "Comstock Act," the statute broadened the 1865 federal mail act to prohibit the mailing of obscene materials.

Religious groups joined the anti-obscenity movement in the 1930s (Kobylka 1991, 24). During that decade, the National Legion for Decency (NLD) and the National Office for Decent Literature (NODL)—both affiliated with the Catholic Church—were created. Formed in 1933, the NLD was dedicated to preserving virtue in the motion picture industry; it coded films based on their moral content and made the results available to the public. The NODL, created five years later, produced lists of books that it regarded as unacceptable for children.

Not until the 1960s, however, when the first major libertarian challenges to obscenity statutes began, did obscenity become a politicized issue in American politics (Kobylka 1991; Daynes 1988). In the late 1950s and throughout the following decade, the U.S. Supreme Court issued several important obscenity decisions, which I examine shortly. But like all politicized issues, debate over obscenity is not confined to courts. Congress considered numerous legislative proposals to restrict or prohibit obscene or pornographic materials.[3] Further, two national commissions have addressed the problem of obscenity and pornography. While they reached markedly different conclusions, each commission's report served to intensify the modern debate on the issue.

In 1968, in response to public concern over the increased availability of pornographic materials, President Lyndon Johnson appointed a Commission on Obscenity and Pornography. The Supreme Court's liberalization of obscenity law during the 1960s gave sexual material a legitimacy not previously enjoyed; it became more prevalent. This led to a backlash by socially conservative groups and defenders of "traditional" values, who attacked the Court for undermining morality (Kobylka 1991, xii).[4]

The commission issued its report in 1970. By a vote of 12 to 5, it recommended the elimination of all legal restrictions on the use by consenting adults of sexually explicit books, magazines, pictures, and films. The commission argued that unless sexual material directly harms others, it should not be restricted but rather tolerated as a matter of individual taste. Three dissenters, two of whom founded leading anti-obscenity organizations,[5] called the report "a Magna Charta for the pornographer" (President's Commission 1970, 456). The Senate voted to reject the commission's findings, and President Nixon vigorously renounced the permissive proposals. He even objected to the illustrations of pornography included in the commission's report.

Sixteen years later under President Ronald Reagan, the Attorney General's Commission on Pornography (Meese Commission) issued differing recommendations. While it did not suggest broadening the legal definition of obscenity, it called for restrictions on "violent" and "degrading" types of pornography that it considered harmful to individuals and society as a whole. Also, the Meese Commission recommended better enforcement of current obscenity laws and increased regulation (short of censorship) of certain forms of pornography that it considered harmful but not legally obscene.[6] Downs (1989) attributes the two commissions' different findings not only to the compositions of the groups (the 1970 commission was staffed largely by relatively liberal social scientists, the 1986 commission by more conservative law enforcement officials), but also to a changed social and political environment that by the 1980s challenged the earlier commission's liberal findings.

While these activities occurred at the national level, it is important to note that most regulation of sexual speech and conduct occurs at the state and local levels. Virtually every state and local government has some type of obscenity statute. In 1989, for instance, over 95 percent of the population resided in states with anti-obscenity laws that employed the Supreme Court's definition of "obscenity" as developed in *Miller v. California* (*Obscenity Law Bulletin* 1989). Throughout the 1980s, some anti-obscenity activists attempted to broaden the regulation of sexually explicit materials beyond that restricted by prevailing obscenity law. An antipornography movement led by two feminist activists, Catherine MacKinnon and Andrea Dworkin, introduced ordinances in Minneapolis and Indianapolis that would have treated pornography (defined as "the sexually explicit subordination of women, graphically or in words") as a civil offense against "harmed" women (see MacKinnon 1985, 1984; Dworkin 1981). Unlike obscenity, which is an area of criminal law and focuses on the moral wrongs caused by sexual materials, Dworkin and MacKinnon proposed to prosecute certain sexual materials because of the relationship between pornography and men's systematic oppression of women. They contend that pornography objectifies women, causes men to act violently toward women, and thus perpetuates an oppressive social relationship.[7] Under the ordinances, the restricted pornographic materials would not be limited to those deemed legally obscene; other material might still be banned. More generally, the proposed ordinances departed from standard First Amendment doctrine that holds that speech restrictions must be viewpoint neutral; speech cannot be restricted because of its political or social implications.

Ultimately, the ordinances failed in both cities. In Minneapolis, the first city to consider such a law, the city council by a 7–6 vote passed the ordinance, but in January 1984 it was vetoed by Mayor Donald Fraser. A similar ordinance passed in Indianapolis, but was struck down as unconstitutional by a federal district court in *ABA et al. v. Hudnut* (1984). Comparable antipornography laws were considered, although never adopted, in other cities (see Brest and Vandenberg 1987).

OBSCENITY LAW

This section provides a general overview of the development of obscenity law in the United States. Of particular importance is the Supreme Court's decision in *Miller v. California* (1973), which brought about a marked change in obscenity law, one that furnished organized interest groups with legal incentives to turn to state courts. The Court provided libertarian groups with the new judicial federalism incentive by abruptly retreating from its liberal holdings of the 1960s. It also provided the federal restriction incentive by its decision to give states and localities increased discretion to restrict sexually explicit materials and expressions, thereby making state courts more important policy makers in this area of law.

Though the First Amendment is written in absolutist terms ("Congress shall make no law . . . abridging the freedom of speech"), the Supreme Court has never interpreted it to protect all speech. Yet by and large, First Amendment doctrine does protect individual expression, especially in the domain of politically oriented speech. Throughout the twentieth century, the Court largely abandoned the traditional notion that only socially valuable speech deserves protection and accepted the idea that all individuals and groups deserve free speech protection except when such speech threatens others with direct and immediate harm (Downs 1989).

The Supreme Court incorporated these principles into a two-tiered theory of speech, which divides expression into protected and unprotected categories.[8] Regulations that affect protected speech are presumed unconstitutional, while those that affect unprotected speech generally are permissible. In obscenity, as in all areas of First Amendment law, the Supreme Court's role is to define the categories of speech and thus the level of constitutional protection they are accorded. The Court never has recognized obscenity to be protected speech.

American obscenity law is based on the British legal tradition. Obscenity was first held an offense under English common law in *Dominus Rex v. Curll* (1727); the first American conviction occurred in 1821 in *Commonwealth v.*

Holmes. As a constitutional matter, American obscenity law derived originally from the British Court of the Queen's Bench's decision in *Regina v. Hicklin* (1868). This case held obscenity to be a crime and defined it in terms of its ability to "deprave or corrupt" those who come in contact with it. *Hicklin* held that the obscenity of a work was to be judged on the basis of isolated parts of the work without examination of its overall worth or objective, and that courts were to consider the concerns of individuals most vulnerable to the objectionable material even if they are from socially peripheral or minority groups (for example, minors or psychological deviants).

Through the early decades of the twentieth century, prosecutors relied on *Hicklin* to gain convictions against books that contained sexual ideas as well as literary or artistic merit, such as D.H. Lawrence's *Lady Chatterly's Lover*. Yet some lower courts brought about liberal innovations in obscenity doctrine that preceded the U.S. Supreme Court's later doctrinal changes. In the early 1930s, a federal district and appellate court held that James Joyce's *Ulysses* was not obscene despite having pornographic passages (*U.S. v. One Book Called "Ulysses"* 1933). Enunciating a new standard, the district court asked if the author of the work had "pornographic intent" and, if not, whether the effect of the work as a whole on the average reader was to "stir the impulses or to lead to sexually impure or lustful thoughts." This liberalized the *Hicklin* test by turning attention away from the effect of isolated passages on the most susceptible readers. Many lower courts adopted the *Ulysses* test (Downs 1989).

Despite these changes, lower courts did not address constitutional (that is, First Amendment) issues but instead examined statutory definitions of obscenity. Through the late 1950s, *Hicklin* provided the prevailing definition of obscenity in most American courts (Schauer 1976). But this precedent ended during the Warren Court era, when the Court took steps to minimize the impact of anti-obscenity laws on free expression. The Court's reconsideration of obscenity came at a time when it liberalized First Amendment law more generally. Paralleling changes in obscenity doctrine, the Court throughout the 1960s and early 1970s granted greater constitutional protection for libel as well as lewd and offensive speech.[9] In short, the Court placed fewer expressions in the unprotected tier of First Amendment law.

In *Butler v. Michigan* (1957), the Supreme Court for the first time addressed the definition of obscenity, and it abandoned the *Hicklin* analysis. Specifically, the justices rejected the focus on isolated passages of an allegedly obscene work and on the work's impact on the "most susceptible persons." The *Butler* decision, however, did not explicitly reject *Hicklin* on First Amendment grounds. But that same year in *Roth v. U.S.*, the Court more clearly abandoned the *Hicklin* approach as too restrictive of free expression. In its place, Justice William Brennan, writing for a five to four majority, established a new test for obscenity: "whether to the average person, applying contemporary community standards, the dominant theme of the material, taken as a whole, appeals to the prurient interest" (*Roth* 1957, 487). The Court made clear that obscenity was not protected speech under the First Amendment, but nevertheless the Court attempted to restrict obscenity prosecutions to a narrower category of material and showed greater regard for free speech and expression values than that found in *Hicklin*. Brennan recognized that "all ideas having even the slightest redeeming social importance . . . have the full protection of the [Constitution]" (*Roth* 1957, 484). The Supreme Court's doctrinal innovations in *Butler* and *Roth* drew on lower-court developments over the previous decades.

Roth and subsequent decisions showed that the Court had difficulty defining obscenity. Indeed, Daynes (1988, 42) suggests that the Warren Court was unable to define obscenity, so it attempted to define what obscenity *was not*. In subsequent years, the justices were required to expound upon numerous concepts central to the definition, such as "dominant theme," "contemporary community standards," and "prurient interest." Following the *Roth* landmark, the Supreme Court as well as lower federal and state courts attempted to clarify the definition of obscenity and draw the line between protected and unprotected sexual speech.

While *Roth*'s primary holding was that the First Amendment does not protect obscenity, the decision did liberalize the *Hicklin* precedent. The Supreme Court's subsequent obscenity decisions were even more libertarian in nature; they broadened standards as to what types of sexual speech the First Amendment protects. Throughout the 1960s, the Supreme Court liberalized both procedural and substantive dimensions of obscenity law (Kobylka 1991, 5). Procedurally, the Court generally made it more difficult to prohibit allegedly obscene material by addressing issues such as scienter (the degree of knowledge that the seller of allegedly obscene material must have to be criminally liable),[10] proper procedures for warrants,[11] the suitability of creating lists of obscene works,[12] and the scope of permissible prior restraints.[13]

Substantively, the Court modified its *Roth* test for the definition of obscenity on several occasions. It is important to note, however, that throughout the 1960s the Court was unable to garner a majority to alter formally the *Roth* test. Reflecting the divisiveness of the obscenity issue, pluralities of the justices decided major opinions.

In *Manual Enterprises v. Day* (1962), Justice John Marshall Harlan said that for a work to be obscene it must be "patently offensive." *Jacobellis v. Ohio* (1964) added that materials proscribed as obscene must be "utterly without redeeming social importance." Thus, government could not censure material that had any measure of redeeming importance. The Court culminated its liberalization of obscenity doctrine in *Memoirs v. Massachusetts* (1966). There, the Court overturned the state court's decision that John Cleland's novel *Fanny Hill* was unprotected by the First Amendment. Justice Brennan extended *Jacobellis* by announcing that the "community" discussed in *Roth* was national in scope, providing a uniform definition of obscenity nationwide. He issued a new three-part test that deemed materials to be obscene only if "(a) the dominant theme of the material taken as a whole appeals to the prurient interest in sex; (b) the material is patently offensive because it affronts contemporary community standards relating to the description or representation of sexual matters; and (c) the material is utterly without redeeming social value" (*Memoirs* 1966, 419-20).

Memoirs shifted the emphasis in obscenity cases to the presence or absence of some minimal level of social value; *Roth* had focused on the presence of prurient appeal. In dissent, Justices Thomas Clark and Byron White argued that the Court had so liberalized obscenity doctrine as to abandon the balancing approach emphasized in *Roth*. Since each prong of the test had to be met, the minimal social value prong became decisive in most cases (Downs 1989). Almost all publications and forms of expression had *some* social value; rarely would the *Memoirs* test yield obscenity convictions. The practical effect of the new test was to protect a broader range of sexually explicit material and to make obscenity convictions more difficult to obtain.

Yet despite liberalizing obscenity doctrine, the Court was still unable to agree on a definition. In *Redrup v. New York* (1967), the Court in a per curiam decision reversed an obscenity conviction. The justices acknowledged their inability to devise a specific definition of obscenity but nevertheless noted that the material at issue in the case was not obscene under the several tests applied in previous cases. Following the decision, the Court in the next four years issued thirty-one summary reversals of obscenity convictions, collectively known as the "Redrup reversals." Finally, the Court extended its liberalization of obscenity law in *Stanley v. Georgia* (1969), where it held that the First Amendment and privacy interests permit the possession of obscene material within the privacy of one's home. By the end of the 1960s, some considered the *Roth* precedent, and specifically its declaration of obscenity as unprotected speech, to be near an end (Engdahl 1969; Katz 1969; Rembar 1968). Daynes (1988, 42) suggests that the Warren Court criteria to define what is obscene "became so broad and unmanageable that the term *obscene* all but disappeared."

To summarize, throughout the 1960s, the Supreme Court expanded the scope of First Amendment protection for sexual speech and expression. Fewer works were considered obscene, and convictions increasingly were difficult to achieve. The Court also took policy responsibility into its own hands, consistently reviewing lower federal and state court decisions. By declaring community standards national in scope, the Court established the legal foundations for an active federal role in obscenity law. These decisions by the Warren Court would appear to have provided interest groups with little incentive to turn to state courts to litigate obscenity cases.

A Changed Legal Context: *Miller v. California* (1973)

However, President Richard Nixon's judicial appointments reshaped the composition of the Court and effectively ended its liberalizing tendencies in many areas of law, including obscenity. Nixon made the opposition to pornography an important issue in his campaign for the presidency. He exerted his greatest influence over obscenity policy by placing four new members on the Court—Chief Justice Warren Burger and Associate Justices Lewis Powell, Harry Blackmun, and William Rehnquist—weakening the Court's libertarian bloc.

In *Miller v. California* (1973), the Supreme Court diverged from the libertarian decisions of previous years and modified the *Roth* test.[14] *Miller*, which dealt with a conviction for sending unsolicited obscene brochures through the mail, saw the Court develop a new majority position on the definition of obscenity for the first time since *Roth*. The five-member majority, which included each Nixon appointee, specified less restrictive standards in determining what material is obscene. Chief Justice Burger issued a three-part test in his majority opinion: (a) whether the "average person, applying contemporary community standards" would find that the work, taken as a whole, appeals to the prurient interest; (b) whether the work depicts or describes, in a patently offensive way, sexual conduct specifically designated by applicable state law; and (c) whether the work, taken as a whole, lacks serious literary, artistic, political, or scientific value" (*Miller* 1973, 24). The Court also noted that juries can judge material based on local "community standards"; material need not be judged based on single, uniform national standards.

What was *Miller*'s impact on obscenity law? Two consequences of the decision are relevant for our purposes. First, *Miller* granted the federal and state governments greater leeway to restrict sexually explicit materials. Some scholars debate the extent to which *Miller* represented more restrictive obscenity doctrine, arguing that the decision did not change the state of obscenity law significantly (Downs 1989; Schauer 1976; Wasby 1976). To be deemed obscene, material must meet all three parts of the *Miller* test. Further, the patent offense test represents a compromise, since Chief Justice Burger noted that only hardcore materials could be prosecuted as patently offensive.

Nevertheless, *Miller* restricted free speech and expression rights in several important respects. Most significant, it rejected the "redeeming social importance" standard of the *Roth-Memoirs* test for the less stringent standard of whether the work lacks "serious" value. Justice Burger noted that the former standard is nearly impossible to meet, since it is possible to find even the most infinitesimal social value in just about anything. *Miller* appeared to make it easier for government to prosecute obscenity. Further, the Court refused to extend the logic of its earlier decisions, especially *Stanley* (1969), which protected the actions of consenting adults (Kobylka 1987, 1062-63).

Empirical evidence appears to support this interpretation, suggesting that *Miller* helped to bring about changes in case outcomes. Kobylka (1991) shows marked changes in the outcomes of obscenity litigation before the U.S. Supreme Court between 1957 and 1987. Table 5.1 updates his findings through 1994.

The Warren Court supported libertarian outcomes in 78 percent of its decisions, compared to only 22 percent in the Burger and Rehnquist Courts. Further, across the entire American judiciary (not just the Supreme Court), appellate court reversals of obscenity convictions declined from 18 to 8 percent between 1972 and 1975 (Obscenity Law Project 1977). While these data do not account for alternative explanations in case outcomes,[15] nonetheless, the evidence suggests that doctrinal changes brought about by *Miller* had immediate and clear consequences.

It is important to note that in addition to issuing a more restrictive definition of obscenity, the Court in *Miller* (1973, 24) also defined more precisely the limitations on prosecutions of sexually explicit material, requiring that prohibited sexual conduct be "specifically defined by the applicable state law." Justice Burger set down some guidelines as to what types of sexual conduct might be labeled obscene. These acts include, but are not necessarily limited to, "(a) patently offensive representations or descriptions of ultimate sexual acts, normal or perverted, actual or simulated" or "(b) patently offensive representations or descriptions of masturbation, excretory functions, and lewd exhibition of the genitals" (*Miller* 1973, 25). By adding the requirement that laws specify exactly what conduct can and cannot be portrayed, *Miller* jeopardized many state statutes as unconstitutionally vague (Schauer 1976). In sum, the Court required that whatever types of sexual conduct the states regulate be described in some detail, although it set out broad parameters of permissible regulations and issued a less libertarian definition of obscenity.

Table 5.1
Outcomes of U.S. Supreme Court Obscenity Cases, 1957–1994

	Libertarian	Proscriptionist	Other
Warren Court (1957–1971) (N=74)	78%	15%	7%
Burger and Rehnquist Courts (1972–1994) (N=54)	22%	54%	24%

Sources: Kobylka (1991), Table 1.1 (1957–1987). Updated through 1994 by author.

The second consequence of *Miller v. California* is that it represented the "Court's intention to leave the determination of obscenity to local authorities and thereby diminish[ed] the oversight role of the federal courts in this area of law" (Kobylka 1991, 7). The Burger Court substituted local for national community standards in determining whether material is obscene and showed a renewed willingness to defer to state and local authorities in controlling sexual materials. Although federal courts continued to remain active in obscenity law, their role was reduced. Indeed, Justice Stevens's highly unusual concurring opinion to the denial of review of an obscenity conviction, quoted at the beginning of this chapter, suggests that *Miller* altered considerably the Supreme Court's propensity to review obscenity convictions. After *Miller*, the final decisions in obscenity cases increasingly were made in lower federal and (more often) state courts. While many state cases dealt with the application of federal doctrine, state judiciaries became more prominent implementers of that doctrine (see, for example, Songer 1988; Murphy 1959). Consequently, groups seeking to affect the judicial policy process had greater incentive to turn toward the relevant institutions—state courts.

To summarize, *Miller v. California* altered significantly the context of obscenity law and provided interest groups with two reasons to turn to state courts. First, the Supreme Court issued a less restrictive definition of obscenity, one that allowed the federal and state governments greater leeway to restrict access to sexually explicit materials. Consequently, the new judicial federalism incentive suggests that groups supporting rights of free speech and expression may turn to state courts to seek broader protection under state constitutional free expression provisions. Second, by enunciating a "local community standards" logic and indicating its unwillingness to continually review lower-court obscenity convictions, the Supreme Court made state courts de facto the final decision makers in most obscenity cases. With state courts more important, interest groups that seek to affect obscenity policy may turn to these tribunals, motivated by the federal restriction incentive.

Post-*Miller* in Federal and State Courts

Miller v. California plainly altered the legal context in which interest groups participated in obscenity cases. Since the decision, lower federal and state courts have continued to wrestle with obscenity and related issues. The U.S. Supreme Court, too, has not completely abandoned the litigation fray. As with most Supreme Court decisions, particularly those decided by a bare majority, *Miller* raised many questions. The Supreme Court has had to address some ambiguous aspects of the decision.

An important consequence of *Miller* is that obscenity prosecutions vary according to local standards, so materials deemed obscene in one state might not be obscene in another. The justices recognized that while permitting local regulations, the Court must in some situations retain a final say on what is considered obscene. In *Jenkins v. Georgia* (1974), the Court rejected the Georgia Supreme Court's ruling that in Albany, Georgia, the movie *Carnal Knowledge* was obscene. Writing for the majority, Justice William Rehnquist noted that "it would be a serious misreading of *Miller* to conclude that juries have unbridled discretion in determining what is 'patently offensive'" (*Jenkins* 1974, 160). In *Pope v. Illinois* (1987), the Court ruled that the third prong of the *Miller* test (that works lack serious literary, artistic, political, or scientific value) should be applied based on standards set by a "reasonable" person, not an "ordinary" person, and that this person be considered from the national as opposed to the local community. *Jenkins* and *Pope* restrained, although by no means retracted, the local community standards logic enunciated in *Miller*.

While some areas of obscenity law continue to be divisive, the Burger and Rehnquist Courts have been more accepting than the Warren Court of restrictions on the availability of sexually oriented materials. Laws that prohibit child pornography have received unanimous support from the justices. The Court first upheld a state ban on child pornography in *New York v. Ferber* (1982).[16] Later, in *Osborne v. Ohio* (1990), the Court upheld Ohio's law banning the private possession and viewing of child pornography. The Court generally has accepted restrictions on the mailing of obscene materials (*Rowan v. U.S. Post Office Dept.* 1970; *U.S. v. Reidel* 1971).[17] It allowed restrictions on adult bookstores as well as nude dancing and other forms of live, sexually oriented entertainment. In *California v. LaRue* (1972), the Court upheld California's prohibition of sexually explicit live entertainment and films in bars. Since *Miller*, the Court has upheld state prohibitions on nude dancing under their authority to regulate liquor under the Twenty-first Amendment (*New York State Liquor Authority v. Bellanca* 1981; *City of Newport v. Iaobucci* 1986). The Court also allowed the closing of an adult bookstore where its premises were used to solicit prostitution (*Arcara v. Cloud Books, Inc.* 1986).

Another way in which communities have sought to limit the availability of obscene and pornographic material is through exclusionary zoning that restricts the operation of adult theaters and nightclubs to certain areas of the community. The Supreme Court first accepted this practice in *Young v. American Mini Theatres* (1976); a five to four majority upheld a Detroit law restricting adult theaters from operating within 1,000 feet of each other and 500 feet of a residential home. In *Young*, the sexually explicit movie shown by the adult theaters did not technically fit *Miller*'s definition of obscenity. But the Court argued that since nonobscene sexually explicit materials possess only minimal social value, limited access to these materials (as opposed to banning them entirely) does not violate the First Amendment.[18] Later decisions upheld other uses of exclusionary zoning to regulate adult entertainment businesses (*City of Renton v. Playtime Theatres, Inc.* 1986) as well as Indiana's statewide ban on totally nude dancing (*Barnes v. Glen Theatre, Inc.* 1991).

Today, the *Miller* doctrine appears safe. Federal courts, interpreting the federal Constitution, remain relatively inhospitable to rights litigants in this area of law. Justices appointed under Presidents Reagan and George Bush, especially Sandra Day O'Connor, Antonin Scalia, and David Souter (and probably Clarence Thomas as well) generally support obscenity restrictions. President Bill Clinton's appointments of Justices Ruth Bader Ginsburg and Stephen

Breyer are unlikely to alter meaningfully the Court's position on most obscenity questions. [19] It is highly likely that the *Miller* doctrine will remain intact for the foreseeable future.

As the Burger and Rehnquist Courts have been less willing to intervene to protect free speech claims against obscenity prosecutions, some litigants turned to state courts and argued that state constitutional free speech and expression guarantees provide greater protection than the U.S. Supreme Court recognizes under the federal Constitution. While numerous state high courts have been willing to base obscenity rulings on their state constitutions, only the Oregon Supreme Court has ruled unambiguously that obscenity is protected under its constitution. In *State v. Henry* (1987), the Oregon Supreme Court made it clear that the Oregon Constitution provides heightened protection for sexually explicit material. The court conducted an extensive historical analysis, concluding that obscenity was not "an original or modern version of an historically established exception to the protection afforded freedom of expression" under Article 1, Section 8 (the free speech clause) of the Oregon Constitution (*Henry* 1987, 11). Since Oregon criminalized only the distribution of obscenity to minors during the nineteenth century, restrictions on obscene materials to consenting adults did not fall within any recognized exceptions to free speech at the time Oregon's Bill of Rights was adopted in 1857. Thus, the court concluded that "in this state any person can write, print, read, say, show or sell anything to a consenting adult even though that expression may be generally or universally considered 'obscene'" (*Henry* 1987, 18).[20]

In the wake of the U.S. Supreme Court's decision in *Miller v. California*, greater opportunities for state constitutional activism arose in obscenity law. The possibility of securing protection through state constitutional free speech and expression clauses may motivate interest groups to enter state courts and assert state law arguments. Reinforcing the new judicial federalism incentive was the Oregon Supreme Court's decision in *Henry*, which may provide encouragement for libertarian groups seeking to mobilize state constitutional law in other state courts.

CONCLUSION

This chapter has provided a basic sketch of the political debate over sexually explicit material and the development of obscenity law in the United States. It has also shown that the United States Supreme Court's decision in *Miller v. California* (1973) provided interest groups that seek to influence obscenity policy with incentives to litigate in state courts. *Miller* brought about two relevant legal changes. First, the Court issued a new definition of obscenity, one that set out broader parameters of permissible regulations of sexually explicit materials and expressions. Libertarian groups, under the new judicial federalism incentive, therefore might respond by seeking to expand free speech protection based on state constitutional law. Second, the Court indicated its unwillingness to continually review state court obscenity decisions, instead deferring increasingly to the state courts. Consequently, state judiciaries are de facto the final decision makers on most matters in obscenity law. The decentralization of policy making provides groups with reason to turn to state courts under the federal restriction incentive, since that is "where the action is."

This assessment of obscenity law allows for consideration of the following question: When the legal context provides clear incentives to do so, to what extent have interest groups turned to state judiciaries to participate in obscenity litigation? The next chapters examine group litigation in state courts in a decentralized area of law.

NOTES

1. Until recent times, "obscenity" and "pornography" were used interchangeably. But they are not identical terms, particularly in American legal discourse. "Obscene" refers to materials considered offensive or repulsive. In common usage, the term is not limited solely to sexual matters, although in American law it is limited explicitly to sexual depictions. "Pornography" refers to depictions of "sexual lewdness or erotic behavior" (Schauer 1976, 1). The term usually is broader than obscenity; pornographic material is not necessarily legally obscene.

2. For more detailed discussion of the various critiques of obscenity, see Downs (1989).

3. On the types of anti-obscenity measures Congress addressed between 1957 and 1985, see Daynes (1988).

4. Whether the Supreme Court's decisions *caused* sexually explicit materials to become more widespread is a complex issue, and not easily resolved. However, what is perhaps more important is that opponents of obscenity and pornography believed that the Court's decisions had this effect, and the opponents responded accordingly.

5. The two were Charles H. Keating, Jr., founder of Citizens for Decency through Law, and Father Morton A. Hill, founder of Morality in Media.

6. The Meese Commission report mixed the language of feminist anti-pornography critiques with traditional moralistic concerns against sexual materials. For commentary on the commission, see Downs (1987), West (1987) and Hertzberg (1986).

7. Downs (1989) provides an excellent analysis of the feminist critique of pornography, as well as the Minneapolis and Indianapolis ordinances. Not all feminists adopt the Dworkin/MacKinnon approach. For debate over the feminist response to pornography, see Strossen (1995) and Brest and Vandenberg (1987).

8. The two-tiered theory is associated most often with the Supreme Court's decision in *Chaplinsky v. New Hampshire* (1942). See also Meiklejohn (1961) and Kalven (1960).

9. See *New York Times v. Sullivan* (1964) (libel against public officials protected unless done with malice); *Cohen v. California* (1971) (greater protection for offensive speech and fighting words). Throughout the 1960s, the Court devoted increased agenda space to First Amendment civil liberties cases, suggesting greater interest in First Amendment law (Pacelle 1991).

10. *Smith v. California* (1959).

11. *Marcus v. Search Warrant* (1961).

12. *Bantam Books v. Sullivan* (1963).

13. *Times-Film v. Chicago* (1961) and *Freedman v. Maryland* (1965).

14. *Miller* is the leading of eight obscenity decisions issued by the Court at the end of the 1972 term. The others are *Paris Adult Theatre v. Slaton, Kaplan v. California, U.S. v. 12 Reels, U.S. v. Orito, Heller v. New York, Roaden v. Kentucky*, and *Alexander v. Virginia*. Each case rejected libertarian claims by a 5-to-4 vote.

15. For example, the explicitness of material reviewed increased over time (Obscenity Law Project 1977, 889).

16. *Ferber* did have four concurring opinions.

17. However, in *Bolger v. Youngs Drug Product Corp.* (1983), the Court struck down another statute restricting the mailing of advertisements for contraceptives.

18. In *F.C.C. v. Pacifica Foundation* (1978), the Court relied on similar reasoning to uphold the authority of the F.C.C. to regulate nonobscene indecent speech on radio broadcasts.

19. However, the Court recently provided a broad endorsement of free speech on the Internet, invalidating provisions of the Communications Decency Act of 1996 that made it crime to send or display "indecent" materials in cyberspace. Although Rehnquist and O'Connor dissented from part of the Court's ruling in *Reno v. American Civil Liberties Union* (1997), the justices were unanimous in extending complete First Amendment protection to on line communications.

20. The Hawaii Supreme Court also provided extensive protection for sexual speech, although its decision was based on the state constitutional guarantee to privacy, not free speech and expression. In *State v. Kam* (1988), the court invalidated the state's obscenity statute as a violation of the explicit privacy provision of the Hawaii Constitution.

6

Obscenity: The ACLU in State Judiciaries

> Wherever liberty is threatened, the ACLU is there. . . . Our nationwide network gives the ACLU's activities an immediacy and a grassroots power unmatched in the field of human rights by any other national organization in the U.S.
>
> —American Civil Liberties Union Annual Report, 1992-93

> One of the problems with obscenity laws is they are vague. If we got involved in all local cases, it would drain our resources.
>
> —Rick Karpel, Director of Legal Affairs,
> Video Software Dealers Association

The U.S. Supreme Court's landmark obscenity decision in *Miller v. California* (1973) provided interest groups with incentives to turn to state courts. *Miller*'s less restrictive definition of obscenity potentially encouraged rights litigants, via the new judicial federalism incentive, to mobilize state constitutional law to seek more expansive protection than that available under federal standards. Groups might also turn to the state level by way of the federal restriction incentive, since the decision indicated the Court's willingness to defer to lower courts rulings, thereby making state judiciaries increasingly the final decision makers. I will show that—impelled by these incentives—interest groups have turned to state courts, but that the trend was attenuated significantly. Leading the way was the American Civil Liberties Union (ACLU), which dominated interest group litigation in the five states.

The next two chapters attempt to explain patterns of interest group litigation over time, across groups, and across states. The findings suggest significant hurdles to consistent litigation in state courts. Only the ACLU, with its nationwide network of affiliates and cooperating attorneys, had the capacity to litigate in many states. For example, the ACLU had scores to hundreds of affiliated attorneys in each state, while other organizations had less than ten nationwide. While the increased group litigation was caused largely by the U.S. Supreme Court's decision in *Miller v. California* (1973), which gave groups reason to turn to state courts, organizational factors conditioned groups' responses to the decision. The ACLU had the resources and, as a purposive group, the organizational incentives to litigate most often in a decentralized litigation environment. I will also show that, until very recently, libertarian organizations were reluctant to mobilize state constitutional law to seek expansive protections.

These findings have important implications. They raise questions about the ability of most organized interests to mobilize the law in the environment of decentralized decision making that characterizes an increasing number of judicial policies. Currently, many organizations appear to lack the incentives and resources to respond to trends in national-state relations in the judiciary by turning to state courts. In the meantime, state courts continue to develop doctrine without their participation.

INTEREST GROUPS IN STATE OBSCENITY CASES

Table 6.1 compares interest group participation in the United States Supreme Court and the intermediate appellate and state high courts of Colorado, Indiana, Minnesota, New Jersey, and South Carolina both before and after *Miller v. California* (1973). The table reveals two important aspects about interest group participation in obscenity cases. First, organized group litigation is much more pervasive in the Supreme Court than in state judiciaries. Groups have been active in 13 percent of the state court decisions since 1960. In contrast, they participated in over 53 percent of the U.S. Supreme Court's obscenity cases (74 percent not counting summary reversals) during this period. It should not be surprising that there is a greater group presence in the Supreme Court, given that it is at the apex of the American judicial system and its precedents apply to the entire nation.

Despite lower rates of interest group participation in state litigation, there is still substantial and important activity at the state level. (Appendix B lists the state court cases with group participation.) Where groups litigated, cases raised important doctrinal issues. With one exception,[1] all raised federal or state constitutional issues. In obscenity law, groups appear to have used state courts to seek policy goals, and in doing so, have addressed important legal issues.

The second and most prominent finding is that interest groups have been much more active in the five state judiciaries after the *Miller* decision. Increased rates of group litigation after *Miller* are more marked in state judiciaries than in the U.S. Supreme Court, particularly when we disregard summary reversals. While this does not necessarily mean that the decision *caused* the observed trends, the fact remains that groups were more active in the post-*Miller* period.

Table 6.1
A Comparison of Interest Group Participation in Obscenity Litigation in the U.S. Supreme Court and Five State Courts, 1960–1994

	U.S. Supreme Court			State Courts		
	Pre-*Miller*	Post-*Miller*	Total	Pre-*Miller*	Post-*Miller*	Total
Percent of Cases with Group Participation	42% (72%)*	78%	53% (74%)	2%	17%	13
Number of Cases with Group Participation	37 (33)	31	68 (64)	1	20	21
Total Number of Cases	88 (46)	40	128 (86)	42	119	161

*Figures in parenthesis do not include summary reversals.

Note: Figures refer to cases in the U.S. Supreme Court and the intermediate appellate and supreme courts of the five states in which an interest group participated as a party, counsel, or amicus curiae.

To understand more fully the dynamics of group litigation in the state courts, Table 6.2 reports in which decades the interest groups entered litigation. Over half of the twenty-one cases occurred in the 1970s; of these cases, only one (*State v. Watkins* 1972) was decided before *Miller v. California*. These data suggest strongly that the Supreme Court's landmark is an important cause of the trends in group litigation. Unlike general trends in interest group litigation in state courts (see Epstein 1994), group participation in obscenity cases has not increased consistently over time. The trend appears issue specific, and thus better explainable in light of *Miller* rather than the general dynamics of interest groups' use of courts.

Table 6.2
Percentage of State Court Obscenity Cases with Interest Group Participation by Decade, 1960–1994

	1960s	1970s	1980s	1990–1994
Percent with Group Participation	0%	57%	19%	24%
Number of Cases with Group Participation	0	12	4	5

Note: Figures refer to cases in the intermediate appellate and supreme courts of the five states (N=21) in which an interest group participated as a party, counsel, or amicus curiae.

Table 6.3 displays the data by state. Save for South Carolina, the percentage of appellate cases with group involvement increased after *Miller*. In the four other states there is no group activity whatsoever between 1960 and 1973. Increased rates of group litigation after *Miller* are most evident in Colorado, Minnesota, and New Jersey.

These data provide a basic picture of interest group participation in obscenity cases in the Supreme Court and the five states. But which organizations litigated? Table 6.4 shows the groups most active in Supreme Court obscenity litigation, both before and after *Miller*. Following Kobylka (1991), groups that argue that government cannot and should not censor sexual materials are classified as *libertarian groups*. In contrast, *proscriptionist groups* support restrictions on sexually oriented materials in the name of public morality.

In the Supreme Court, Kobylka (1991) argues, material organizations mobilized in the wake of *Miller* to protect their members' interests. Indeed, the

American Booksellers Association (ABA), Association of American Publishers (AAP), and American Library Association (ALA) each were much more active after the Supreme Court landmark. Because these groups mobilized, Kobylka (1991) maintains, the ACLU was able to deemphasize obscenity after *Miller* and turn its attention to other issues on its broad agenda. Among the proscriptionist groups, Citizens for Decency through Law (CDL) and Morality in Media (MM) consistently were the two most active litigators.

Table 6.3
Interest Group Participation in State Court Obscenity Litigation by State, Pre- and Post-*Miller*

State	Pre-*Miller*	Post-*Miller*	Total
Colorado	0% (0 of 1)	33% (6 of 18)	32% (6 of 19)
Indiana	0% (0 of 5)	2% (1 of 47)	2% (1 of 52)
Minnesota	0% (0 of 13)	39% (7 of 18)	23% (7 of 31)
New Jersey	0% (0 of 19)	18% (4 of 22)	10% (4 of 41)
South Carolina	25% (1 of 4)	14% (2 of 14)	17% (3 of 18)
Total	2% (1 of 42)	17% (20 of 119)	13% (21 of 161)

Note: Figures indicate the percentage of cases in the intermediate appellate and supreme courts of the five states in which an interest group participated as a party, counsel, or amicus curiae.

Table 6.5 reveals the most active litigators in the states. Organized group litigation is dominated by one libertarian organization, the American Civil Liberties Union. The national organization and its affiliates were active in thirteen of the twenty-one cases (62 percent) with group participation. The ACLU is the only group to have litigated in all five states. Yet although the most active organization, patterns of ACLU litigation vary markedly across states. The ACLU mobilized most substantially in Minnesota and New Jersey (see Table 6.6). In

Colorado, Indiana, and South Carolina, the group has not litigated as consistently.

Table 6.4
Interest Groups Most Active in U.S. Supreme Court Obscenity Litigation, 1960–1994

Group	Pre-*Miller*		Post-*Miller*	
	%	N	%	N
Libertarian Groups				
ACLU	23.9 (39.1)	21 (18)	27.5	11
ABA/MC	0	0	35	14
AAP	12.5 (22.7)	11 (10)	42.5	17
ALA/Freedom to Read Foundation	2.3 (2.3)	2 (2)	40	16
Proscriptionist Groups				
CDL	18.2 (30.4)	16 (14)	42.5	17
MM	2.6 (4.8)	2 (2)	15	6

* Figures in parenthesis do not include summary reversals.

Key:

AAP	Association of American Publishers
ABA	American Booksellers Association
ACLU	American Civil Liberties Union
ALA	American Library Association
CDL	Citizens for Decency though Law
MC	Media Coalition
MM	Morality in Media

Note: Figures refer to U.S. Supreme Court obscenity cases in which the interest groups participated as a party, counsel, or amicus curiae.

Table 6.5
Interest Groups Most Active in State Court Obscenity Litigation, 1960–1994

Group	Pre-*Miller*		Post-*Miller*	
	%	N	%	N
Libertarian Groups				
ACLU	2	1	10	12
ABA/MC	0	0	3.3	4
Proscriptionist Groups				
CDL	0	0	1	1
MM	0	0	1	1
NFLF	0	0	2	2

Key:

ABA American Booksellers Association
ACLU American Civil Liberties Union
CDL Citizens for Decency though Law
MC Media Coalition
MM Morality in Media
NFLF National Family Legal Foundation

Note: Table presents the percentage of obscenity cases in the intermediate appellate and supreme courts of the five states in which the interest groups participated as a party, counsel, or amicus curiae.

These data reveal a variety of interesting trends and raise important questions. First, why were interest groups more active in state appellate courts in the post-*Miller* period? The last chapter examined legal incentives brought about by *Miller* that may have led groups to mobilize in state courts. One possible explanation for the increased rates of group participation is that the groups were motivated by the federal restriction incentive. Since *Miller* indicated the Court's unwillingness to continually review lower-court obscenity cases, state appellate courts increasingly were the de facto final decision makers on most obscenity questions. With federal appellate avenues closed, groups had to turn to state courts.

Table 6.6
ACLU Participation in State Court Obscenity Litigation, Pre- and Post-*Miller*

State	Pre-*Miller*	Post-*Miller*	Total
Colorado	0% (0 of 1)	6% (1 of 18)	5% (1 of 19)
Indiana	0% (0 of 5)	2% (1 of 47)	2% (1 of 52)
Minnesota	0% (0 of 13)	33% (6 of 18)	19% (6 of 31)
New Jersey	0% (0 of 19)	14% (3 of 22)	7% (3 of 41)
South Carolina	25% (1 of 4)	7% (1 of 14)	11% (2 of 18)
Total	2% (1 of 42)	10% (12 of 119)	8% (13 of 161)

Note: Figures indicate the percentage of cases in the intermediate appellate and supreme courts of the five states in which the ACLU participated as counsel or amicus curiae.

However, the new judicial federalism incentive suggests a second possible explanation for libertarian groups' increased use of state judiciaries. If this motivated groups to turn to the states, then *Miller*'s most important effect was not that it decentralized policy responsibility but rather that it served as a signal to libertarian organizations to mobilize state constitutional law in response to the Supreme Court's retrenchment on free expression protection under the First Amendment. If so, libertarian groups would be expected to offer rights claims that seek broader protection on state constitutional grounds than is available under federal standards. Where libertarian groups did not offer such state law arguments, then they were not motivated by the new judicial federalism incentive.

A third explanation for the increased use of state courts focuses on the organizational threshold. Perhaps the link between *Miller* and increased rates of state litigation is spurious and instead growing resources or changing priorities during the early 1970s impelled groups to enter the litigation fray. If this is the case, then organizational factors rather than the *Miller* decision primarily account for the observed patterns of group litigation. This explanation can be discounted, however, if there is evidence that groups active after *Miller* had the organizational incentives and capacity to litigate in state courts before the decision, but did not.

A second question to examine is, Why did some organizations litigate more often than others? In particular, why was the ACLU the most active litigator? In a study of group participation in Supreme Court obscenity cases, Kobylka (1991, 162) asserts that "in localizing the obscenity determination, *Miller* led to decentralized group litigation. To cover the field once occupied by the ACLU, numerous groups representing narrow interests began to litigate."

While such a response occurred in the Supreme Court, clearly it did not in these five state judiciaries. The ACLU did not exit but rather mobilized in most state courts.[2] The ACLU itself recognized that "as a result of the Supreme Court's attitude [in *Miller v. California*], many affiliates have found themselves defending numerous individuals against pornography charges."[3] To understand why the ACLU was the most active litigator and why certain ACLU affiliates participated more often than others, attention focuses naturally on organizational factors, since *Miller* affected all groups in all states. An examination of groups' organizational settings will help us to identify factors that conditioned their responses to the decision.

The remainder of this chapter and the next chapter examine group litigation on obscenity in a variety of settings. Given its prominent role in state obscenity litigation, the rest of this chapter is devoted entirely to analysis of the ACLU and its affiliates. The next chapter examines libertarian groups that represent commercial and professional interests, as well as proscriptionist organizations.

AMERICAN CIVIL LIBERTIES UNION

Why was the ACLU by far the most active litigator in the five states? The answer, in large part, is because it could be. The ACLU is the largest and most active public interest litigation organization in the United States. Roger Baldwin founded the ACLU in 1920. Throughout the century, the organization has grown considerably in size and scope (Walker 1990). In addition to the national office, the ACLU has an extensive network of semiautonomous state and local affiliates. It has affiliates in all fifty states and maintains some 200 local organizations. It also runs several special projects through the ACLU Foundation, including the Arts Censorship Project, which is concerned with obscenity and related matters.

The ACLU's resources give it a capacity to litigate in courts at all levels nationwide. In addition to its extensive affiliate structure, the ACLU has a network of thousands of volunteer cooperating attorneys, which the group relies on for 65 percent of its legal work (O'Connor and Epstein 1989, 12). I will show that the ACLU has a resource base that truly is unmatched, at least in the obscenity litigation fray. Through its affiliates, staff, and cooperating attorneys, the group can track locally based litigation and develop legal expertise in the many state court systems.

On obscenity and other First Amendment issues, the ACLU generally favors a strict interpretation of the amendment's free speech and expression guarantee, which would allow little or no limit to these freedoms. Pursuit of this goal led the group, in 1977, to defend the right of the American Nazi Party to parade in Skokie, Illinois, a predominately Jewish suburb of Chicago. While consistent with the general agenda of the organization, the defense of the Nazis outraged many ACLU members. Between 1977 and 1978, the ACLU lost 60,000 members, ending years of consistent growth (O'Connor and Epstein 1989, 12).[4]

Since then, the group largely has recovered from its membership losses. Today, it has approximately 300,000 members nationwide. It has an extremely active litigation agenda that includes many First Amendment issues, such as obscenity. Consistent with the purposive orientation of the ACLU, the group enters obscenity litigation primarily because of its implications for free speech and expression values:

> The issue of free speech . . . is a very, very important issue for the members and the people that actually work for the ACLU affiliates and the national office. As obscenity fits within free speech, then of course it is very important. (Jane Bell [1995], Staff Attorney, ACLU of Colorado)

> I cannot [speak] directly to obscenity and pornography, but free speech values are . . . the most important to our members. . . . My members are very strongly opposed to censorship. (Steven Bates [1995], Executive Director, ACLU of South Carolina)

> Free speech is very important. For our members, the issue is the power of government. (Sheila Kennedy [1995], Executive Director, Indiana Civil Liberties Union)

Of course, simply because the ACLU opposes censorship does not necessarily mean that it will participate in obscenity litigation. Resources vary significantly across ACLU affiliates. Other factors also condition the willingness to litigate. The ACLU has the broadest issue agenda among the groups most active in obscenity litigation; sexual speech is not its sole concern. Its constitution declares that the ACLU seeks to "maintain and advance civil liberties, including freedoms of association, press, religion, and speech, and the rights to the franchise, to due process of law, and to equal protection of the laws for all people throughout the United States and its possessions." The group has litigated on each of these issues.

While all ACLU affiliates share identical or similar general policy positions on sexually oriented speech and expression, the priority of this issue compared to others on its broad agenda varies from affiliate to affiliate. Such variation is made possible by the ACLU's decentralized decision-making structure. In the 1950s most litigation decisions were made by the national legal department in New York, but "the inability of the national staff to manage the growing volume of business, combined with growing pressures from the local affiliates for greater freedom, produced a rapid decentralization" (Sorauf 1976, 42). Decentralized decision making in the organization was most pronounced during the 1960s and 1970s. Since the early 1980s, the national office has exerted somewhat greater control over affiliates, but even now "the national ACLU conducts very little litigation. Most of it occurs in the state affiliates" (Moore 1995).

Organizational decentralization, and specifically the affiliates' freedom to choose their own cases, allows priorities to develop according to local conditions. One report notes that "while the ACLU's policies are decided by its board of directors, which cases are taken and which issues are given priority are determined at the local level" (*National Law Journal* 1983, 9). Indeed, there is significant variation in rates of obscenity litigation across state affiliates: the organization mobilized after *Miller* most substantially in Minnesota and New Jersey, while trends in the other states are less conclusive. Why did the ACLU litigate most actively in these two states? Differences in organizational resources and issue priorities must be accounted for when explaining variations in the group activity across states. The remainder of this chapter investigates ACLU litigation in the five states. The examination begins with the Minnesota and New Jersey affiliates, and then turns to the remaining groups which were less active in the litigation fray.

Minnesota

The Minnesota Civil Liberties Union (MCLU) is the most active state court litigator in this study. The organization mobilized clearly in the post-*Miller* period. It dominated state appellate obscenity litigation in Minnesota, participating in a third of the post-*Miller* cases (see Table 6.6).[5] In addition, the organization litigated in seven published federal court cases. The following analysis address two primary questions. First, why did the MCLU mobilize in the post-*Miller* period? Second, why was it so much more active than other ACLU affiliates?

What accounts for the MCLU's mobilization after *Miller*? One explanation focuses on the organizational threshold. Perhaps the resources or priorities of the group changed over time for reasons unrelated to *Miller*, thereby allowing the group to litigate. The evidence, however, suggests that this is not the case. Before *Miller*, the MCLU had the resources to litigate in state appellate courts and it was involved in debate over obscenity. While no single indicator of organizational resources is in itself sufficient, several taken together suggest that the MCLU possessed the necessary litigation resources. For the entire time period of this study, the ACLU had a formal organizational presence in Minnesota, which allowed it to track local litigation and develop expertise in state courts. Also, there is ample evidence of MCLU litigation in federal and state courts before 1973 on issues other than obscenity.[6]

Despite having not litigated appellate obscenity cases, the organization was active on obscenity before the *Miller* decision. The MCLU litigation docket reveals that as early as 1953, the organization challenged a St. Paul obscenity ordinance as a violation of First Amendment free speech rights when a bookseller was cited for selling a paperback novel called *The Women's Barracks*. A municipal court agreed with the challenge and ordered the charges dismissed. In 1968, the MCLU filed an amicus curiae brief in a St. Paul municipal court opposing, as a prior restraint on speech, an order to close an adult bookstore until it could prove that it would not violate "the concept of decency and good taste." In *Minneapolis Police Department v. Twin Sister Movie*, MCLU staff attorney Michael Wetherbee filed an amicus brief opposing the state's asking the court to rule that the movie *Twin Sisters* was obscene, or that there was probable cause to deem it obscene, for the purpose of obtaining a search warrant. In these and other cases, such as *Sexual Freedom in Denmark v. Valerick and Minneapolis Police Department* and *State v. Grierson*, the MCLU played an active role in opposing state proscription of sexually explicit materials.[7] Compared to the other ACLU affiliates, the MCLU was exceptionally active in obscenity litigation even before *Miller v. California*. In sum, before the decision, the group had the capacity to litigate and was involved actively in the debate over obscenity. As a result, the post-*Miller* mobilization does not appear to be due primarily to a changed organizational threshold. This suggests that the incentives brought about by *Miller v. California* led to MCLU's mobilization in state courts.

A more complete understanding of *Miller*'s effect on the MCLU requires an investigation of why the organization litigated and the arguments it presented in state cases. Of the MCLU's six appearances in state appellate courts, five occurred in the 1970s, relatively soon after the decision (see Appendix B). This suggests that *Miller* had a rather direct and immediate impact on the MCLU. The group litigated in state courts primarily to represent criminal defendants charged with obscenity violations. Of the five state cases during the 1970s, the MCLU initiated a suit only once (*Koppinger v. City of Fairmont* 1976). It represented defendants in the remaining cases.

Of primary importance, though, is that in none of the state cases during the 1970s did the MCLU rely solely or primarily on state constitutional arguments. The organization argued the cases primarily on First Amendment and other federal constitutional grounds. When it did offer state law arguments, it did not seek broader protection than that available under federal standards. For example, in *Alexander v. City of St. Paul* (1975), MCLU attorney Randall Tigue argued that the city's removal of Alexander's license to operate a movie theater because one of his employees entered a guilty plea to showing an obscene film violated First Amendment freedom of speech and press guarantees. In an amicus brief, the MCLU argued in *City of Duluth v. Wendling* (1975) that the seizure of the only copy of a film without a prior adversary hearing as to whether the film is obscene violated the freedoms of speech and press, as guaranteed by the First and Fourteenth Amendments to the U.S. Constitution. Thus, while the MCLU litigated in state courts after *Miller*, it did not seek broader protection based on state constitutional grounds. This evidence suggests that the MCLU was motivated by the federal restriction incentive.

Further support for this conclusion is that, when it had the choice to initiate cases, the MCLU almost always chose federal courts. Executive Director Michael Moore (1995) noted that "[i]n the past, we have focused on federal courts." In fact, in three of the four published cases where the group initiated a suit, and therefore had a choice between federal and state court, it chose federal court.[8] Thus, the group entered state appellate courts primarily to represent defendants in criminal cases. Similar evidence emerges from the group's record in state trial courts.[9] The MCLU appears to have turned to state courts since they were increasingly the de facto final decision makers as a result of *Miller*.

As noted, the MCLU has been active in federal court obscenity litigation. It participated in six published federal district and circuit court cases in the post-*Miller* period, as well as one in the U.S. Supreme Court.[10] Interestingly, the MCLU brought cases in federal courts despite the Eighth Circuit's hostility to the group's libertarian policy claims. Moore noted that across a range of issues, "we have not had very good luck in federal courts." He described the Eighth Circuit, staffed by Reagan and Bush appointees, as "weak, fundamentalist, and conservative" (Moore 1995). Indeed, the Eighth Circuit has reached proscriptionist outcomes in all of its published post-*Miller* obscenity decisions.

Not surprisingly, then, the MCLU has had little success in federal obscenity cases. For example, in *UMBA v. City of Minneapolis* (1985), the court rejected the Upper Midwest Booksellers Association's (UMBA) argument (MCLU attorney Randall Tigue represented the group) that a district court erred in severing the invalid portion of a Minneapolis ordinance designed to regulate the manner in which sexually explicit material deemed "harmful to minors" is displayed for sale. According to the UMBA, the court instead should have struck down the entire law. In *Blatnik v. Ketola* (1978), the court rejected the MCLU's challenge to an ordinance that prohibited nudity in on-premises liquor establishments.

The group did fare slightly better in the federal district court. In *Alexander v. City of Minneapolis* (1982), the court struck down a Minneapolis zoning ordinance that prohibited adult bookstores, theaters, and massage parlors from operating within 500 feet of residential districts, churches, or educational buildings. The city passed the ordinance in the wake of the U.S. Supreme Court's decision in *Young v. American Mini Theatres* (1976), which for the first time permitted restrictive zoning of nonobscene pornography. However, the district court ruled that the Minneapolis ordinance went beyond merely restricting locations and unduly limited public access to material protected by the First Amendment.

In the wake of generally unsuccessful efforts to advance their libertarian goals in federal courts, the MCLU appears prepared to emphasize state litigation, and particularly to mobilize state constitutional law. Michael Moore told me that "in the future, we will focus on state courts." The motivation for turning to state courts is that arguments can be advanced on both federal and state constitutional grounds. Said Moore (1995), "[Y]ou get two bites at the apple in state courts."[11]

The MCLU joined the ACLU Arts Censorship Project as amicus curiae in *State v. Davidson* (1992), which is one of very few obscenity cases in the five states to feature multiple-group involvement from both the libertarian and proscriptionist camps. The MCLU asserted two independent state constitutional claims. It argued that Minnesota's obscenity statute violated the due process guarantee of the state constitution by using local rather than statewide community standards to determine obscenity. Indeed, it was for this reason that a state appellate court had ruled the obscenity statute unconstitutional, declaring that the state constitution's due process clause grants more expansive protection than the U.S. Constitution.

The MCLU also argued that obscenity is not unprotected under the Minnesota Constitution. This argument not only cited but also relied directly on the reasoning of the Oregon Supreme Court in *State v. Henry* (1987). In declaring that obscenity was not unprotected by the Oregon Constitution's free speech clause, the Oregon high court relied on the historical argument that at the time the state constitution was adopted, obscenity was not an exception to free speech. In *Davidson*, the MCLU conducted a similar historical analysis, found no obscenity exception in Minnesota, and asserted that "as a result, the historical analysis in *Henry* is applicable and should be persuasive in construing" the free speech clause of the Minnesota Constitution.[12] The Minnesota Supreme Court, however, rejected both of MCLU's independent state law claims and overturned the lower court's expansive state law ruling.

To summarize, the MCLU's mobilization in state courts appears due primarily to the legal incentives provided by *Miller v. California*. In the post-*Miller* period, the group entered state courts primarily to represent criminal defendants and asserted rights claims based primarily on federal (not state) constitutional grounds. When given the choice between federal and state courts, the MCLU typically chose the former. Indeed, the group's executive director noted that the organization generally has preferred the federal courts. This evidence suggests that the federal restriction incentive provided the principal motivation for the MCLU to enter state judiciaries. With the final word in many obscenity debates increasingly in the hands of state courts, the MCLU had reason to enter that arena. By no means did the group respond to *Miller* by immediately turning to state courts and state law to seek expansive protections. However, in recent years the group did look to state law as a viable alternative to federal law for the development of its libertarian agenda on obscenity.

So far, the analysis has focused on why the MCLU mobilized in state courts after *Miller*. But why has the group been so much more active on obscenity than any other ACLU affiliate in this study? Here, attention turns to the organizational threshold.

The MCLU clearly had sufficient resources to litigate in state courts both before and after *Miller*. The group currently has three staff attorneys and a pool of about 150-200 cooperating attorneys. Additionally, the MCLU has long had an activist reputation on issues of obscenity and pornography. Compared to the other affiliates, it held an absolutist view of the reach of the First Amendment. The following comparisons of the views of MCLU officials with those of staff in other state affiliates are instructive:

> You can't "properly" have people in the community tell you what's acceptable to be in their community. . . . Bookstores cannot be censored. That's all there is to it. (Matthew Stark, Former Executive Director, MCLU [quoted in Downs 1989, 69])

> We don't talk about any difference between obscenity and pornography [both are protected speech]. (Michael Moore [1995], Executive Director, MCLU)

Staff and members in other affiliates held less absolutist positions. Wenk (1995) suggested that members of the ACLU of New Jersey are less concerned with restrictions on obscene and pornographic communications than they are with restrictions on political speech. According to Jane Bell (1995) of the ACLU of Colorado:

> There are always the issues that sit behind obscenity . . . gender discrimination and child abuse. Those are two areas that must be considered with the obscenity question. We are against any kind of gender discrimination and of course we do not support child abuse in any way. If a child is hurt substantially, either physically or psychologically, especially by somehow becoming involved in the making of obscene or pornographic movies or videos . . . then the ACLU in no way supports that.

Much more than other ACLU affiliates, the MCLU rejected as illegitimate *any* efforts to control sexually explicit materials or expressions. This conclusion, based on my interviews, is consistent with Downs's account of the MCLU. He "questioned the M[CLU]'s understanding of free speech because it did not recognize the dangers inherent in some expression; [it] pursu[ed] instead an absolutist ideal of liberty." In contrast, "the Indiana Civil Liberties Union was more credible in this regard" (Downs 1989, 142). Given the MCLU's unwavering issue position, the group naturally viewed obscenity as a higher priority than did other affiliates. Consequently, it was more likely to devote scarce resources to obscenity litigation.

Why was the obscenity issue so important to the MCLU? While many factors likely play a role, certainly Minnesota's long history of strong and politicized debate over sexually explicit material is important in understanding the MCLU's perceived threat to its libertarian ideals.[13]

Downs (1989) described the history of the proscription of sexually oriented material in Minnesota's largest city, Minneapolis. Like many other urban areas, the city's pornography business grew in the 1960s. In response, politicians and neighborhood groups mobilized against pornography and other forms of "moral deviance" such as homosexuality and prostitution. Numerous efforts were made to prohibit sexually explicit material through measures such as obscenity and indecency laws, restrictive zoning ordinances, and laws requiring opaque covers on certain magazines. At the University of Minnesota, Catharine MacKinnon and Andrea Dworkin developed a feminist critique of pornography and proposed to the Minneapolis City Council the nation's first modern antipornography ordinance. While Mayor Donald Fraser vetoed the ordinance passed by the council, debate over the ordinance polarized the community. Downs (1989, 91) characterized the tenor of the debate in Minneapolis: "The dominant public discourse attending the anti-pornography ordinance . . . was marked by excessive zeal and incivility toward reasonable opponents. The ordinance's supporters were the major offenders in this regard, although the MCLU's intransigent, knee-jerk opposition compounded the problem." The novel and radical approach of the Minneapolis pornography ordinance undoubtedly accentuated debate in comparison to "typical" obscenity issues. Nevertheless, the discussion is instructive in suggesting why obscenity and related issues were particularly important to the MCLU. The organization operated in an environment in which numerous attempts to ban sexual expressions have been made in the name of moral integrity. Consequently, obscenity rose to a priority status for the MCLU.

The MCLU's organizational threshold impelled it to litigate much more than other ACLU affiliates. The group possessed considerable litigation resources and viewed obscenity as an important issue on its broad agenda. As a result, resources were devoted to obscenity litigation; it participated in cases both before and after *Miller*. Yet it was only after *Miller* decentralized policy making on obscenity and made state appellate courts more vital policy makers that the organization participated in those courts.

To summarize, with legal incentives to turn to state courts and the organizational resources and incentives to do so, the MCLU litigated regularly after *Miller*. The group's resources were well suited to obscenity litigation. Not only did it have sufficient numbers of attorneys, but also the state's leading pornography lawyer, Randall Tigue, was an MCLU attorney, which gave the organization particular expertise in this area of law (see Wasby 1988). Even when the organization did not litigate formally, the MCLU had links to the expert counsel who argued several other cases in state and federal courts.

New Jersey

The dynamic nature of ACLU litigation in New Jersey illustrates how changing priorities influence the behavior of an organization with a broad issue agenda. The ACLU of New Jersey mobilized initially in the wake of *Miller* to oppose the extension of obscenity laws. It participated in three appellate obscenity cases, all during the 1970s. However, as the perceived threat posed by *Miller* and obscenity prosecutions in general lessened over time, the ACLU increasingly focused on other issue areas.

Various explanations may account for the ACLU of New Jersey's mobilization in state courts after *Miller v. California*. The mobilization could have been caused by a changing organizational context unrelated to *Miller*. The evidence, however, does not support this conclusion. Before 1973, the ACLU of New Jersey had sufficient litigation resources. There had been an organizational presence in the state for many years. A state affiliate was incorporated in New Jersey in 1961, and before this time the state was served by the New York and Greater Philadelphia ACLU chapters. There is also ample evidence of federal and state appellate litigation in the pre-*Miller* years on issues other than obscenity.[14]

Further, before *Miller* the ACLU of New Jersey was involved in obscenity debates. For example, in *Levine v. Fort Lee Board of Education*, an ACLU cooperating attorney contested a ban on the use of a school auditorium to show a film that contained nudity, profanity, and drug abuse. That same year, ACLU represented in juvenile court a minor charged with exhibiting an indecent film at a high school dance. While neither case went to trial, these instances illustrate the ACLU's concern with obscenity and related issues even before *Miller*.[15]

Thus, the group's mobilization in state courts appears due primarily to *Miller* rather than a changed organizational setting. In the wake of the decision, the ACLU of New Jersey mobilized to protect its libertarian policy interests. Government and proscriptionist forces, such as religious organizations, in New Jersey saw *Miller* as an opportunity to enforce obscenity law more vigorously. State Attorney General George Kugler and the state's county prosecutors met the week after the Supreme Court issued *Miller* to plan a crackdown on pornography. Kugler declared that X-rated films "are in for a rough time in New Jersey."[16]

As in Minnesota, the ACLU entered New Jersey courts—at both the trial and appellate levels—to represent criminal defendants. In spring 1973, just before the Supreme Court issued *Miller*, state law enforcement officials conducted a mass obscenity raid in Union County. Numerous cases emerged from the raid; ACLU cooperating attorneys represented the defendants in trial courts. While only one of these cases reached the appellate level (*State v. Blecker* 1978), the ACLU devoted significant resources to the defense.[17] Eventually, charges in most of the cases were dropped when the defendants agreed to enter a pretrial intervention program, but not before ACLU attorneys prepared to challenge the constitutionality of the state's obscenity law.

The group participated in three appellate cases within six years of the *Miller* decision; it represented defendants in each case. In every case, the ACLU did not mobilize state constitutional law, but instead relied solely on federal constitutional arguments to assert rights claims. In *State v. Carmel* (1979), for instance, ACLU attorneys argued that the seizure of Joseph Carmel's stock, without a prior adversary hearing, was a prior restraint on speech in violation of the First Amendment. The attorneys also contended that the seizure violated Carmel's rights to procedural due process, once again relying solely on federal constitutional (Fourteenth Amendment) grounds to assert a rights claim. This evidence suggests that the group was motivated primarily by the federal restriction incentive. This finding is interesting and somewhat unexpected. Despite New Jersey courts' tradition of activism and the view that they play an important role in the new judicial federalism (Tarr and Porter 1988; Caldeira 1985), the ACLU advanced only federal constitutional claims in state litigation.

Why did the ACLU of New Jersey not assert rights claims based on state constitutional law? My interviews reveal a general preference for federal courts, at least under some circumstances. Staff attorney Marsha Wenk (1995) noted that "on cutting edge issues, New Jersey courts offer broader protections than federal courts. This makes state courts more attractive and we turn there." However, "where federal and state protections are equivalent, we generally go to federal courts . . . they are quicker, easier, and more efficient . . . you avoid local political disadvantages [found in state courts]."

The ACLU of New Jersey appears most willing to enter state courts and to assert rights claims based on state constitutional law when it offers broader protection than federal law. But on issues where federal and state protections are analogous, the group favors federal courts. Obscenity is one of those issues. In *State v. DeSantis* (1974), the New Jersey Supreme Court authoritatively construed the state obscenity statute to include the *Miller* test for obscenity. Thus, federal courts and New Jersey courts implement the same legal standard in obscenity cases. While this evidence, by itself, is far from conclusive, it certainly suggests that the group prefers to litigate obscenity cases at the federal level.

Examination of the sole instance in which the group initiated a challenge against an obscenity law further supports this conclusion. In 1975, the group represented plaintiffs challenging a 1796 state fornication law as a violation of the First Amendment guarantee of free expression. Actors and producers of the film *Deep Sleep* were indicted under the law in a Passaic County court. The ACLU filed the suit, which ultimately failed, in federal district court.[18] The only other instance of federal court litigation by the ACLU of New Jersey was in joining the national office on an amicus brief before the U.S. Supreme Court in *Cryan v. Hamar Theatres, Inc.* (1974). However, the Court did not hear this case, remanding it instead to a New Jersey appellate court for further consideration in light of the recent *Miller* decision. The ACLU did not pursue the case further.

Thus, it appears that the federal restriction incentive impelled the ACLU of New Jersey into state courts after the *Miller* decision. Yet since 1979 the group has participated in no appellate obscenity cases at the state or federal levels. Why has it not litigated? It is certainly not due to a lack of resources. Currently, the group has two paid staff attorneys and a pool of cooperating attorneys that numbers in the hundreds.[19] Instead, the lack of continued involvement on the issue reflects primarily the lessened threat that obscenity prosecutions pose in New Jersey. Marsha Wenk (1995) reported that New Jersey does not prosecute obscenity as vigorously as the federal government and that much of the available sexually explicit material is not legally obscene. Indeed, in 1976, ACLU of

New Jersey Executive Director Stephen Nagler noted that the apparent rising tide of censorship in the state was probably just a periodic peak in the "ebb and flow" of "public morals regulators who come out of the woodwork."[20]

Given the lack of vigorous prosecution in the state, obscenity is no longer as important for the ACLU of New Jersey. Although the organization's general issue position has not changed, the lessened threat posed by obscenity prosecutions has resulted in obscenity becoming a lower priority for the ACLU of New Jersey, allowing it to devote resources to other issues on its broad agenda. In recent years, the group has increasingly emphasized civil rights for gays, lesbians, and people with AIDS, and nontraditional issues like poverty and welfare. In the area of free speech and expression, the group has tended to focus on cases involving "political" speech. For example, of the seven free expression cases the ACLU of New Jersey litigated in 1991, two involved political expression in shopping malls, one involved the dismissal of a teacher for expressing controversial ideas in the classroom, and another challenged a New Jersey Supreme Court rule prohibiting court employees from engaging in "political activities." In contrast, the ACLU of New Jersey was involved in eight obscenity cases (at both the trial and appellate levels) in 1977 alone.[21] This change in litigation behavior lends insight into the fluidity of issue priorities for groups, like the ACLU, with a broad issue agenda.

In Minnesota and New Jersey, the ACLU mobilized, at least temporarily, in state courts in response to the legal incentives provided by the U.S. Supreme Court in *Miller v. California*. However, the ACLU did not mobilize as clearly in Colorado, Indiana, and South Carolina. Attention now turns to these affiliates to explain why they did not participate often in state obscenity litigation.

Colorado

The ACLU of Colorado did not mobilize markedly in the wake of *Miller*. It participated directly in only one state appellate obscenity case, *In re Title* (1994). In that case, the organization filed an amicus curiae brief challenging the wording of an ultimately unsuccessful state referendum that sought to require Colorado courts to proscribe obscenity as vigorously as the U.S. Supreme Court permits under *Miller*. To determine whether material is obscene, Colorado courts require that a work be judged based on a community "tolerance" standard, which allows fewer restrictions than the "acceptance" standard used in the federal courts and most state judiciaries.[22] While the group had the resources to litigate in state courts and clearly viewed obscenity as an important issue, the presence of other actors offering libertarian arguments in state courts allowed the ACLU to remain out of the litigation fray.

While no single indicator of organizational resources is in itself sufficient, several taken together suggest that the ACLU of Colorado has had adequate resources to litigate since 1960. The ACLU incorporated an affiliate in Colorado in 1952; it had a formal organizational presence in the state throughout the entire time period under study. Currently, the affiliate has a paid staff of six members, two of whom are attorneys. According to a staff attorney (Bell 1995), the pool of approximately 125 volunteer attorneys generally is sufficient to handle a normal caseload. The group has litigated on issues other than obscenity in both federal and state courts, before and after *Miller*.[23] With a formal organizational presence and a track record of litigation, the ACLU of Colorado appears to have had at least a minimal litigation capacity.

Further, the ACLU of Colorado participated in disputes over the proscription of sexual material. Affiliate records indicate that it first litigated on obscenity in 1966, when members of the San Francisco Mime Troupe were arrested for "using filthy language and performing lewd acts" during a satirical minstrel show. ACLU cooperating attorneys represented the defendants in a Denver municipal court.[24] In 1970, the ACLU represented defendants challenging the state's lewdness statute, but like the Mime Troupe case, this case did not reach the appellate level.[25]

In the post-*Miller* period, the group was prepared to oppose the proscription of sexually explicit material in the state. In the wake of *Miller*, the ACLU worked with the local Media Coalition (MC) to oppose the expansion of obscenity laws. At the January 13, 1975, meeting of the ACLU of Colorado, MC attorney Peter Ney discussed the state of Colorado obscenity law and obtained ACLU support in the event that there were efforts to expand the law.[26] On several occasions, the group publicly opposed state legislative efforts to enact and enforce anti-obscenity measures. For example, state ACLU Executive Director James Joy spoke out against an anti-obscenity bill passed by the state legislature in 1981, a year after the Colorado Supreme Court invalidated the previous obscenity statute in *People v. New Horizons, Inc.* (1980). Joy noted that "each year there seems to be a ritualistic attempt to stamp out smut in Colorado [and the legislature is] saying, 'People of Colorado, you cannot be trusted. You cannot select what you want to read, see and hear.'"[27]

For many years, then, the group had sufficient resources and clearly was concerned with attempts to proscribe sexual material. Yet until 1994, the ACLU of Colorado did not litigate in state or federal appellate courts. The organizational threshold alone cannot explain the lack of litigation, particularly in the post-*Miller* period. However, an examination of other actors in Colorado courts helps to explain why the ACLU did not litigate.

The primary reason that the organization did not mobilize in the wake of *Miller* appears to be the fact that there were other libertarian actors in Colorado courts, specifically the Mountains and Plains Booksellers Association (MPBA) and Arthur Schwartz, a nationally known member of the "obscenity bar."[28] Arthur Schwartz or the MPBA (along with the Media Coalition) have been involved in 44 percent (eight of 18) of the Colorado Supreme Court obscenity decisions since *Miller*.[29] With them in the litigation fray, the ACLU knew that its libertarian position was well represented before the courts, and therefore did not have to enter obscenity cases. I draw this conclusion for two reasons. First, as comparative analysis demonstrates, the absence of other libertarian actors impelled the MCLU and ACLU of New Jersey into the litigation fray. Like them, the ACLU of Colorado had the resources to participate in obscenity litigation. But it did not have to expend those scarce resources since other actors mobilized in response to *Miller*, a luxury the Minnesota and New Jersey affiliates did not enjoy.

Second, by working closely after *Miller* with the MC and MPBA, the ACLU of Colorado kept abreast of obscenity litigation without becoming involved directly. There appears to have been an implicit cooperation between the ACLU and material groups in Colorado, much as there was on the national level. In the early 1970s, material groups participated in the ACLU-sponsored National Coalition Against Censorship, but most later left it to form MC. The latter group was devoted to litigation, while the former focused on public education. A similar division of labor appears to have occurred in Colorado.

The breadth of the ACLU's issue agenda is important in understanding its litigation behavior. Clearly, the ACLU of Colorado was concerned with the ongoing obscenity debate; it worked outside of the courts with other libertarian organizations to prevent obscenity prosecutions. Yet since other actors mobilized in Colorado courts in the post-*Miller* period, the ACLU of Colorado did not have to devote scarce resources to obscenity cases. The group was able to conserve its resources and litigate on other issues.[30]

More recently, obscenity has not been a priority for the ACLU of Colorado, in part because it does not view prosecutions as a major threat. According to Bell (1995), "I don't think obscenity is being prosecuted that strongly in this state; . . . we get complaints on all sorts of issues and I haven't seen [many] on obscenity." This view is echoed by Arthur Schwartz (1995), who noted that "there are very few state court prosecutions going on right now." Indeed, the ACLU's sole foray into the state courts—its amicus brief in *In re Title* (1994)—represented an attempt to ensure that obscenity prosecutions do not proliferate. The ACLU's overriding concern was the potential consequence of voter approval of a constitutional amendment requiring state courts to apply the *Miller* standard in obscenity cases. The group argued that the "amendment, if approved, would effectively nullify this Court's decisions in *735 East Colfax* and *Ford*, and mandate a reversion to the narrower, less protective standards of community 'decency' or 'acceptance,' which have not proved adequate to protect free expression in the past" (ACLU Foundation of Colorado amicus brief in *In re Title* [1994], p. 3).

Indiana

Like the ACLU of Colorado, the Indiana Civil Liberties Union (ICLU) participated in only one obscenity case in state appellate courts, *Fordyce v. State*

(1991). The lack of consistent litigation by the ICLU was due both to the group's insufficient resources and its need to attend to a broad issue agenda. Given the number of issues on which the ICLU litigates, it could not devote the resources to participate regularly in obscenity litigation.

The ICLU certainly has been concerned with restrictions on sexual speech and expression. According to Legal Director Richard Waples, the group tracks most state and federal court obscenity litigation in Indiana. He noted that at the state and local levels, governments in Indiana have actively sought to prohibit access to sexually explicit material through direct proscription, zoning, and other means (Waples 1995a). Debate over obscenity often has been intense in the state. In recent years, two important U.S. Supreme Court cases emerged from Indiana, *Fort Wayne Books v. Indiana* (1989) and *Barnes v. Glen Theatre, Inc.* (1991). In both cases, the ICLU joined the national ACLU on amicus briefs in the Supreme Court.

While not typically active on obscenity, the ICLU mobilized to challenge what was likely the greatest threat to its libertarian policy position, Indianapolis's antipornography ordinance. In fact, the ICLU was "the only organized political opposition to the ordinance" (Downs 1989, 115). In addition to opposing the ordinance publicly and testifying against it before the city council, the ICLU filed an amicus brief in support of Media Coalition's constitutional challenge to the ordinance in federal district court. The local counsel in the suit, Sheila Kennedy and Richard Kammen, both have ties to the ICLU. Currently, Kennedy is the organization's executive director. Kammen, a member of the First Amendment Lawyers Association, periodically consults with the ICLU (Waples 1995a).

Thus, obscenity clearly has been an important issue for the ICLU. The group has tracked litigation, joined the national organization on amicus briefs in the Supreme Court, and occasionally entered litigation directly. Further, the groups' legal director viewed Indiana as a particularly active state in attempting to prohibit sexual speech and expression. Why, then, did the ICLU made only one venture into state court obscenity litigation?

The answer focuses on the organizational threshold, particularly resources. According to staff:

> There are a lot of issues to attend to, and we can't do everything. . . . So we don't go out looking for [obscenity cases]. (Cheri Harris [1995], Staff Attorney, ICLU)

> I wouldn't say that we have enough resources; . . . we would like to litigate more. (Richard Waples [1995a], Legal Director, ICLU)

In contrast to the ACLU of Colorado, resource scarcity appears to have directly affected the ICLU's entry into obscenity litigation. While the ACLU has had an organizational presence in Indiana since before 1960, its forays into state appellate courts were rare until relatively recently. Between 1960 and 1980, the

ICLU participated in only six state appellate cases.[31] Currently, the organization has two paid staff attorneys and a volunteer pool of about eighty members (Harris 1995; Waples 1995a). While these appear to be adequate litigation resources, they are far from abundant, particularly given the group's broad issue agenda. The organization could not devote its litigation resources solely, or even primarily, to obscenity cases. While the ICLU viewed anti-obscenity efforts as a threat, limited resources and the need to attend to a variety of other legal issues restricted the group's ability to enter obscenity litigation with any consistency.

It is also important to note that the ICLU has not taken as absolutist a position on obscenity as other affiliates, most notably the MCLU. For instance, Downs (1989, 115) noted that "unlike MCLU Director Matthew Stark in Minneapolis, [ICLU Executive Director Michael] Gradison conceded the validity of obscenity law and the [*New York v.*] *Ferber* [1982] case's doctrine on child pornography, as well as such regulatory measures as zoning and opaque covers." This insight helps to explain the ICLU's orientation toward obscenity litigation. The group accepted some governmental attempts to restrict or prohibit sexually explicit materials and expressions. Unlike its counterpart in Minnesota, the Indiana affiliate has not taken an absolutist position on issues of sexual speech and expression. Therefore, organizational priorities did not impel it to enter the litigation fray to challenge all laws that restricted access to sexual materials. The group was willing to challenge only some of these laws. Compared to the MCLU, obscenity appears to be a less crucial issue; the ICLU instead has devoted scarce litigation resources to other issues.[32]

Easing ICLU's decision not to enter state courts consistently was the presence of members of the obscenity bar in state cases. Waples noted that there are strong criminal defense lawyers in the state. The leading pornography lawyer in Indiana is Richard Kammen, who as mentioned consults occasionally with the ICLU. Kammen argued seven state obscenity cases in the post-*Miller* period, including several that presented constitutional claims.[33] The presence of Kammen and others in the litigation fray allowed the ICLU not to litigate when it otherwise might have.[34] These actors presented libertarian arguments similar to the type that the ICLU likely would have put forth if it had litigated. For example, in *Albright v. State* (1986), Kammen brought a challenge to Indiana's obscenity statute under the U.S. and Indiana Constitutions. In *State v. Sappenfield* (1987), he argued that Indiana's Racketeer Influenced and Corrupt Organizations (RICO) provision, as applied to a violation of the obscenity statute, was unconstitutionally vague and a violation of the Fourteenth Amendment due process guarantee. The ICLU has been able to keep abreast of this litigation but allocated scarce resources elsewhere.

Though not active consistently in obscenity litigation, the sole instance of ICLU participation in a state appellate case is a doctrinally important one. In *Fordyce v. State* (1991), the ICLU filed an amicus brief arguing that obscenity is not unprotected under the Indiana Constitution. The group mobilized state constitutional law to seek more expansive protection than that recognized under federal standards. Waples noted that he "sens[es] a greater receptivity in state courts" and while state courts are "not champions of civil liberties and civil rights . . . there is [now] an opportunity there to create state constitutional law." He suggested that state constitutions on their face offer broader protections than their federal counterpart and that the trend for state courts to use their constitutions to create independent law is likely to continue in the future (Waples 1995a, 1995b).

Like the MCLU in *State v. Davidson* (1992), the ICLU in *Fordyce* cited *State v. Henry* (1989) and conducted a similar historical analysis of anti-obscenity laws in Indiana at the time of the ratification of the state constitution. The Indiana appellate court noted ICLU's reliance on *Henry*: "By this precedent [*State v. Henry*], Fordyce and the ICLU would have us apply the Oregon analysis to conclude that the framers of Indiana's current constitution did not intend for obscenity to be an exception to the free speech guarantee" (*Fordyce* 1991, 361). The court in fact did conduct a similar historical analysis, but rejected the claim that obscenity was not an exception to the Indiana Constitution's free speech guarantee.

In sum, the ICLU's limited resources and broad issue agenda primarily account for its lack of obscenity litigation in both state and federal courts. The evidence does not suggest that one factor is clearly more important than the other. The ICLU seldom litigated during the years immediately following *Miller*, and since then, it has monitored obscenity cases but generally avoided directly entering litigation.

South Carolina

Both cases in which the ACLU participated in South Carolina courts (*State v. Watkins* was heard twice by the state supreme court) were argued by Laughlin McDonald of the ACLU's Southern Regional Office, headquartered in Atlanta. The South Carolina affiliate of the ACLU, however, never litigated an obscenity case at the appellate level. Unlike other ACLU affiliates, the lack of litigation in South Carolina reflects sheer resource scarcity. Whereas other state affiliates set issue priorities in the face of scarce resources, the South Carolina chapter has been unable to litigate consistently on any issue without the aid of the national office. In short, resource scarcity itself explains the lack of ACLU participation in obscenity litigation in South Carolina.

By any indicator of resources, the ACLU of South Carolina has been organizationally weak. A state chapter was not formed until 1968, so throughout most of the pre-*Miller* period there was no formal organizational presence in South Carolina. During the first few years, the affiliate was operated entirely by volunteers. The ACLU did have a staff attorney during most of the next decade, although according to Executive Director Steven Bates (1995), the attorney was merely a "caretaker."[35] During this period "the organization really had a staff attorney and no staff." As late as the early 1980s, the South Carolina ACLU had a volunteer attorney pool of only eight members (*National Law Journal* 1983). Currently, the group has only 20-30 cooperating attorneys, which is approximately a third the size of the next smallest volunteer pool among the five affiliates examined. Finally, in the pre-*Miller* period, the ACLU of South Carolina was the only state affiliate to have litigated in no published state or federal appellate cases.

Much more than the other affiliates, resource scarcity influences the organization's litigation decisions. Referring to the choice to enter litigation, Bates noted that "the key determinant is: can we find an attorney to give the time when we need the time?" The lack of available attorneys constrained severely the ACLU's litigation potential in South Carolina. Bates asserted that not having a staff attorney for many years restricted the ACLU's ability to litigate on a broad range of issues and to recruit a larger pool of cooperating attorneys. Exacerbating this problem is the fact that South Carolina courts rarely award attorney's fees in criminal cases. Bates acknowledged that, for private practice attorneys, this limits the attractiveness of volunteering for the ACLU and that it also "colors our decision to use state courts."

The ACLU of South Carolina "generally picks two or three issues a year and focuses on them instead of a broad range of issues." Nominally, the affiliate had goals similar to those of other state affiliates. However, it could not act on most of these goals given the sheer lack of a resource base. On the few issues on which the ACLU has litigated with any frequency (particularly voting rights), it has done so in concert with the national office. Says Bates, "the national staff plays a big support role" in providing money, lawyers, and other resources.

This is not to suggest that the ACLU of South Carolina is indifferent to attempts to prosecute obscenity. In 1970, it joined in on an appeal of a state court order to ban the film *I Am Curious Yellow*. Nearly twenty years later, the organization filed suit in the Richland and Greenville Judicial Circuits to overturn the ban on the sale of rap group 2 Live Crew's album *As Nasty as They Wanna Be*.[36] But compared to other ACLU affiliates, the South Carolina chapter had virtually no resources with which to litigate. As the interview evidence reveals, this fact is critically important in the group's decision making process. Since minimal resources are necessary to litigate and during most of the period under study the ACLU of South Carolina lacked this organizational prerequisite, the *Miller* decision had little effect on the group's behavior. Regardless of the legal incentives, the ACLU of South Carolina simply was unable to enter the courts.

CONCLUSION

The American Civil Liberties Union is widely regarded as among the most active and vigilant supporters of civil rights and civil liberties in the United States. For decades, the ACLU has been the heart of attempts to expand liberties and advance the cause of social and political equality (Walker 1990; Murphy 1979). No organization in America has been as crucial to the development of civil liberties law in the twentieth century.

True to its reputation, the ACLU was the most active group litigant in obscenity cases in the five states. No other organization responded as clearly to *Miller v. California*'s incentives to turn to the states. Yet perhaps surprisingly, ACLU affiliates were largely inactive in some states. Only in Minnesota and New Jersey did the organization mobilize clearly in state courts in response to *Miller*. The group seldom participated in courts in Colorado, Indiana, and South Carolina.

The analysis in this chapter suggests that organizational factors, particularly resources, are extremely important in explaining the ACLU's use of state courts, at least after legal precedent provided incentives to turn to the states. Much of the variation in patterns of group litigation reflects differences in affiliates' resources and priorities. The ACLU had greater litigation resources than any other group involved in obscenity litigation, a point that will become evident in the next chapter. Yet the resources of ACLU affiliates varied significantly across states. The lack of obscenity litigation by the ACLU of South Carolina demonstrates that when a group (even one organized at the state level) lacks sufficient access to attorneys, it simply cannot litigate. To be sure, all ACLU affiliates faced varying degrees of resource scarcity (see Table 6.7) and consequently had to establish priorities among the issues on their broad agenda. Given the perceived threat from proscriptionist forces and the affiliate's staunch anticensorship position, the Minnesota Civil Liberties Union viewed obscenity as an issue of primary importance. Indeed, the MCLU was more active than the other affiliates in obscenity litigation.

The breadth of the ACLU's issue agenda means that in the face of resource scarcity, affiliates must pick and choose among cases and issues. This allows issue priorities to develop at the local level. Each affiliate, save for South Carolina's, appears to have had sufficient resources to participate at least occasionally in state litigation for much of the time period under study. Yet only two affiliates entered obscenity cases regularly. Resource scarcity, the need to attend to other issues, and (in the case of the ACLU of Colorado) the presence of other actors in the litigation fray conditioned the groups' willingness and ability to enter state courts.

While organizational resources and priorities did influence group litigation efforts, the analysis in this chapter also demonstrates the importance of legal incentives. The U.S. Supreme Court's decision in *Miller v. California* decentralized decision making in obscenity law. With the Supreme Court less willing to review lower-court convictions, state courts increasingly became the de facto policy makers of last resort. It was not until after the *Miller* decision that the MCLU and ACLU of New Jersey litigated in state appellate courts. Analysis of material groups and proscriptionist organizations in the next chapter will examine further the importance of the *Miller* decision.

Table 6.7
ACLU Litigation Resources in Five States

State	Affiliate?	Staff Attorneys	Cooperating Attorneys
Colorado	Yes	2	125
Indiana	Yes	2	80
Minnesota	Yes	3	150-200
New Jersey	Yes	2	Hundreds
South Carolina	Yes	1	20-30

Sources: Interviews with group officials; group files; *Encyclopedia of Associations* (various years). Figures for cooperating attorneys represent approximate numbers.

When ACLU affiliates did enter state courts, they appear to have been motivated primarily by the federal restriction incentive. ACLU of South Carolina Executive Director Steven Bates (1995) put it this way: "I'm not sure we are in state courts by choice." In most instances of state court litigation in the immediate wake of *Miller*, the ACLU represented defendants and relied primarily on federal constitutional arguments to advance rights claims. Libertarian groups had to go "where the action is," and *Miller* pushed the ACLU into state appellate courts. Only relatively recently have some affiliates asserted rights claims based on independent state constitutional grounds.

While the ACLU was the dominant group litigator, other libertarian as well as proscriptionist organizations also participated in state and federal court cases. These groups differ from the ACLU on a variety of potentially important dimensions. Not all exist primarily to litigate, nor do they have as broad an issue agenda as the ACLU. The next chapter examines state court litigation by libertarian groups like the American Booksellers Association and proscriptionist groups like Citizens for Decency through Law and Morality in Media. It explores how groups in various organizational contexts responded to *Miller v. California*.

NOTES

1. The exception is *In re Title* (1994), a challenge to the wording of a proposed state constitutional amendment that sought to require Colorado courts to proscribe obscenity as vigorously as permitted by the U.S. Supreme Court. While it did not raise a constitutional issue, clearly the case had important policy implications in Colorado.

2. Kobylka (1991) argues that groups can respond to Court decisions in one of three ways: they can exit the arena, increase their efforts (mobilize), or continue to use the legal system.

3. *Civil Liberties*, January 1975, p. 2.

4. For more detailed discussion of the ACLU's defense of the Nazis in Skokie, see Downs (1985) and Gibson and Bingham (1985).

5. While I classify the MCLU as active in one third of Minnesota's state appellate obscenity cases, it is likely that the group played an indirect role in many other cases. Randall Tigue, past president of the MCLU and a cooperating attorney for the organization, is also the primary pornography lawyer in Minnesota. According to Downs (1989, 54), Tigue is the personal counsel for the Alexander family, the leading pornography suppliers in Minneapolis.

Tigue declined my interview requests. However, MCLU Executive Director Michael Moore told me that the organization regularly works closely with Tigue. Tigue was primary counsel in three state court (*Knudtson v. City of Coates* [1994]; *State v. White* [1990]; and *State v. Bonynge* [1990]) and four federal court (*Alexander v. City of Minneapolis* [1991, 1989]; *Doe v. City of Minneapolis* [1990]; and *Wolff v. City of Monticello* [1992]) obscenity cases for which I was unable to identify direct MCLU participation. In the interest of validity, I do not classify these cases as instances of MCLU involvement. But either classification scheme produces the same substantive conclusions about MCLU litigation patterns.

6. See *In re Discharge of Bruce W. Johnson* (1970); *State v. Witherall* (1970); *State v. Target Stores* (1968); *State v. Miller et al.* (1968); *State v. Edwards* (1970); *State v. Dailey* (1969); *State v. Hartman* (1965); *Lykken v. Vavreck* (1973); *Kosydar v. Wolman* (1972); *Koelfgen v. Jackson* (1972).

7. Source: MCLU files (copy on file with author).

8. The federal court cases that MCLU sponsored are *UMBA v. City of Minneapolis* (1985), *Blatnik v. Ketola* (1978), and *Alexander v. City of Minneapolis* (1982). The state court case is *Koppinger v. City of Fairmont* (1976). In addition, MCLU joined as amicus in two other suits initiated in federal court, *Schneider v. City of Ramsey* (1992) and *Frejlach v. Butler* (1978).

9. See *Bogen v.* Sheedy; *Parkway Theatre Corp. v. City of Minneapolis*; *City of Minneapolis v.* LaLonde; Higgins, *and Kouri*; *Jochim v. City of Minneapolis*; *City of Minneapolis v. Opsahl et al.*; *Sparks v. City of Minneapolis*; *Jones v. City of Minneapolis*. In each case, the MCLU represented defendants in state courts. Sources: ACLU Litigation Docket (various years); MCLU files.

10. The Eighth Circuit cases are *UMBA v. City of Minneapolis* (1985), *Blatnik v. Ketola* (1978), and *Frejlach v. Butler* (1978). The district court cases are *Schneider v. City of Ramsey* (1992), *UMBA v. City of Minneapolis* (1985), and *Alexander v. City of Minneapolis* (1982). The other instance of MCLU participation in federal court is an amicus brief that it filed together with the national ACLU in *Alexander v. U.S.* (1993).

11. Sources: Interview with Moore; group files.

12. MCLU amicus brief in *State v. Davidson* (1992, 13).

13. The purpose of this analysis is to provide a context within which to understand the MCLU's litigation. It is not intended to completely account for the organization's priorities or resources.

14. *State Board of Education v. Board of Education of Netcong* (1970); *Roman v. Sharper* (1969); *Board of Education of Union Beach v. New Jersey Education Association* (1968); *Robinson v. Cahill* (1972); *Essex County Welfare Board v. Cohen* (1969); *Provenzano v. U.S.* (1964).

15. Source: ACLU Litigation Docket, 1972.

16. *New York Times*, 30 June 1973, p. 69.

17. The other cases in which the ACLU represented defendants were *Cranford v. Mauri*, *Plainfield v. Rosetti*, *Hillside v. Medina*, *Plainfield v. Lemma*, *Kenilworth v. Doslik*, *State v. Twerdak*, *State v. Turchin*, *Roselle v. Miditz*, *State v. Stein*, *Roselle v. Levine*, *State v. Zurustky*, *State v. Polonski*, *State v. Lewis*, *State v. Honig*, *State v. Schulman*, and *State v. Polanski*. Source: ACLU Litigation Docket (various years).

18. Source: *Civil Liberties Reporter (ACLU of New Jersey)*, February 1975, p. 2. The opinion was unpublished.

19. Sources: group files; interview with Marsha Wenk.

20. *New York Times*, 24 October 1976, Section 11, p. 1.

21. Sources: ACLU of New Jersey Litigation Docket, 1991, 1977.

22. *People v. Ford* (1989); *Tattered Cover v. Tooley* (1985).

23. Before *Miller*: *Passmore v. Birkins* (1969); *Brick v. Board of Education* (1969); *Ohlson v. Phillips* (1969); *Hosack v. Smiley* (1967). After *Miller*: *In re Nelson* (1973); *People v. Gibson* (1974); *Bernzen v. City of Boulder* (1974); *Goedecke v. State* (1979); *Lujan v. Colorado State Board of Education* (1982); *Ashlock v. District Court* (1986); *People v. Pozo* (1987); *Evans v. Romer* (1993).

24. Source: *Civil Liberties*, Nov. 1966, #241, p. 1.

25. Source: ACLU Archives, Mudd Library, Princeton University (copy on file with author).

26. Source: ACLU Archives. Ney was also an ACLU cooperating attorney. However, he litigated obscenity cases as an attorney for MC and the Mountains and Plains Booksellers Association (MPBA).

27. United Press International News, 24 February 1981.

28. Kobylka (1991, 87-88) notes the emergence of an identifiable obscenity bar in the post-*Miller* period.

29. Booksellers interests (MC, ABA, and/or MPBA) participated in *In re Title* (1994), *People v. Ford* (1989), *Tattered Cover v. Tooley* (1985), and *Pierce v. City and County of Denver* (1977). Arthur Schwartz argued *Seventy-Two Fifty Corporation v. Adams* (1990), *People v. Ford* (1989), *People ex rel. Tooley v. Seven Thirty Five East Colfax* (1985), *People v. New Horizons* (1980), and *People v. Hildebrandt* (1976).

30. In recent years, the group has focused on other areas of criminal law, as well as civil rights issues (Bell 1995). See, for example, *State v. Freedom from Religion Foundation* (1995); *University of Colorado v. Derdeyn* (1993); *Bock v. Westminster Mall Company* (1991); *People v. Rister* (1990); *Colorado Civil Rights Commission v. Travelers Insurance Co.* (1988); *People v. Pozo* (1987); *People v. Drake* (1988).

31. *Fair Share Organization v. Kroger Company* (1961); *Crim v. State* (1973); *In re Hauptly* (1974); *Yunker v. Porter City Sheriff's Merit Board* (1978); *Garlin v. State* (1975); and *Owens v. Kohlmeyer* (1978).

32. Like the ACLU of Colorado, ICLU has focused on other areas of criminal law and civil rights issues (Harris 1995). See, for example, *Gallagher v. Indiana State Election Board* (1992); *In re Lawrance* (1991); *Cooper v. State* (1989); *Doe v. Smith* (1988); *In re Mental Commitment of M.P.* (1987); *In re Hauptly* (1974).

33. The cases in which constitutional claims were raised are *Austin v. State* (1988), *State v. Sappenfield* (1987), *Albright v. State* (1986), and *Saliba v. State* (1985). Kammen also helped to argue *Fort Wayne Books v. Indiana* (1989) on remand from the U.S. Supreme Court.

34. Several cases were argued by John Weston and Robert Eugene Smith, members of the obscenity bar who are affiliated with the Adult Film Association of America and First Amendment Lawyers Association.

35. All quotes in the remainder of this section are taken from the Bates interview (1995).

36. Source: ACLU of South Carolina Litigation Docket.

7

Obscenity: The Organizational Threshold and Group Litigation

The American Civil Liberties Union (ACLU) was the most active interest group litigator in obscenity cases in the five states. The ACLU mobilized in state courts after *Miller v. California* (1973), although organizational factors conditioned responses to the decision. In particular, affiliates' resources and priorities emerged as the most important factors explaining variations in litigation behavior among ACLU affiliates. However, the ACLU was not the only interest group to litigate in state court obscenity cases. Attention now turns to these other organizations. Unlike the purposive ACLU, other libertarian groups are material organizations—they enter litigation primarily to defend the commercial and vocational interests of their members. In addition to libertarian groups that support free speech and expression values, proscriptionist organizations, which generally support restrictions on access to sexual material, also have been active in the litigation fray. This chapter will examine state court litigation by material and proscriptionist groups, and will attempt to explain why these groups have been far less active than the ACLU. Analysis in this chapter focuses primarily on the organizational factors, specifically resources and priorities, that differ among the interest groups.

MATERIAL ORGANIZATIONS

Unlike the purposive ACLU, which litigates for primarily political or ideological reasons, material groups are involved in obscenity cases to represent their members' vocational and commercial interests. Nevertheless, material groups, like the ACLU, do attempt to shape judicial policy. Only with legal doctrine favorable to their members' interests can the organizations realize their goals.

The American Booksellers Association (ABA) was the most active commercial organization in state obscenity litigation. The ABA is the major national trade association of booksellers, with about 4,000 members (including owners of the profitable "chain" operations), who account for over 80 percent of the sales of books of general interest by bookstores nationwide (ABA brief in *Virginia v. ABA et al.* 1988). The ABA seeks to maintain and improve connections between the sellers and publishers of books and to increase the sale of materials that are profitable to ABA members. Obscenity prosecutions, or even their threat, potentially affect the efficiency and profitability of ABA member organizations. To maintain and advance its commercial interests, ABA litigates in its members' interests and maintains a Foundation for Free Expression.

The ABA and numerous other material groups litigated primarily through the Media Coalition (MC). MC was created the Sunday following the *Miller* decision in 1973 by representatives of the Association of American Publishers, the Council for Periodical Distributors Association, the Magazine Publishers Association, the Motion Picture Association of America, and the International Periodical Distributors Association. The ABA later joined the MC (Kobylka 1991, 136). The MC acted to coordinate the numerous trade associations that seek to defend First Amendment rights to distribute books, magazines, recordings, and videotapes. In litigation, MC filed cases and amicus curiae briefs to defend producers and distributors of what the groups viewed as constitutionally protected works.

MC is an anomaly among material organizations. Its member organizations seldom are active in the political fray, and—as we shall see—rarely enter obscenity litigation without MC. But the sole purpose of MC is political: to enter litigation to protect the commercial interests of members from infringements by obscenity prosecutions.

These material organizations, Kobylka (1987) argues, replaced the purposive ACLU as the dominant libertarian litigators in obscenity law because of *Miller*. While that may be the case in the United States Supreme Court, it is not so in state judiciaries. In the last chapter, I showed that the ACLU was the dominant litigator in the five states (see Table 6.5). Why did material groups not replace the purposive ACLU in state obscenity litigation after *Miller*, as they did in the U.S. Supreme Court? The answer focuses on the organizational threshold. The material groups' narrow issue orientation and fewer resources restrained them from litigating consistently at the state level.

In the five states, material groups litigated only in Colorado. The Mountains and Plains States Booksellers Association (MPBA) and the Media Coalition (MC) participated in four cases in Colorado (see Appendix B). Material groups were involved in only two other cases arising in the five states. In Minnesota, the Upper Midwest Booksellers Association (UMBA), a regional affiliate of ABA, challenged in federal court a Minneapolis law that regulated the manner in which sexually explicit material deemed "harmful to minors" is displayed for sale (*UMBA v. City of Minneapolis* 1985). Also, MC filed a suit in federal district court challenging the constitutionality of Indianapolis's antipornography ordinance (*ABA v. Hudnut* 1984, 1985).

While there is little state court litigation by material groups, it is important to note that all occurred after *Miller v. California*. Because the *Miller* precedent made trial courts more important, material groups responded to the decision by entering more trial court litigation on behalf of their members (Kobylka 1991, 45). Much of the litigation that occurred was brought by the MC, which of course did not even exist until after the *Miller* decision in 1973.

Yet save for Colorado, in none of the five states did material groups litigate as frequently as the ACLU. The organizational context appears to provide the strongest explanation for these patterns of litigation. The litigation goals of all material groups are in some respects narrower than that of purposive organizations like the ACLU. Material groups litigate primarily to advance and/or defend the commercial or vocational interests of their members. While concerned with all obscenity laws to some degree, they are interested specifically in those cases that directly affect the interests they represent. This limits and specifies their range of concerns. In contrast, the ACLU nominally is concerned with the censorship of any form of expression, whether or not the censorship impinges on the interests of a particular social or economic sector.[1]

Given narrower litigation goals, the material groups are less interested than the ACLU with litigation arising in particular contexts. For example, the Minnesota Civil Liberties Union (MCLU) participated in cases involving the public display of nudity (*Koppinger v. Fairmont* 1976); other affiliates challenged state lewdness statutes. These types of obscenity questions generally were of less concern to the ABA and other material organizations, whose litigation efforts focused on subjects more directly relevant to their members, such as the regulation of sexually explicit depictions in television, movies, or print.[2]

In addition, resource scarcity limits material groups' capacity to engage in state court litigation. The ABA has twenty regional affiliates, but none have permanent counsel. Together, the ABA and MC never had more than five staff attorneys nationwide. Interestingly, when ABA affiliates litigated, they relied on attorneys associated with the ACLU. In Colorado, the Mountains and Plains Booksellers Association retained Peter Ney and Daniel Recht, both ACLU volunteer attorneys, as private counsel for obscenity litigation (*Pierce v. City and County of Denver* 1977; *People v. Ford* 1989). In Minnesota, Randall Tigue of the Minnesota Civil Liberties Union represented the Upper Midwest Booksellers Association in *UMBA v. City of Minneapolis* (1985).

The MC currently has two staff and an annual budget of $350,000; these resources do not allow the group to litigate on a regular basis. Of course, one reason that MC has had few litigation resources is that litigation is not an organizational priority for the material groups that established and fund MC. Member organizations of MC have considerable resources (for example, AAP has 38 staff and a $5,000,000 budget; American Library Association has 275 staff and a $31,000,000 budget). But since they do not exist for distinctly political purposes; these groups become involved in politics principally to protect their members' interests. Association of American Publishers (AAP)—Freedom to Read Foundation Director Richard Kleeman noted that "[o]ur stand has over the years led us into some litigation . . . [b]ut to define this relatively minor part of our activities as engaging in 'obscenity politics' would be a major overstatement, since we do many other things as well" (Letter to author, August 5, 1995).

Limited resources provide greater incentive for organizations to litigate most frequently where they are likely to have the greatest policy impact: in federal courts, especially the United States Supreme Court. The MC, for instance, participated in more litigation in the Supreme Court than in any other court. Kleeman noted that AAP does not litigate often in state courts precisely because it is not prepared to litigate on obscenity matters on a regular basis.[3] Even if they desired to litigate more often, many material organizations would find it a difficult task, as they lack the resources to enter state courts consistently.

Unlike the ACLU, material organizations did not represent defendants in obscenity cases in these five states. In every instance, the material groups participated either by initiating lawsuits or filing amicus curiae briefs. Therefore, an examination of their choice of judicial forums is instructive for understanding the groups' willingness to turn to state courts.

There appears to be general bias toward federal courts, as most groups viewed the federal judiciary as more inclined than state courts to protect individual rights. A member of a material organization asserted that "instinctively we go to federal courts. It's a federal right we are trying to vindicate, so that's where we feel we should be."[4] The MC brought a constitutional challenge to the Indianapolis pornography ordinance in federal district court. When the Upper Midwest Booksellers Association, a regional affiliate of the ABA, contested the constitutionality of a Minneapolis ordinance that prohibited the display of any "sexually explicit material harmful to children," it too went to federal court.

Only in Colorado did material groups choose to bring cases at the state level. Why is so much of material group participation in Colorado?[5] Given the state supreme court's broad grant of free speech protection under state law, the groups expended resources to protect this preferred policy from attack by proscriptionist forces. The willingness of material groups to turn to Colorado courts suggests that, when state law is more receptive than federal precedent to their policy positions, groups will turn to state courts. Multiple indicators reveal that Colorado courts are more receptive than their federal counterparts. The Colorado Supreme Court favored the libertarian position in 61 percent of its post-*Miller* obscenity decisions.[6] In contrast, the Tenth Circuit has made no libertarian decisions in its published obscenity cases. David Miller, legal director of the ACLU of Colorado, noted that the Tenth Circuit "has always been a conservative court."[7]

On a doctrinal level, the Colorado Supreme Court consistently claimed that the free speech provision of its constitution grants broader protection than the

First Amendment. In obscenity law, the state high court's use of a community "tolerance" rather than "acceptance" standard when employing the *Miller* test for obscenity has rendered it, according to libertarian litigators, more protective of speech rights (Bell 1995; Schwartz 1995).[8] For example, Arthur Schwartz (1995) asserted that "the law in Colorado is such that unless the material is so bad that it defies description or involves children or extreme sadomasochistic conduct, [government] can't even pursue it."

With the Colorado Supreme Court's broad interpretation of the state constitutional free speech provision, material groups mobilized state constitutional law to seek more expansive protection than that available under the *Miller* precedent. While the ABA and/or MC argued on both federal and state constitutional grounds, they consistently referred the state high court to its previous decisions that declared the state speech protections broader than under federal standards. For example, in *Pierce v. Denver* (1977), MC attorney Peter Ney represented a book department manager who filed a complaint attacking the constitutionality of a Denver obscenity ordinance. Pierce argued that "the Colorado Constitution . . . seems to be even more protective of the right to freedom of expression than the First Amendment."[9] Particularly interesting is *Tattered Cover v. Tooley* (1985), in which the MC challenged a state law making it illegal to display for sale "sexually explicit material harmful to children." The MC argued that the law was vague and difficult for their members to apply and that any method of separating the books and magazines so that children would be unable to view sexually explicit material would interfere with adults' exercise of their rights of free speech and expression as guaranteed by both the federal and Colorado constitutions. In advancing the state law claims, the MC asserted that the state constitution provides greater protection for speech than its federal counterpart. Note that in the same year, the UMBA challenged a similar Minneapolis ordinance, but it chose to initiate the case in federal district court. The UMBA's arguments, unlike MPBA, relied solely on federal constitutional provisions; it did not mobilize state law to seek more expansive speech protection.[10]

Like the Indiana Civil Liberties Union (ICLU) in *Fordyce v. State* (1991), not until after *State v. Henry* (1987) did the MPBA argue that the state constitution completely protects obscene expressions.[11] In *People v. Ford* (1989), MPBA brought a suit challenging the constitutionality of the state's obscenity statute.[12] It asserted a First Amendment argument, but also argued that "the lack of a Colorado tradition of prohibiting obscenity indicates that the constitutional framers intended to provide unlimited constitutional protection to freedom of speech" (*Ford* 1989, 1063). Here, the MPBA suggested that the court reject its conclusion just four years earlier in *People v. Seven Thirty-Five East Colfax* (1985) that obscenity is unprotected by the state constitution's free speech provision.

Like the ICLU, the MPBA urged a state appellate court to accept a historical analysis similar to that the Oregon Supreme Court accepted in *Henry*. And, like the court in Indiana, the Colorado high court rejected this invitation. It questioned the Oregon Supreme Court's historical analysis and also concluded that at the time of the framing of the Colorado Constitution, there was ample evidence of limits on sexually explicit expression. Consequently, obscenity was a historical exception to free speech in Colorado.

To summarize, the analysis shows that material groups' narrower range of interests and limited resources explain why they have not been as active in state courts as the ACLU. The MC, ABA, and other groups did not devote the resources that were necessary to participate regularly in numerous state courts. When they did litigate in Colorado courts, the groups appear to have been motivated by the new judicial federalism incentive. They initiated cases in state, not federal courts, and mobilized state law to seek broader rights protections than those available under federal standards.

PROSCRIPTIONIST ORGANIZATIONS

Proscriptionist organizations used state appellate courts much less often than libertarian groups. In part, this is due to the strictures of criminal law and the necessarily supplemental role that proscriptionist groups play in the prosecution of obscenity. Since most obscenity cases are criminal prosecutions, and governments prosecute these cases, the opportunity for proscriptionist groups to participate in litigation is limited primarily (although not exclusively) to filing amicus curiae briefs. However, organizational factors were also important in explaining the lack of a strong proscriptionist presence. While many proscriptionist organizations attempted to affect policy through participation in appellate cases, they confined activities largely to the U.S. Supreme Court and, less often, lower federal appellate courts. Forays into the states were rare.

Between 1960 and 1994, Citizens for Decency through Law (CDL) and Morality in Media (MM) consistently were the most active proscriptionist groups in the United States Supreme Court (Kobylka 1991). CDL is the "legal arm of the anti-obscenity movement" (O'Connor and Epstein 1989, 53). It was founded in 1957 by Charles H. Keating, an anti-obscenity activist, who later was one of the three dissenting members of the President's Commission on Obscenity and Pornography. Keating recognized obscenity and pornography as major issues, but thought that "government attorneys would generally lack the experience and resources to successfully litigate these matters" (O'Connor and Epstein 1989, 53). The group's purpose was to assist law enforcement agencies and legislatures in enacting and enforcing statutes, ordinances, and regulations controlling obscenity, pornography, and other materials that it believes are harmful to children.

To achieve these goals, CDL provided free legal assistance, including legal research, briefs, model legislation, and courtroom assistance for obscenity prosecutions. It also entered appellate cases as amicus curiae "to bring a national perspective to local litigation" (O'Connor and Epstein 1989, 54). On occasion,

CDL attorneys have provided direct representation in obscenity prosecutions. But since they side with the government, they must attain the permission or cooperation of prosecutors. In *Flynt v. Ohio* (1981), the state hired CDL attorney Bruce Taylor to represent it in a case against *Hustler* magazine. (Ohio hired Taylor in part because he had been the city prosecutor in Cleveland when *Hustler* publisher Larry Flynt was arrested.)

In 1989, after Charles Keating became involved in controversy over the savings and loan crisis, CDL reorganized itself and changed its name to the Children's Legal Foundation. The new organization, which claims no ties to Keating, continues to focus on obscenity and pornography issues and has expanded its activities to include musical lyrics and Satanism (Corn 1990). Bruce Taylor, CDL's general counsel for ten years, now is president and chief counsel of the National Law Center for Children and Families, a proscriptionist organization that has participated in obscenity litigation.

Morality in Media (known as "Operation Yorkville" until 1968) was created in 1962 "to educate and alert the public to the problems of illegal pornography, and to encourage communities to express themselves in a unified, organized way to law enforcement officials, urging vigorous enforcement of obscenity law."[13] MM's founders were three Manhattan clergymen who were concerned about the availability of "salacious publications" to youth (Kobylka 1991, 50). The group's leader for many years was Morton A. Hill, a Jesuit priest who was appointed by Lyndon Johnson to the President's Commission on Obscenity and Pornography. Like Keating of the CDL, he dissented from the commission's libertarian policy recommendations.

MM opposes obscene and pornographic material primarily because it believes that exposure to the material can lead to moral depravity and affect behavior: "From its inception, Morality in Media has worked to alert and inform private citizens and public officials about the destructive effects of pornography and the extent of the traffic of obscenity. Vigorous enforcement of obscenity laws is encouraged to combat this onslaught. . . . Morality in Media believes that vocal, unremitting, organized public expression will stop the exploding pornography traffic that is corrupting children and all of society."[14] Today, MM has a national office in New York City, as well as six state groups and forty-five local chapters (*Encyclopedia of Associations* 1994, 1892). It claims 11,500 members.

In the wake of *Miller*, both CDL and MM used two primary judicial strategies to attain their proscriptionist goals.[15] The first was to assist prosecutors by providing them with information and expertise. To overcome the strengths of libertarian groups and the obscenity bar, the groups tried to bring expertise to the proscriptionist side, since local prosecutors often are inexperienced in obscenity litigation.

A primary strategy of CDL was to become actively and directly involved in local obscenity trials and to provide staff and assistance to prosecutors handling litigation. According to Kobylka (1991, 106), CDL had four full-time attorneys and five others maintained on part-time retainers. The resources allowed the organization to participate at least periodically in trial court litigation. On occasion, CDL attorneys (especially Bruce Taylor) were invited by the prosecutors to argue cases at trial. Typically, however, CDL assistance to prosecutors was in the form of teaching them how to handle cases and counter the arguments of libertarian opponents. By educating prosecutors, the organization could help secure convictions without actually having to enter every trial court case. This helped to save scarce resources.

While direct participation in trials was less common for CDL attorneys, Bruce Taylor assisted as counsel in some obscenity prosecutions in Indiana.[16] His direct assistance to prosecutors was a bone of contention for defense attorneys. For instance, in the appellate phase of *Sedelbauer v. State* (1983), Sedelbauer argued that the trial court committed an error of law in allowing Taylor to act as a special prosecutor. The appellant's brief noted that "because CDL wants to stop all adult bookstores and sexually oriented material, regardless of the legal definition of obscenity . . . to allow a person with this background and affiliation to participate in a trial such as this . . . is highly prejudicial and a denial of due process and equal protection under the law."[17] The appellate court did not accept this argument.[18]

Further examples of CDL activity in Indiana illustrate less conventional means of judicial lobbying. In *Austin v. State* (1988), members of a local CDL chapter attempted to pressure the trial court judge by writing letters and engaging in other forms of direct communication regarding her conduct in obscenity trials and the appropriate sentence in the event of a conviction. On appeal, Austin argued that by not disclosing the letters she received from CDL, the trial court judge denied Austin the opportunity to request her recusal or disqualification from the trial. The appeals court rejected Austin's argument, holding that without direct information that the letters compromised the judge's impartiality, the court must assume no error. Nevertheless, the court did not look kindly upon CDL's strategy, declaring that "needless to say, we do not condone the alleged actions of 'Citizens for Decency through Law' to the extent that its members would attempt to influence a trial court by means of ex parte communications."[19] Another common CDL strategy was to organize anti-obscenity rallies and then to refer to those rallies in obscenity trials as evidence of contemporary community standards. Certainly, such lobbying strategies are ethically questionable. But they demonstrate CDL's attempts to influence the implementation of the *Miller* doctrine in state trial courts through low-cost strategies that required few organizational resources, which is especially important since the group lacked the resources necessary for consistent participation in formal litigation.

Morality in Media attempted to aid in the prosecution of obscenity by creating the National Obscenity Law Center (NOLC) in 1976. NOLC is a clearinghouse of information available to prosecutors on all aspects of obscenity law. In addition to files on legal memoranda, articles, statutes, and briefs, NOLC publishes *Obscenity Law Bulletin*, which digests cases, statutes, and other legal developments in obscenity law at all levels of government. Unlike CDL, MM rarely participated directly in trial court litigation. But there have been a few exceptions. In a New Jersey case, *Lordi v. UA New Jersey Theatres, Inc.* (1969), MM founder Father Morton Hill testified at trial concerning community standards of obscenity in an attempt to enjoin the showing of the film *I Am Curious Yellow*. More recently, MM was a direct party in F.C.C. broadcast indecency cases in the federal courts.[20]

Thus, both CDL and MM attempted to aid to prosecutors in trial courts. In addition, a second judicial strategy CDL and MM employed was to attempt to shape law through appellate courts, primarily by filing amicus briefs. Their activity in state appellate courts, however, has been rare. Of the states I examine, CDL and MM each participated in only one appellate case. CDL leader Charles Keating and General Counsel Bruce Taylor, along with attorneys James Clancy and Richard Bertsch, filed an amicus brief in the Colorado Supreme Court in *People v. New Horizons, Inc.* (1980). Given that the state high court on several occasions since *Miller* had invalidated state or local obscenity laws, CDL's amicus brief is not surprising. The brief noted that "amicus have a fervent desire to see that fair and powerful laws exist to help this country eliminate a problem which has historically been repulsive to the overwhelming majority of our people."[21] The group attempted to ensure that the anti-obscenity law pass constitutional scrutiny by urging the court to "protect the statute from frivolous attack" and reminding it that "the Courts should not engage in unnecessary faultfinding on philosophical grounds."[22]

Through its state chapter, MM filed an amicus brief in the Minnesota Supreme Court in *State v. Davidson* (1992). Like the CDL in Colorado, MM filed its brief in the context of a challenge to the constitutionality of a state obscenity statute. Here, the state appellate court had declared the definition of "obscene" in the state statute inconsistent with the due process guarantees of the Minnesota Constitution because it relied on local and not statewide community standards. MM argued that the definition "in the Minnesota Obscenity Statute—and in every other Federal, State and Local Obscenity Law—[is not] unconstitutionally vague under the Minnesota Constitution, regardless of wether [*sic*] a local or statewide standard is required."[23]

While CDL and MM have not been particularly active in litigation in these five states, they were involved in extrajudicial activities. Most notably, CDL was an active proponent in the passage of the Indianapolis pornography ordinance. The Indianapolis CDL formed in 1984, just before debate over the pornography ordinance began. The group, along with other religious and neighborhood organizations in the city, lobbied the city council to pass the ordinance and organized busloads of members to attend council meetings.

The Minnesota chapter of MM claims to have played "a key role" in the passage of an amendment to the Minnesota Obscenity Statute that conformed its definition of obscenity to that established by the U.S. Supreme Court in *Miller*.[24] During debate over the proposed pornography ordinance in Minneapolis, the MM initially supported the measure (Brest and Vandenberg 1987). However, the group later rescinded its support, suggesting instead that existing obscenity laws should be enforced.[25]

If proscriptionist organizations, particularly CDL, responded to *Miller* by decentralizing their lobbying efforts, then why were they involved only rarely in state appellate litigation?[26] Once again, organizational considerations provide the strongest explanations. For MM, the lack of litigation reflects almost entirely resource scarcity. Although MM and its affiliates follow obscenity litigation, the affiliates have no permanent legal counsel. At the national level, Kobylka (1991) reported, MM's NOLC had only two staff attorneys. This apparently has changed little. MM General Counsel Paul McGeady was reluctant to discuss the group's resources, telling me that "Currently, we don't have many [staff attorneys] but that [the number of attorneys] is information we don't want in general release."[27] While I was unable to specify the group's precise resource capacity, the evidence strongly suggests that staff are at a premium and that MM cannot litigate regularly in federal or state appellate courts.

Given the lack of attorneys, MM's direct judicial participation focused on the federal courts "because that's where you get the biggest impact." The organization continues to litigate in the United States Supreme Court and the D.C. Circuit, the latter primarily in broadcast indecency cases. However, McGeady does recognize the importance of state courts, telling me that federal courts "have limited jurisdictions and for the most part law is made in the state [courts]."[28]

CDL's lack of state appellate litigation flows from both resource scarcity per se and pursuit of a different strategy in state courts. Unlike MM, CDL turned directly to state courts in the wake of *Miller*. Yet it focused on the trial and not appellate level. Given the structure of criminal law, CDL and all proscriptionist organizations occupy a supplemental role in the prosecution of obscenity. This is not to say, however, that CDL (like MM) did not attempt to shape obscenity doctrine through appellate litigation. Indeed, both organizations in the post-*Miller* period filed amicus briefs, particularly before the U.S. Supreme Court and other federal courts.[29] Amicus participation is not only well suited to the proscriptionist organizations' litigation posture but also is a relatively cheap form of organizational involvement; it requires little expenditure of organizational resources.

Indeed, the fact that CDL and MM were active on obscenity in ways other than formal participation in litigation reveals the importance of having the specific resources needed to enter state courts, namely, access to attorneys. McGeady's comments and CDL's lobbying of trial courts show that the groups did recognize the importance of state litigation. But unable to enter the courts consistently, the groups had to develop and rely on strategies that were better suited to their available resources. CDL and MM occasionally entered appellate cases, but neither relied on this as the primary lobbying tactic. On the few occasions they entered litigation, they chose to focus on the federal courts.

Thus, limited resources provides an important, though certainly not the only, explanation for the groups' lack of participation in state appellate litigation. This discussion of proscriptionist organizations has focused so far only on CDL and MM. However, the resurgence of antipornography campaigns in the 1980s brought about an increase in the number and scope of proscriptionist organizations active in the debate. Some have litigated in state judiciaries and presented important doctrinal arguments to courts.

In particular, the National Family Legal Foundation (NFLF) has been an active opponent of using state constitutions to expand individual rights. The group "seeks to preserve the integrity of families and the innocence of our children by promoting a healthy and safe environment for families, free from obscenity and the sexual crimes which inevitably accompany its widespread dissemination."[30] NFLF Executive Director Alan Sears directed the Attorney General's Commission on Pornography, which in 1986 issued a report calling for legal restrictions on violent and degrading forms of pornography. Len L. Munsil, the group's legal counsel, wrote about what he perceived to be the dangers associated with the increased use of state constitutions to strike down laws that withstand federal constitutional scrutiny (Twist and Munsil 1989).

In *State v. Davidson* (1992), NFLF and the Minnesota Berean League[31] filed an amicus brief that attacked both the state appellate court's methods and its conclusions in using state constitutional due process provisions to strike down the Minnesota obscenity statute for definitional vagueness. The groups argued that

> [a]lthough the court purported to base its decision on Minnesota's constitutional due process guarantees, there is no explanation or discussion of the differences between the process due under the state constitution compared to the federal constitution. In fact, the arguments adopted by the appeals court, if correct, would apply equally to make all obscenity laws void for vagueness under the federal due process clause. But of course the court could not simply rule the use of contemporary community standards vague under the U.S. Constitution because the Supreme Court has already rejected that approach. (NFLF amicus brief in *Davidson* 1992, 3-4)

The NFLF contended that state courts need to bring more evidence to bear if they wish to expand protections under state constitutions:

> Although it is certainly true that state courts are free to expand their "individual liberty" provisions to protect activity beyond that protected by the federal constitution, they should be required to support such an interpretation with some evidence that such a result was intended by the provision's authors. Minor textual differences are not sufficient; . . . there is nothing in Minnesota constitutional history or precedent to support the conclusion that Minnesota's constitution provides any protection for obscene material. An unexplained state constitutional decision . . . in contradiction to years of established precedent, disserves the legitimate use of state constitutions to protect rights separately from the federal constitution. It opens up state courts to the charge of judicial policy making, and writing laws (or repealing them) instead of undertaking the legitimate judicial function of interpreting laws. (NFLF amicus brief in *Davidson* 1992, 8-9)

The NFLF's argumentative posture in *Davidson* is an important one. The group emphasized primarily the methodology rather than the outcome of the appellate court's constitutional analysis. The brief argued not only to reverse the lower court but also for the limited (and more "principled") interpretation of state constitutions in rights cases. The group presented arguments to counter those of libertarian organizations concerning the proper interpretation of state constitutional rights provisions. In fact, the NFLF justified filing a brief because the organization's "experience with obscenity law and the use of state constitutional grounds to attack obscenity statutes puts NFLF in a unique position to assist this court in analyzing the issues presented."[32]

NFLF's only other instance of participation in these five states, also in the Minnesota Supreme Court, arose in a very similar situation. In *Knudtson v. City of Coates* (1994), the group filed an amicus brief arguing that a Minnesota appellate court erred in holding that a city ordinance that bars nude dancing in licensed liquor establishments violated the free speech protections of the Minnesota Constitution. As in *Davidson*, a lower court invalidated a law by declaring the guarantees in the Minnesota Constitution more expansive than those in the federal Constitution. *Knudtson*, however, dealt not with obscenity per se, but rather with the extent to which government may prohibit nonobscene nude dancing.[33] In both *Davidson* and *Knudtson*, the state supreme court overturned lower court rulings; the high court was unwilling to interpret the state constitution to grant broader protection in these instances.

The NFLF's entry into state litigation reveals how emerging debate over the interpretation of state constitutions has expanded the scope and nature of group conflict. As libertarian interests, motivated by the new judicial federalism incentive, sought expansive rights under state constitutions, proscriptionist organizations turned to state courts to counter the threat posed by their opponents. In obscenity law, libertarian groups introduced a new policy conflict by mobilizing state constitutional law. In response, some proscriptionist groups entered state courts and argued that they should not expand the scope of protection based on state constitutions.

DISCUSSION

Neither material nor proscriptionist groups litigated often in state obscenity cases. This chapter assessed these groups' use of state courts and showed that no other organization has been as active as the ACLU. Material groups' relatively narrow range of interests and scarce litigation resources explain why they did not participate consistently in litigation across a variety of states. Proscriptionist groups, too, did not litigate often in state appellate courts because of limited resources. Both CDL and MM recognized the importance of state courts. However, their participation at the appellate level focused primarily on the U.S. Supreme Court. Only in a few instances did they file amicus briefs in state appellate courts.

Organizational considerations help to explain the differing responses by libertarian groups to *Miller* in federal and state courts. In the Supreme Court, material groups mobilized after the landmark to protect their commercial and economic interests. This mobilization allowed the national ACLU to deemphasize obscenity and turn to other issues on its broad agenda, since the ACLU knew that libertarian arguments would be presented to the Court by other organizations (Kobylka 1991). But in state courts, material organizations were much less active, which potentially created a void in organized opposition to anti-obscenity efforts. While material organizations (especially the MC) did focus increasingly on trial courts in the wake of *Miller*, their ventures into state judiciaries were few and far between. As a result, some ACLU affiliates (with sufficient resources) increased their level of activity. The ACLU became the dominant litigator in state obscenity cases in part because no other libertarian organization had the resources and organizational incentives to be active in the litigation fray. Indeed, the experience in Colorado is the exception that proves this rule. Where material groups did mobilize, the ACLU of Colorado was able to avoid litigation. This implicit coordination of efforts among groups that present the same view stems from the desire to conserve scarce resources.

Thus, at the same time the national ACLU deemphasized obscenity, some affiliates entered the litigation fray. This shift is testament to the group's resources and organizational flexibility. Unlike all other organizations active in obscenity cases, the American Civil Liberties Union possessed the capacity to litigate in the several state court systems (see Table 7.1). Whereas unitary groups faced significant expenses and logistical difficulties, the ACLU—organized at all levels of government—was better suited to litigating across states and levels of courts. Its established presence in every state allowed it to track litigation, develop expertise in state courts, and cultivate networks of volunteer attorneys. The ACLU's decentralized structure and, most important, its network of volunteer cooperating attorneys permitted the group to participate to an extent unrivaled in obscenity litigation. Access to attorneys emerges as a vital resource in explaining entry into state litigation. Cooperating attorneys allowed the ACLU to enter cases with little or no resource expenditure, and are important in explaining why the group was much more active than the other organized litigants. Further, since the ACLU focuses much of its political activities on the courts, its resources largely were allocated to litigation.

The importance of organizational goals and resources in explaining litigation behavior does not mean that the probability of winning is unimportant. ACLU affiliates, for example, routinely consider the prospects for success when deciding whether to take on a case. The two libertarian organizations that participated most frequently in state courts—the MCLU and MPBA—generally were successful (see Table 7.2). Had they been less successful, they might have been more reluctant to enter obscenity cases.

Table 7.1
Resources of Interest Groups Active in Obscenity Litigation

Group	Affiliate	Staff Attorneys	Cooperating Attorneys
ACLU	50	100+	Thousands
ABA/MC	20	Fewer than five	0
CDL	50	4	0
MM	45	2	0

Key:

ACLU	American Civil Liberties Union
ABA/MC	American Booksellers Association/Media Coalition
CDL	Citizens for Decency through Law
MM	Morality in Media

Sources: Interviews with group officials; group files; *Encyclopedia of Associations* (various years). Figures listed are the groups' nationwide resources. Figures for cooperating attorneys represent approximate numbers.

Table 7.2
Success of Libertarian Groups in State Obscenity Cases

Group	Success Rate
Mountains and Plains Booksellers Association (Colorado)	75% (3 of 4)
American Civil Liberties Union of Colorado	100% (1 of 1)
Indiana Civil Liberties Union	0% (0 of 1)
Minnesota Civil Liberties Union	67% (4 of 6)
American Civil Liberties Union of New Jersey	33% (1 of 3)
American Civil Liberties Union of South Carolina	0% (0 o 0)

But staff in organizations that were relatively inactive in state litigation *said* that resource considerations drove their litigation decisions. While interview responses should not be blindly accepted as valid, this evidence is supported by several independent measures of resources. Further, it is understandable that considerations other than potential success influenced group decisions on whether to pursue litigation. Groups lacking the organizational incentives or requisite resources (such as attorneys, time, and money) simply could not enter litigation, regardless of the prospects for success. In short, organizational resources and priorities, rather than the probability of winning, account for a center finding: that some groups seldom or never entered state obscenity cases.

In addition to organizational threshold, the analysis of obscenity litigation demonstrates the importance of legal doctrine in providing incentives to litigate at the state level. The U.S. Supreme Court's decision in *Miller v. California* altered the context of litigation by decentralizing decision making on obscenity. With the Supreme Court less willing to review lower-court convictions, state courts increasingly became the de facto policy makers of last resort. It was not until after *Miller* that groups with the resources to litigate in state courts did so. Other groups lacked the resources to use state courts consistently, but still recognized the increased importance of state judiciaries. This is illustrated by CDL's attempts to aid local prosecutors and lobby trial judges.

When libertarian groups initiated litigation, the general preference for federal courts and federal law is clear. Except in Colorado, where state courts are among the most libertarian in the nation on the issue of obscenity, groups turned to federal courts more often than their state counterparts, when given a choice. Staff in most affiliates typically viewed federal courts as more receptive to individual rights and preferred to litigate at the federal level. Even when they entered state litigation, in many cases libertarian groups did not advance independent state law claims. This is finding is somewhat puzzling, since libertarian groups had nothing to lose by asserting independent state law claims as part of their typical layered legal arguments. Their reluctance to do so no doubt reflects the dominance of federal law in state courts for many years (see, for example, Esler 1994).

Although they generally preferred federal to state courts, several group officials mentioned that increasingly they planned to turn to state courts and state constitutions in the future. In recent years, libertarian groups increasingly based rights claims on independent state constitutional grounds. While few cases featured state law arguments, these are doctrinally important cases.

Groups' recent reliance on state constitutional law no doubt reflects the general maturation of state constitutional jurisprudence in recent decades. However, a complete explanation must also account for the central role of *State v. Henry* (1987). No group claimed that the state constitution protected obscenity until the Oregon Supreme Court decided *Henry*. Following this, the MPBA in *People v. Ford* (1989), the MCLU in *State v. Davidson* (1992), and the ICLU in *Fordyce v. State* (1991) each presented virtually identical arguments to their state courts, relying almost exclusively on *Henry* as precedent.

The material organizations' arguments in Colorado nicely illustrate *Henry*'s impact. Material groups always contended that the Colorado Constitution protects sexual communications more broadly than the federal Constitution. But they had not gone so far as to argue that the state constitution completely protects obscenity. However, following *Henry*, the MPBA asserted that "the lack of a Colorado tradition of prohibiting obscenity indicates that the constitutional framers intended to provide *unlimited* constitutional protection to freedom of speech" (*People v. Ford* 1989, 1063 [italics added]). In support, the MPBA cited *Henry* and relied on a historical analysis similar to the one conducted by the Oregon Supreme Court.

Facilitating groups' reliance on *Henry* are textual similarities between the free speech clause of the Oregon Constitution and those of Colorado, Indiana and Minnesota. Article 1, Section 8 of the Oregon Constitution provides that "no law shall be passed restraining the free expression of opinion, or restricting the right to speak, write, or print freely on any subject whatever; but every person shall be responsible for the abuse of this right." The Oregon Supreme Court noted that its free speech clause is textually broader than the First Amendment on two grounds. First, in addition to granting freedom of speech and press, it separately precludes laws retraining the free expression of opinion. Second, the free speech clause "covers 'any subject whatever' and does not contain any express exception for obscene communications" (*Henry* 1987, 11).[34] The Colorado, Indiana, and Minnesota constitutions protect all subjects.[35] In addition, the Indiana Constitution protects the "free interchange of thought and opinion," although the Colorado and Minnesota constitutions lack comparable clauses separately protecting the free expression of opinion. The textual similarities would appear to assist the MPBA, MCLU, and ICLU in applying the logic of the *Henry* decision in their states.

But while textual similarities may facilitate state law arguments, note that in New Jersey, whose constitution also explicitly protects "all subjects," groups did not advance similar state constitutional arguments.[36] Indeed, in some respects, the Oregon free speech clause resembles those in most states. Only nine state free speech clauses do not protect "any subject" or "all subjects," and only West Virginia's has an express exception for obscene communications. Thus, although it may appear textually based, the Oregon justices went far beyond the actual text to derive their position in *Henry*, conducting a historical inquiry into the status of obscenity as an exception to free speech at the time of the framing of the Oregon Constitution.

Nevertheless, the MPBA, MCLU, and ICLU's reliance on *Henry* reveals an interesting and important aspect of state constitutional policy making. Certainly, *State v. Henry* did not formally alter obscenity law in Colorado, Minnesota, or Indiana. Nevertheless, the Oregon Supreme Court did provide precedent for the libertarian groups, which (albeit unsuccessfully) attempted to adopt the Oregon court's innovative state constitutional decision in other states. *Henry* provided an argumentative foundation for litigants in other states whose rights claims likely would fail on federal constitutional grounds. While this phenomenon may not have lead to a meaningful increase in the frequency of group litigation in state courts, it is significant from a doctrinal perspective. The groups were agents in an attempted diffusion of an innovative state constitutional decision (see Porter and Tarr 1982; Gray 1973; Walker 1969). As libertarian groups and other litigants increasingly based rights claims on independent state constitutional grounds, proscriptionist organizations—particularly the NFLF—turned to state courts to respond to their libertarian counterparts, thereby expanding the scope of conflict in state obscenity litigation. Libertarian and proscriptionist group involvement helped to extend discourse on state constitutional law, clarify the meaning of state constitutional free speech provisions, and induce courts to consider the appropriate role of their constitutions in protecting rights.

CONCLUSION

This analysis sheds light on the dynamic nature of litigation in a federal judicial system. As the relative importance of the federal and the state courts changes, so too does the efficacy of litigation strategies. We would expect interest groups to be sensitive to these changes and to respond accordingly. Thus, when *Miller v. California* made state courts more important actors in obscenity law, groups litigated increasingly at the state level.

However, other factors conditioned the ability of groups to respond to *Miller* by turning to state courts. While interest groups may be able to amass the resources to participate in a handful of important Supreme Court cases, a decentralized litigation environment requires that groups enter many more cases across a variety of states. The evidence suggests that the organizational threshold to enter state litigation is quite high. It may be difficult for groups to participate actively in the judicial process as policy responsibility is dispersed among the state courts. Indeed, many organizations were unable or unwilling to respond to *Miller* by participating often in state courts.

If the U.S. Supreme Court continues its trend of accepting fewer cases, decentralizing policy making in many areas of law, and impeding access to federal courts through procedural hurdles, interest groups that attempt to affect public policy increasingly will be faced with incentives to turn to the states. However, these findings suggest that it will be difficult for many groups, especially national organizations that do not have affiliates with sufficient access to attorneys at the state and local levels, to amass the resources necessary to litigate regularly in a decentralized litigation environment. To the extent that interest groups shape judicial agendas, doctrinal debate, and case outcomes, the opportunity to influence judicial policy may be lost or severely restricted for many organizations.

Nevertheless, while interest groups' use of state courts was sporadic, it may still have had important implications for doctrinal development. In recent years, debate on obscenity and other rights issues has focused increasingly on the interpretations of state constitutions. Both libertarian and proscriptionist organizations have recognized this and have debated the proper interpretations of state constitutional speech and expression protections.[37] In this way, groups have played a role in the development and clarification of state constitutional law.

Examination of interest group participation in obscenity cases, coupled with the analysis of takings litigation, allows for an evaluation of the conditions under which major litigating organizations are likely to litigate at the state level. The concluding chapter reviews the findings of the analysis of takings and obscenity litigation, assesses the importance of legal incentives and organizational thresholds, and considers the implications of these findings for judicial policy making and the protection of rights in a decentralized litigation environment.

NOTES

1. Of course, the ACLU's broad issue orientation allows it to allocate resources to other issue areas under certain conditions. Material groups do not enjoy this exit option. When their interests are at stake, they are pressured to act (see Kobylka 1991).

2. Unlike the ACLU, for instance, the ABA and MC did not file amicus briefs in the U.S. Supreme Court in *Barnes v. Glen Theatre, Inc.* (1991), Indiana's nude dancing case.

3. Letter to author, August 5, 1995.

4. This group official requested anonymity.

5. Computer searches on Lexis and Westlaw reveal that the ABA and/or MC initiated litigation in only three other state cases nationwide. Two are in Tennessee (*Davis-Kidd Booksellers, Inc. v. McWherter* [1993] and *Leech v. ABA* [1979]) and one is in Pennsylvania (*ABA v. Rendell* [1984]). There are other instances of state court litigation, but they involve either amicus participation (for example, *People v. Wiener* 1994) or cases originally initiated in federal courts that were certified to state courts on questions of state law (for example, *ABA et al. v. Webb* 1985). In contrast, ABA and MC sponsored three Colorado Supreme Court obscenity cases.

6. The mean for the five state court systems is 33 percent.

7. Anne Kornhauser, "Rocky Mountain Harmony," *The American Lawyer*, June 1988, p. 49.

8. See also amicus brief, MPBA et al. in *In re Title* (1994); MPBA brief in *People v. Ford* (1989); MC brief in *Tattered Cover v. Tooley* (1985).

9. *Pierce v. City and County of Denver* (1977), plaintiff's brief, p. 8.

10. Since the ordinances were slightly different, the federal constitutional arguments offered by the two ABA affiliates were not identical. Nonetheless, the decision by MC to bring suit in a Colorado court and UMBA in federal court is telling.

11. In cases prior to *People v. Ford*, the MPBA argued that the state constitution's speech protections were broader than federal protections, but the groups did not go so far as to argue that the state constitution completely protected obscene speech.

12. *MPBA v. Early* was one of three cases consolidated for appeal as *Ford* in the state supreme court.

13. Source: Group literature (on file with author).

14. Source: Group literature.

15. Except where otherwise noted, this discussion relies heavily on Kobylka (1991, 55-57).

16. I was able to identify Taylor's participation in Indiana courts but in none of the other four states. This may reflect Indiana's proximity to Taylor's home state, Ohio.

17. *Sedelbauer v. State* (1983), appellant's brief, p. 13.

18. See *American Film Distributors v. State* (1981) for another challenge to Taylor's participation in an Indiana obscenity trial.

19. *Austin* (1988), fn 4.

20. Telephone conversation with Paul McGeady, general counsel of MM, August 21, 1995. See, for example, *Action for Children's Television v. FCC* (1993).

21. Amicus brief of Charles Keating et al., *People v. New Horizons, Inc.* (1980, 27).

22. CDL amicus brief, p. 14.

23. MM of Minnesota, Inc., amicus in *State v. Davidson* (1992, 1).

24. MM amicus brief in *State v. Davidson* (1992, ii).

25. MM of Minnesota's lack of active participation in debate over the pornography ordinance may be due to the ideological and philosophical tenor of the debate (see Kobylka 1991, 61-62). Feminist antipornography groups, whose social and ideological visions differ markedly from MM's emphasis on traditional social and moral values, dominated debate in Minneapolis. In this setting, cooperation with feminist organizations would be difficult. In contrast, the pornography debate in Indianapolis featured no organized women's groups and had a decidedly more conservative tone (Downs 1989). CDL could take an active role supporting the ordinance in a political environment more compatible with its viewpoints.

26. A Lexis search identified two other instances of CDL participation in state appellate courts nationwide: *Commonwealth v. Wasson* (1992) and *Cain v. Commonwealth* (1969). MM has been involved in only one other case, *Morality in Media of Western New York, Inc. v. City of Buffalo Common Council* (1984).

27. Telephone conversation with Paul McGeady, general counsel of MM, August 21, 1995.

28. Telephone conversation with McGeady, August 21, 1995.

29. For example, *FW/PBS, Inc. v. City of Dallas* (1990, 1986); *Dworkin v. Hustler Magazine, Inc.* (1989); *Carlin Communications, Inc. v. F.C.C.* (1984); *Penthouse v. McAuliffe* (1983).

30. NFLF amicus brief in *State v. Davidson* (1992, 1).

31. The Berean League is a St. Paul–based religious organization that has been active in attempting to proscribe sexually explicit material. The conviction in *Davidson* began when the organization's Winona Chapter investigated the availability of obscenity in Winona. The Berean League has joined on amicus briefs in several recent U.S. Supreme Court obscenity cases.

32. NFLF amicus brief in *Davidson* (1992, 1).

33. In *Barnes v. Glen Theatre, Inc.* (1991, 566), the U.S. Supreme Court permitted the regulation of nonobscene nude dancing, commenting that this form of expression is only within the "outer perimeters of the First Amendment."

34. Of course, the First Amendment also contains no express exception for obscenity.

35. Colorado Constitution, art. 1, sec. 10: "No law shall be passed impairing the freedom of speech; every person shall be free to speak, write or publish whatever he will on any subject, being responsible for all abuse of that liberty"; Indiana Constitution, art. 1, sec. 9: "No law shall be passed, restraining the free interchange of thought and opinion, or restricting the right to speak, write, or print, freely, on any subject whatever: but for the abuse of that right, every person shall be responsible"; Minnesota Constitution, art. 1, sec. 3: "[A]ll persons may freely speak, write and publish their sentiments on all subjects, being responsible for the abuse of such right."

36. New Jersey Constitution, art. 1, sec. 6: "[E]very person may freely speak, write and publish his sentiments on all subjects, being responsible for the abuse of that right." Of the five states examined, only the South Carolina Constitution, which is patterned after the First Amendment, does not explicitly protect "any" or "all" subjects. Article 1, sec. 2 provides that "the General Assembly shall make no law . . . abridging the freedom of speech or of the press."

37. This trend is not limited to the five states in this study. See, for example, *People v. Wiener* (1994).

8

Conclusion: Interest Groups and Rights in a Decentralized Litigation Environment

In recent decades, battles over constitutional rights and liberties increasingly have been fought out in state judiciaries. As the United States Supreme Court turned more conservative beginning in the early 1970s, it halted the Warren Court's liberal activism of previous decades. The Court discouraged the use of federal court forums, relegating cases increasingly to state judiciaries. The justices also restricted or refused to expand the scope of many rights under the federal Constitution. In response, some rights advocates have encouraged litigants to seek broader protection based on state constitutions than the Supreme Court recognizes under federal standards. As a result of these changes, state courts now have greater policy responsibility in many diverse areas of law, including criminal justice, education, apportionment, censorship, welfare assistance, interstate commerce, and labor-management relations (Porter 1982, 3-4).

This study has been an effort to assess the impact of the changing trends in judicial federalism on the litigation activities of organized interest groups. I examined the role of major litigating organizations in state judiciaries by addressing two primary questions. First, under what conditions are major litigating organizations most likely to participate in state litigation? Second, when in state courts, do interest groups seek more expansive protection for individual rights under state constitutions than is required by federal standards?

Based on scholarly studies of interest group litigation and my interviews with group officials, two sets of factors, legal incentives and an organizational threshold, were identified as important for understanding group litigation in state courts. To assess the explanatory capacity of these factors, I examined interest group participation in five states since 1960 in eminent domain and obscenity litigation. This concluding chapter evaluates the importance of legal incentives and organizational thresholds by reviewing the findings that emerged from the analysis of takings and obscenity law. Few national organizations litigated with any consistency in state courts in either area of law. Importantly, however, groups did not litigate *for different reasons*. Some groups lacked legal incentives to enter state litigation; others lacked the resources to do so. The presence of both a legal incentive and sufficient resources is extremely important, and perhaps necessary, for groups to enter state litigation on a regular basis.

These findings are potentially quite significant. As rights battles increasingly are fought out at the state level, interest groups that seek to bring about legal and social change must litigate in a greater number of state cases to achieve a comparable policy impact. But in takings and obscenity litigation, from 1960 to 1994, limited resources prevented many organizations from entering litigation on a regular basis. Many interest groups appear ill prepared to respond to trends in judicial federalism by litigating at the state level. This finding raises serious questions about the capacity of organized interests to participate in a decentralized policy-making process that affects their interests.

SUMMARY OF FINDINGS

Table 8.1 presents a comparison of litigation in the five states by the interest groups most active in U.S. Supreme Court takings and obscenity cases. It shows clear differences in the use of state courts across issue areas. National organizations litigated in a higher percentage of state obscenity cases, at least after *Miller v. California* (1973), than they did on takings issues. Even by a frequency measure, national organizations participated in more obscenity cases, despite the much greater number of takings cases in the state courts.

To explain these data and assess the importance of legal incentives and organizational thresholds, the remainder of the chapter reviews and evaluates this study's findings. Both legal incentives and organizational factors are extremely important for understanding the willingness and ability of national organizations to participate regularly in state-level litigation. Neither factor, however, is by itself sufficient to impel groups to litigate consistently in state courts.

Legal Incentives

I hypothesized that major litigating groups are most likely to enter state courts when they have a distinct legal incentive to do so. The U.S. Supreme Court may provide this incentive in one of two forms. First, Supreme Court decisions restricting the scope of individual rights may motivate interest groups to turn to state courts to seek greater protection under state constitutions than is available under federal law. I called this the *new judicial federalism incentive*. Second, the Court may relegate to state courts policy responsibility on issues of law, thereby escalating the importance of state courts as judicial policy makers.

Groups that seek to affect policy may have reason to turn to state courts because increasingly they are the de facto policy makers of last resort. I called this the *federal restriction incentive*. If the U.S. Supreme Court does not provide one or both of these incentives, then groups are much less likely to turn to state courts on a regular basis.

Table 8.1
Participation by National Organizations in State Court Takings and Obscenity Litigation, 1960–1994

	Takings	Obscenity		
		Pre-*Miller*	Post-*Miller*	Total
Percent of Cases with Group Participation	1%	2%	15%	12%
Number of Cases with Group Participation	12	1	18	19

Note: Figures indicate cases from the intermediate appellate and supreme courts of the five states in which a national organization or affiliate participated as a party, counsel, or amicus curiae. Appendices A and B list the cases.

In fact, in both takings and obscenity litigation, groups seldom litigated in state courts when they lacked a legal incentive. I began by examining takings law. In recent years the U.S. Supreme Court has actively addressed regulatory takings issues and has become more receptive to the rights claims of property owners whose private property is affected by government regulations. The Supreme Court's increased receptivity to takings claims, as well as the lack of more expansive state constitutional protection, left property rights organizations without a strong legal incentive to turn to state courts. Property rights organizations' only incentive to enter state cases was due to the requirement that compensation claims against state or local governments for regulatory takings be initiated in state courts.

Lacking strong legal incentives, interest groups only seldom entered state takings cases. While organizational factors played a part, the lack of a legal incentive emerged as the principal explanation for the paucity of litigation by national organizations. The legal context affected all groups, regardless of their resources. The Sierra Club, which had affiliates in every state and considerable access to attorneys, did not litigate significantly more often than groups with fewer resources. Groups generally did not view state judiciaries as important enough to justify litigation on a regular basis. Of course, some property rights organizations did enter state courts because of the Supreme Court's decisions requiring regulatory takings claims against state and local governments to be initiated in state courts. This provided property rights groups some reason to turn to state courts under the federal restriction incentive. Yet it led groups into state courts only occasionally, not on a consistent basis.

Similar findings emerged from an analysis of obscenity litigation. Before *Miller v. California* (1973), the U.S. Supreme Court actively reviewed lower-court obscenity convictions. It had liberalized obscenity doctrine so much that by the end of the 1960s, commentators predicted the "end of obscenity" (Engdahl 1969; Rembar 1968). In this context, interest groups seldom litigated at the state level, instead focusing their efforts on the U.S. Supreme Court. Even the American Civil Liberties Union (ACLU) rarely entered state courts before *Miller*, despite having the organizational capacity to do so in most states.

Thus, groups seldom litigated when they lacked a legal incentive. In contrast, the analysis of obscenity law showed that when provided legal incentives, groups litigated in state judiciaries, contingent on their resources. *Miller v. California* left little doubt about the future of obscenity litigation. Groups on both sides of the debate realized that policy making was decentralized and therefore state courts were more important actors. The Supreme Court's decision in *Miller* furnished two reasons for libertarian groups to turn to state judiciaries. First, by enunciating a "local community standards" logic to determine whether material is obscene, the Court decentralized policy making and state courts increasingly had the final word in obscenity cases. This provided impetus, via the federal restriction incentive, to turn to the state level. Second, the Court issued a less restrictive definition of obscenity that was inimical to the policy interests of libertarian organizations. This legal change potentially encouraged libertarian groups to turn to state courts, via the new judicial federalism incentive, to assert state constitutional arguments seeking broader speech and expression protection than that granted under the *Miller* doctrine.

Chapters 6 and 7 showed that groups turned to state courts after *Miller*. While entry into state litigation was attenuated by organizational goals and resources, a point to which I return shortly, the *Miller* decision did lead groups to mobilize in state judiciaries. Libertarian groups appear to have been motivated primarily by the federal restriction incentive. The ACLU entered state courts mainly to represent defendants charged with violating obscenity statutes. It argued most cases primarily on federal, not state, constitutional grounds. Except in Colorado, where the state constitution provided greater speech protection than did federal standards, groups generally initiated cases in federal courts, when given the choice. Save for cases in Colorado, then, interest groups were reluctant to bring cases in state courts and to mobilize state constitutional law.

To summarize, the presence of a legal incentive helps to explain the willingness of major litigating organizations to enter state courts. Without such incentive, groups seldom participated in state litigation. This illustrates one way in which interest groups were attentive to the context in which they took political action. Groups involved in obscenity cases reacted to changes in the legal environment that altered the efficacy of different litigation strategies. Since, after *Miller*, state courts were more important decision makers in obscenity law, groups were prompted to turn to these forums. In contrast, trends in takings law provided little reason to litigate at the state level.

These findings suggest that the United States Supreme Court can play an important role in providing incentives or disincentives for organizational action in state judiciaries. Where the Court chooses not to address legal issues regularly or restricts the scope of rights under the federal Constitution, interest groups may have greater incentive to turn to the states. Thus, despite general trends of increased group litigation over the past several decades (see Epstein 1994), there likely is significant variation across policy areas in interest groups' propensity to litigate in state courts. Where the Supreme Court provides little incentive to turn to the states, as in takings law, major litigating organizations are less likely to enter state judiciaries. Of course, legal incentives are not only "top-down"; state court decisions may also influence group litigation behavior. By interpreting their constitutions to protect rights more broadly than the federal constitution, state courts may motivate groups to litigate at the state level, just as the Colorado Supreme Court's obscenity decisions led the Media Coalition and other bookseller interests to bring suits in Colorado courts.

This book examined how legal incentives are connected to the arguments interest groups presented in litigation. When in state courts, groups and other litigants may assert constitutional claims based on the federal Constitution, state constitutions, or both. I hypothesized that, when motivated by the new judicial federalism incentive, groups may more likely to seek expansive protections based on independent state constitutional grounds. Understanding *why* interest groups enter state courts is crucial to assessing their overall impact on judicial policy. Indeed, as repeat players in the judiciary, the significance of groups may be more closely related to the kinds of arguments they present to courts than to the number of times they litigate (Epstein and Kobylka 1992, 306).

I examined groups' propensity to assert state constitutional arguments that seek to expand protections beyond the standards of parallel provisions of the federal Constitution. The role of lawyers and litigants in the new judicial federalism often is downplayed or overlooked. While Gardner (1992, 810-11) suggested that lawyers often do not assert independent state constitutional arguments because they do not help win cases, the fact remains that for courts to address state constitutional issues, typically litigants must raise those claims. By basing rights claims on state constitutions, interest groups can be important agents in the development of state constitutional law, much in the way they have been instrumental in bringing about legal developments in the U.S. Supreme Court (for example, Epstein and Kobylka 1992; Vose 1972).

But in both obscenity and takings law, organized interests seldom turned to state judiciaries to seek protection under state constitutions. The Pacific Legal Foundation (PLF) and Mountain States Legal Foundation (MSLF) litigated in state courts because the Supreme Court's ripeness decisions required certain regulatory takings claims to be initiated in state courts. Affiliates of the American Civil Liberties Union (ACLU) mobilized in the wake of *Miller* primarily to represent defendants in obscenity prosecutions. In both situations, the groups advanced rights claims based exclusively or primarily on the federal Constitution.

Indeed, my interviews revealed a bias among group officials toward federal courts and federal law. Importantly, this bias traverses the liberal-conservative ideological divide. The ideologically liberal ACLU in obscenity cases and conservative MSLF in takings cases both indicated a general preference for the federal judiciary. This suggests that the institutional setting of federal courts vis-à-vis state judiciaries is important in explaining the preference for the former. According to the groups seeking to expand individual protections, the federal judiciary typically is more insulated from majoritarian impulses and more protective of rights, whether the protections sought have liberal or conservative ideological implications.

The belief that state courts are less likely to protect rights—and the groups' consequent litigation behavior—sheds light on the important relationship between federalism and rights. The aversion to state litigation reflects a long-held suspicion of state-level policy making. In the judiciary, federal courts are seen as having a special status on issues of rights (Jacobsohn 1996). Some argue that the federal courts' superior judges and staff, greater resources, and insulation from popular pressures make them better protectors of federal rights (Yackle 1994; Neuborne 1977) and, for much the same reasons, that state courts are unlikely to champion rights through state constitutions (D'Alemberte 1996; see also Gardner 1992). At the heart of the critique of state courts is that they cannot effectively protect rights because they are tied too closely to majoritarian political pressures.

Such attitudes are consistent with the Madisonian distrust of state-level policy making. Unlike many of his contemporaries, James Madison believed that the central problem of rights in a republican government was not to protect people from their rulers, but rather to protect individuals and minorities from popular majorities acting through their elected representatives. He argued in *Federalist #10* that rights are in most jeopardy where government responds most immediately to the passions and interests of its constituents—in the democratic polities of the states rather than the extended republic of the national government.[1] Consistent with the arithmetic logic of his theory of factions, oppressive majorities more easily can gain control of government in the smaller, less diverse states (Hamilton, Madison, and Jay 1961).[2]

According to Madison, the national government would check the actions of the states and ensure that they did not deprive the people of individual rights, particularly property rights. Madison did not anticipate the pivotal role that the judiciary would come to occupy on rights issues, instead believing that Congress would restrain local majorities (Rakove 1991, 139-42). Nevertheless, his vision of national-state relations is consistent with contemporary criticisms of state courts in at least one important respect. Where rights are involved, the politically insulated, deliberative bodies of elites at the national level are needed to check more democratic forces in local communities.

The distrust of state political institutions, including courts, has found its way into important components of contemporary constitutional theory. The Fourteenth Amendment, and the Supreme Court's piecemeal incorporation of the Bill of Rights' protections to restrict state actions, marked the realization of Madison's concern about the tyranny of local majorities (Rakove 1991, 142-43). Justice Stone's renowned Footnote Four in *U.S. v. Carolene Products* (1938), by suggesting the need for special constitutional protection to minorities because of their underrepresentation in the political process, further enhanced the centralization of constitutional rights. The logic of Footnote Four restricted the actions of local communities and implied that the constitutional security of political minorities is doubtful at the subnational level, and therefore required federal constitutional protection (Jacobsohn 1996, 39-40).

In short, the interest groups' suspicion of state courts reflects a long tradition in American political and constitutional theory. But despite the popularity of this perspective, it cannot account completely for the rights agenda of recent decades. The new judicial federalism is especially puzzling. Why would litigants turn to state courts and state law to vindicate rights? Apparently, there is more to the protection of liberty than the consolidation of policy responsibility in federal courts.

In fact, contrary to the lessons of much of modern constitutional theory, libertarian groups involved in obscenity litigation recognized, and in some cases pursued, opportunities for expansive protection in state courts. This suggests a very different understanding of the role of state courts—that they may be instrumental to the protection of rights. Indeed, despite his skepticism of state-level policy making, even Madison recognized the critical role of the states. In *Federalist #51*, he argued that the dividing of power between two distinct governments (the federal system) and then subdividing it into separate departments (separation of powers) would give greater protection for rights by dispersing factional conflict. The states, then, are essential to the "double security" provided by a federal political arrangement (Hamilton, Madison, and Jay 1961).

From this perspective, federalism may be beneficial to rights protection for several reasons. Decentralized decision making allows for experiment and creativity. Numerous state courts addressing rights questions fosters legal innovations through trial and error, and the Supreme Court can draw on the innovations of state judiciaries (Beasley 1996, 108-11). And most important, the ability to vindicate rights by appealing to either federal or state constitutions provides the "double security" of which Madison wrote. Since the U.S. Supreme Court's interpretations of the federal Constitution at least nominally afford a "floor" of rights for all citizens, decentralized policy making provides relatively safe opportunities for rights advocates to seek developments at the subnational level. As Justice Brennan (1977) recognized, state supreme courts may raise the "ceiling" of individual protection for citizens in their states. A decentralized litigation environment may have distinct advantages for those seeking enhanced individual protections.

But simply because state courts *may* provide greater individual protections does not necessarily mean that they *will*. How can rights advocates best achieve their goals in state judiciaries? The perspectives of interest group officials provide insight as to how this question might in part be answered. For groups asserting rights claims, a consistent concern was that, in contrast to the insulated, elite cadre in federal courts, state courts were less insulated from the political fray. Group officials noted that state courts were "more distant from the actor [government]" (Seby 1995) and that federal court litigation can avoid the "local political disadvantages [found in state courts]" (Wenk 1995). Such comments suggest that institutions insulated from majoritarian pressures—such as the federal courts—may be more likely to protect rights than those tied more closely to the political milieu.

From the perspective of those asserting rights claims, the advancement of a rights agenda in state judiciaries may require greater institutional independence.[3] In this regard, the increased use of merit selection and retention procedures (Missouri Plan) in recent decades may be a step in the right direction (D'Alemberte 1996). There is some evidence that these procedures foster judicial independence (Glick 1978; Watson and Downing 1969) and—perhaps—a willingness to provide more expansive civil liberties protection through state constitutional interpretation (Beavers and Waltz 1997).

While my interviews and case analysis showed a general reluctance to litigate in state courts and to assert rights claims based on independent state law grounds, in the exceptional instance of Colorado, where the state supreme court provided broad speech protection under the state constitution, interest groups chose to bring obscenity cases in state courts and to rely on the state constitution as authority.[4] The fact that the Media Coalition and Mountains and Plains Booksellers Association asserted rights claims based on independent state constitutional grounds in Colorado courts is consistent with Gardner's (1992, 810) observation that lawyers will rely on state constitutions if it helps win cases. In pursuit of their policy goals, the groups were willing to mobilize state law when it appeared more protective than federal law.

In recent years, interest groups participated in an emerging state constitutional discourse on obscenity law. Four of the five obscenity cases with group participation since 1990 dealt primarily with the scope of rights guaranteed by state constitutions. The mobilization of state constitutional law certainly is related to the Supreme Court's *Miller* decision and the hostility of federal courts to First Amendment claims. However, a more proximate legal incentive was the Oregon Supreme Court's decision in *State v. Henry* (1987). The Oregon court held that the free speech clause of the Oregon Constitution, unlike its federal counterpart, does not recognize obscenity as a category of unprotected speech. Consequently, sexually explicit speech receives full constitutional protection in Oregon, in the same way that political speech is protected. This decision illustrates the creativity and double security afforded by a dual constitutional system. And libertarian groups' responses demonstrate how the decision provided the basis for similar rights claims in other states. *Henry* furnished libertarian groups with an argumentative model to apply in other state courts. As these groups began to assert rights claims based on state constitutional grounds, proscriptionist organizations mobilized to discredit the use of state constitutions to protect sexually explicit speech, thereby expanding the range of interests in the litigation fray. By bringing cases and asserting legal arguments on both sides of the issue, organized interests played an important role in the process whereby state judiciaries were called upon to address and clarify the scope of protections afforded under state constitutions. Both libertarian and proscriptionist groups likely will continue to debate the appropriate scope of state constitutional protection for sexually explicit speech.

Organizational Threshold

Legal incentives are extremely important in explaining patterns of group litigation in state judiciaries. U.S. Supreme Court decisions may alter the efficacy of different litigation strategies and motivate groups to turn to the states, as was the case in obscenity law. However, a legal incentive is by itself insufficient to impel groups into state litigation on a regular basis. I hypothesized that an organizational threshold is also necessary. Resources are the central component of this threshold. Groups with state and local affiliates and, most important, substantial access to attorneys are better able to litigate in a variety of state court systems. The analysis of obscenity law starkly illustrated the importance of organizational factors in explaining litigation behavior.

Miller v. California brought about legal changes that made state courts more important policy makers in obscenity law. With clear legal incentives, groups turned increasingly to state judiciaries after *Miller*. However, this trend toward state court litigation was attenuated significantly by organizational factors, especially resources. Most groups simply lacked the capacity to litigate consistently in numerous state courts. The clear exception was the ACLU, which emerged as the dominant litigator in state courts. Only it had the resources and also the organizational incentives to litigate across most of the states.

Citizens for Decency through Law's (CDL) response to *Miller* illustrates the significance of organizational resources, especially access to attorneys. The organization recognized the importance of state courts after *Miller* and initiated strategies to respond to the changed legal environment. Members of the affiliates lobbied state trial courts in attempts to ensure the vigorous enforcement of obscenity laws. General Counsel Bruce Taylor assisted local prosecutors in obscenity trials and trained them on how best to conduct trials. CDL responded to the incentives to focus on state litigation.

However, unlike the ACLU, the CDL did not have the resources to litigate formally in several state appellate courts. Of the five states examined, CDL participated as amicus curiae in only one appellate case. Since it had no more than four full-time staff attorneys during the time period examined, the group simply did not have the capacity to litigate more often.

Of course, resources are not the only component of the organizational threshold. For instance, a complete understanding of variations in state obscenity litigation must account for the fact that, compared to the ACLU, litigation is not a priority for material organizations such as the American Booksellers Association (ABA). Further, the importance of the obscenity issue varied across ACLU affiliates. Since the ACLU has a broad issue agenda, affiliates devoted scarce resources to what they perceived to be the most pressing issues. The Indiana and New Jersey affiliates (the latter after the late 1970s) generally allocated resources to other issues, whereas the Minnesota Civil Liberties Union focused greater attention—and litigation resources—on obscenity. In Colorado, the ACLU's choice was easier. With other libertarian actors in the litigation fray, the ACLU knew that its arguments were being presented to the courts and therefore could turn to other issues on its agenda.

Thus, like a legal incentive, organizational factors helped to explain patterns of group litigation in state courts. When groups lacked adequate resources, they were unable to litigate consistently. Particularly in obscenity litigation, limited resources prevented many organizations from litigating more often. Resources were also an important, though not the principal, explanation for the lack of participation in state takings cases.

While the organizational threshold helps to determine whether and to what extent interest groups enter state cases, having enough resources is not in itself sufficient to impel groups into the litigation fray. Before *Miller*, the ACLU in each state except South Carolina had adequate resources to litigate but did not, lacking legal incentives to do so. Comparable findings emerged from the examination of takings litigation. Some groups, most notably the Sierra Club, had the capacity to enter state litigation yet seldom did because they lacked the legal incentives.

The fact that organizational resources account for variations in patterns of group litigation is not theoretically surprising. Scholars have long recognized that some litigants have distinct advantages—including greater resources—than others (Galanter 1974). But in the decentralized litigation environment, this finding is substantively important and has potentially far-reaching implications. As policy responsibility in the American judiciary is decentralized, it abides less in the U.S. Supreme Court and more in the many state court systems.[5] However, no single state court decision has the nationwide policy impact of a comparable decision by the U.S. Supreme Court. This simple fact presents interest groups with significant difficulties. In the environment of decentralized policy making that characterizes an increasing number of areas of law, groups have greater incentive to turn to fifty state court systems instead of just one U.S. Supreme Court. Such a litigation strategy requires much greater resources to track local litigation, to develop expertise in the state court systems, and to participate in more cases. The crucial role of organizational factors in attenuating the trend toward state litigation doubtless extends far beyond the case of obscenity law.

Interest groups turn to the courts in attempts to shape the law. While their ability to influence judicial policy is not completely understood, certainly interest groups can act as catalysts of legal change and provide courts with the stimuli (such as cases, information, and legal arguments) that can promote such change (Epstein and Kobylka 1992, 30). However, the capacity of groups to act even as catalysts of legal change is contingent upon their ability to enter the courtroom. In a decentralized litigation environment, with policy responsibility divided among the states, it may be difficult to affect policy on a nationwide basis. Sporadic participation in a few state cases, even if successful, may yield little overall policy impact. Nevertheless, this is the dilemma groups confront. Faced with resource scarcity, interest groups' opportunities to participate in and potentially affect policy development may be severely restricted or lost.

Of course, many organizations, even if they possessed the resources, likely would not litigate in each and every state. They may pick their battles more carefully and enter only those state cases that are particularly important in terms of doctrinal innovation or policy impact. Yet no matter how innovative a decision, for instance, by the Minnesota Supreme Court, that decision directly affects only Minnesota, not New Jersey, South Carolina, Colorado, or any other state. In short, the resources needed to influence policy on a broad scale in a decentralized litigation environment are much greater than those necessary to do so through a more centralized lobbying strategy that focuses on the U.S. Supreme Court.

A possible objection to this interpretation might be that organizational goals rather than resources provide the most valid explanation for the paucity of state litigation by national organizations. Since the impact of state court decisions are limited in scope compared to federal court (especially U.S. Supreme Court) decisions, perhaps groups did not view most state appellate cases as significant enough to justify participation. While true to some degree, this is the very predicament groups encounter in a decentralized litigation environment. They must enter a greater number of state-level cases, no one of which has the policy impact of a comparable decision by the Supreme Court. But this does not mean that groups no longer seek to shape the law as policy responsibility is decentralized. My interviews revealed that group officials, particularly those involved in obscenity cases, would have liked to litigate more often in state courts. But the costs associated with participating in the judicial process nationwide were prohibitive for most groups.

In both obscenity and takings law, particularly the former, limited resources presented a substantial obstacle for groups that sought to litigate in state courts. One consequence may be that fewer and perhaps a less diverse range of interests are formally brought to bear in a decentralized policy-making process. Of course, it is important to recall that numerous concentrated interests, particularly business organizations, litigated once or twice in state takings cases and were not examined thoroughly in Chapter 4. Through these organizations, interests were represented before state judiciaries. Nevertheless, whether we examine all interest groups or only national organizations, rates of participation were lower in state supreme courts than in the U.S. Supreme Court in both obscenity and takings cases.

This should be no surprise to students of federalism. In *Federalist #10*, James Madison argued that at the federal level, the size of the nation and the diversity of factions would prevent any one interest from gaining domination of national politics. In contrast, the lack of economic and social diversity in most states would lead to domination by one or a few interests (Hamilton, Madison, and Jay 1961). While my analysis did not directly address this argument, in broad contours the findings are compatible with Madison's observations. Limited resources prevented many national organizations from mobilizing the law in state judiciaries. While this does not ensure that interests that did participate dominated policy making, it does reveal less "diversity of factions" in state courts than in their federal counterparts, at least in obscenity and takings law.

The impediments to group participation in state litigation also suggest that rights advocates may be hampered in their attempts to realize the opportunities of the new judicial federalism. State constitutions allow state courts to grant broader protection for rights than the Supreme Court recognizes under the national Constitution. Yet these rights are not self-executing. They depend on litigants to mobilize the law and assert rights claims in the courts. Aside from the willingness of state judges to protect rights, then, those seeking expansive interpretations of rights may not find them as readily in state courts as they once did in federal courts due to the fact that interest groups (and perhaps other repeat players in the judicial process) lack the resources and incentives to litigate in numerous state courts over an extended period of time.

Organized groups have been an important, though by no means the only, mechanism by which the interests of one-shot litigants are represented before the courts. By bringing cases, pursuing appeals, and asserting legal arguments, groups can serve as catalysts of legal change and potentially influence the development of precedents. Interest groups provided a crucial support structure for the U.S. Supreme Court's increased attention to and expansion of federal rights during the Warren Court era. As rights questions increasingly are the province of state judiciaries, however, the willingness and ability of major litigating organizations to continue to play a central role in the litigation fray is in some doubt.

Thus, a decentralized litigation environment is in some ways a double-edged sword for rights advocates. The increased importance of state judiciaries provides opportunities for more expansive protections under state constitutions. Yet with policy responsibility diffused among fifty state court systems, interest groups and other actors seeking broad individual protections may be hampered in their efforts to achieve their goals. Many groups appear to lack the resources or organizational incentives to bring cases and pursue appeals on a repeated and strategic basis.

The ability to litigate successfully in state courts is enhanced by the presence of affiliates to track local litigation and access to attorneys who are licensed to practice in the states and are familiar with state laws, rules, and the procedures of state courts. It is important to recognize that these resources are somewhat different from those required to litigate in the United States Supreme Court. Consequently, some interest groups may be better suited than others to respond to the trends in judicial federalism. In other words, the decentralization of policy responsibility does not affect all groups equally. The influence of any organizational litigant is likely diminished as policy responsibility devolves to the state level and the group must attempt to affect judicial policy through state-by-state litigation campaigns. But some organized litigants are more disadvantaged than others by these trends.

In obscenity litigation, the ACLU became the dominant group litigator in state courts after *Miller v. California*, even though it was not the most frequent participant in Supreme Court litigation (see Kobylka 1991). Organizational resources explained much of the variation in patterns of group litigation after *Miller*. The ACLU's dominance in mobilizing the law at the state level reflected the fact that it had *much* greater resources than any other group active on obscenity issues. The ACLU had well over 5,000 volunteer cooperating attorneys nationwide (Ennis 1980); the other groups active in obscenity litigation relied on less than ten counsel. The ACLU was best able to overcome the obstacles associated with decentralized litigation and had the capacity (through not necessarily the willingness) to participate in obscenity cases in most states. This finding underscores the fact that the ACLU's resources are truly exceptional. In an era in which policy responsibility in many areas of law is relegated increasingly to state courts, not only the quality of attorneys but also their sheer numbers are vital. The organization's relatively decentralized structure and network of cooperating attorneys allows it to litigate in both state and federal courts on a wide variety of issues. Likely, no other nongovernmental organization can match the ACLU's capacity to mobilize the law nationwide.

Groups with the resources and incentives to litigate in state courts regularly have greater opportunities to influence policy. What types of groups are advantaged by the trends in judicial federalism? My findings suggest an intriguing and ironic consequence of decentralized policy responsibility. Most observers associate the growing importance of state courts in recent decades to the rising conservatism of the federal judiciary. U.S. Supreme Court decisions that have narrowed individual protection under the federal Constitution encouraged litigants to bring state constitutional claims in state judiciaries (Linde 1980; Brennan

1977). The Court's procedural decisions restricting access to federal courts were a component of the ideologically conservative agendas of the Burger and Rehnquist Courts (Yackle 1994; Neuborne 1977).

However, it appears that among the national organizations, ideologically *liberal* interest groups are best able to mobilize the law in state judiciaries. Admittedly, few groups have the capacity to litigate consistently in a variety of state court systems. Yet groups with the necessary resources, particularly subnational affiliates and access to attorneys, are predominately liberal organizations. The ACLU and Sierra Club, as this study demonstrated, and perhaps the National Association for the Advancement of Colored People (NAACP), at least before its recent financial troubles, are able to litigate in state courts nationwide. In contrast, many conservative interest groups that devote substantial resources to litigation (such as the PLF and MSLF) are legal foundations. They lack the grassroots structure and large volunteer attorney pools of some of their liberal counterparts.

Of course, this by no means guarantees that the outcomes of the state judicial process will reflect liberal interests. Indeed, conservative interests still may favor decentralized policy making because numerous concentrated groups, such as businesses, likely have greater incentive and capacity to mobilize at the state level (Olson 1965). Regardless of its effects on major litigating organizations, decentralized policy responsibility may benefit conservative causes.

While my study has not addressed that issue directly, some of the findings are relevant. Not surprisingly, a large number of business interests participated as amicus curiae in state takings cases. Businesses comprised 31 percent of the amici in state courts, compared to only 6 percent in U.S. Supreme Court takings cases. It appears that business interests do mobilize and may be well represented in state courts. However, further analysis challenges this conclusion. While 31 percent of the amici were businesses, 34 percent represented the interests of governments. In eminent domain disputes, then, business interests appear to have been matched toe-to-toe by competing governmental interests, at least in these five states. Obviously, the evidence is only suggestive, but it implies that businesses, and perhaps other concentrated interests, do not necessarily dominate in state courts in all areas of law.[6]

In any event, many—if not most—national organizations may lack the resources to litigate regularly in state courts. Interest groups can and perhaps will respond to trends in federalism by allocating greater resources to litigation. Yet for some groups with severely limited resources, this is not possible. Other organizations, especially material groups that engage in a wide variety of both political and nonpolitical activities, must face the tough question of whether it is productive to devote greater resources to litigation. Money and other resources dedicated to litigation cannot be used for other purposes.[7] Whether organizations ultimately allocate greater resources to litigation is a question of strategy that will entail, among other things, assessing the efficacy of litigation in lower courts. However, regardless of groups' decisions, trends in federalism require consideration of these issues. Unless they change priorities and the amount of resources allocated to litigation, most groups will not be able to play as central a role in a policy-making process that affects their interests.

To summarize, the analytic framework set out in Chapter 2 helped to explain patterns of interest group litigation in state judiciaries. Specifically, legal incentives and the organizational threshold both emerged as very important, and perhaps necessary, conditions for consistent use of state courts. In takings law and obscenity law before *Miller*, where groups had little reason to turn to state courts, they seldom litigated. The examination of obscenity litigation in the post-*Miller* period revealed that even when groups had incentives to litigate, many did not do so regularly due to, among other things, limited resources. Few organizations involved in takings and obscenity litigation possessed the resources and incentives to participate regularly in state litigation (see Figure 8.1).

Among all the groups examined in this study, the Minnesota Civil Liberties Union (MCLU) best illustrated the coupling of legal incentives and an organizational threshold. The MCLU was active in debates over the censorship of sexual material since at least the early 1950s and ranked the issue among its most important. Further, staff attorneys and the large pool of volunteer cooperating attorneys gave the MCLU the resources necessary to litigate regularly in state courts. With sufficient organizational resources, the MCLU was the most active group in obscenity litigation after—but not before—*Miller v. California* provided incentives to turn to state courts.

CONCLUSION

As a result of the trends in judicial federalism of the past quarter century, federal courts occupy a less central role in the American judicial policy-making process. Particularly on issues of constitutional rights and liberties, state courts—interpreting both federal and state constitutions—increasingly make the final decisions on many debated legal questions. This is likely to continue to be the case for the foreseeable future. In many areas of law, then, organized interest groups have greater incentives to pursue their policy goals in state courts.

This study is the first to specifically examine the impact of trends in federalism on interest group litigation. My interviews and analysis have shown that a legal incentive and an organizational threshold are extremely important in explaining patterns of interest group litigation in state courts. Even when there is incentive to participate in state cases, scarce resources prevented many interest groups from litigating. Further, groups generally were reluctant to mobilize state law to seek broader protection than that required by federal standards. In takings and obscenity litigation, most rights claims were based primarily on federal constitutional guarantees. Only recently in obscenity litigation did groups rely on state constitutions to assert rights claims.

Figure 8.1
Assessing the Conditions under which Interest Groups Litigate in State Courts

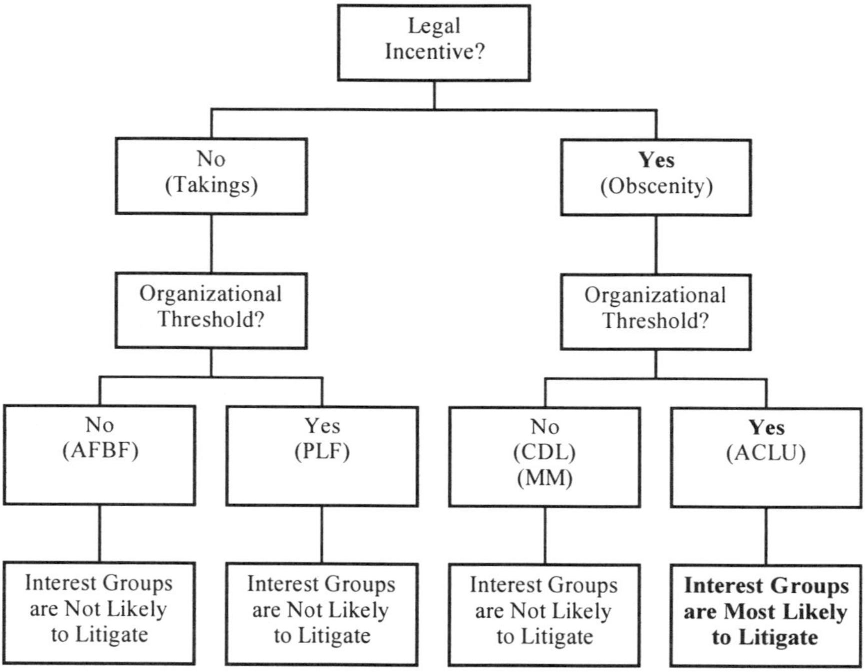

Key:

ACLU	American Civil Liberties Union
AFBF	American Farm Bureau Federation
CDL	Citizens for Decency through Law
MM	Morality in Media
PLF	Pacific Legal Foundation

This study has important theoretical and policy implications, and suggests profitable avenues for future research. A more general understanding of interest groups' use of state courts requires examination of other issue areas and a greater number of states. It would be interesting, for instance, to investigate groups' reliance on independent state constitutional claims in areas such as criminal search and seizure, where state courts have been more willing to interpret their constitutions to provide greater protection than is required by federal standards (see Collins, Galie, and Kincaid 1986).

More generally, this study demonstrated the importance of analysis of litigation across levels of courts. Most studies of group litigation, and the judicial process more generally, examine only federal or state courts in isolation from one another. This is unfortunate. American federalism offers players in the judicial process opportunities for creativity and the strategic use of multiple points of access to the courts to further their goals. A better understanding of how legal actors manipulate these opportunities will lend insight into institutional choice in a dual-court system.

Finally, the study highlighted the role of limited resources in preventing groups from entering litigation and attempting to shape the law in a way that is conducive to their policy goals (Galanter 1974). The trend of decentralized policy responsibility in the judiciary suggests that in the future, resources may have an even greater impact on interest group litigation. Since the U.S. Supreme Court decides relatively few cases and is at the apex of the American judicial system, many groups are able to amass the resources to participate in Supreme Court cases that affect their interests. But in state (and lower federal) courts, the effects of limited resources will most clearly manifest themselves behaviorally. Future studies would do well to further explore the limits to the ability of groups and other litigants to mobilize the law in a decentralized litigation environment.

Interest group litigation in state courts largely has been neglected in the study of law and politics. While more understandable in an era when the U.S. Supreme Court actively addressed most major questions of constitutional rights and liberties, doubtless that era has ended, at least for the foreseeable future. Some interest groups have attempted to respond to the trends in federalism by litigating in state courts. It is time for the attention of scholars who seek to understand how groups affect public policy to respond accordingly.

NOTES

1. Primarily for this reason, Madison doubted the efficacy of the Bill of Rights, which initially restricted the actions of only the national government. He believed that unless it could prevent tyranny at the state level and restrict the impulses of local majorities, the Bill of Rights would be largely inconsequential (Rakove 1991).

2. For an alternative view, see Rapaczynski (1985), who argued that the maintenance of a dominant power elite is much easier at the national than the state level, and thus the possibilities for oppression of minorities are greater at higher levels of government.

3. Neuborne (1977) observed that state appellate courts that most closely approximate the independence of the federal courts appear to be most vigorous in protecting individual rights.

4. Incidentally, Colorado relies on the Missouri Plan to select and retain appellate court judges.

5. This discussion describes tendencies in a decentralized litigation environment. Given its role at the apex of the American judicial hierarchy, the U.S. Supreme Court never completely abdicates policy responsibility in any area of law. Likewise, even when the Supreme Court frequently addresses legal questions, lower federal and state courts always are important in implementing Supreme Court decisions (see Johnson and Canon 1984).

6. I do not wish to infer too much from these data. In Galanter's (1974) terminology, many takings disputes pit repeat players (such as businesses and corporations) against other repeat players (governments). The structure of conflict in takings law, which often places these two categories of repeat players in contention, suggests that businesses are unlikely to be the dominant litigators.

However, whether business litigants are as well matched in state courts in other areas of law is debatable. For instance, in many areas of tort law, where businesses often face one-shot litigants, the repeat player advantages may allow business interests to exert greater control over litigation.

7. Even organizations such as the ACLU and Sierra Club, which have large volunteer attorney pools, face similar dilemmas. Groups commit time and other resources to developing and maintaining their networks of volunteer attorneys. Steven Bates (1995), of the ACLU of South Carolina, noted that one of the most important benefits of having a staff attorney was that it allowed the group to develop a larger volunteer attorney pool. With the growing importance of state courts, groups may deem it necessary to devote more of their scarce resources to develop affiliates and expand volunteer attorney networks.

Appendix A

National Organizational Participation in State Court Takings Litigation

Case	Organizational Participation
Beard v. South Carolina Coastal Council (1991)	Sierra Club (amicus) South Carolina Wildlife Federation (amicus)
Central Baptist Theological Seminary v. City of New Brighton (1992)	Sierra Club (amicus) St. Paul Audubon Society (amicus)
City of Thorton v. Farmers Reservoir & Irrigation Co. (1978)	Colorado Farm Bureau Federation (amicus)
County of Freeborn v. Bryson (1973)	Sierra Club (party)
County of Pine v. State (1979)	Sierra Club (amicus)
Grand Land Co. v. Township of Bethlehem (1984)	New Jersey Farm Bureau (amicus)
In re Egg Harbor Associates (1983)	New Jersey Builders Association (amicus)

Case	Organizational Participation
Jafay v. Board of City Commissioners of Boulder City (1993)	American Planning Association (amicus) Colorado Chapter of American Planning Association (amicus)
Lucas v. South Carolina Coastal Council (1991)	Pacific Legal Foundation (amicus) Sierra Club (amicus) South Carolina Wildlife Federation (amicus)
New Jersey Builders Association v. Dept. of Environmental Protection (1979)	New Jersey Builders Association (party) New Jersey Farm Bureau (amicus)
Southern Burlington County NAACP v. Mt. Laurel (1983)	American Planning Association (amicus)
State v. Christopher (1969)	Sierra Club (amicus)

Appendix B

National Organizational Participation in State Court Obscenity Litigation

Case	Organizational Participation
Alexander v. City of St. Paul (1975)	MCLU (sponsor)
City of Duluth v. Sarette (1979)	MCLU (sponsor)
City of Duluth v. Wendling (1975)	MCLU (amicus)
In re Title (1994)	ABA/Foundation for Free Expression (amicus) ACLU of Colorado Foundation (amicus) ALA Freedom to Read Foundation (amicus) Colorado Library Association (amicus) CPDA/IPDA (amicus) Feminists for Free Expression (amicus) MPBA (amicus) Motion Picture Association of America (amicus) Recording Industry Association of America (amicus)
Knudtson v. City of Coates (1994)	National Family Legal Foundation (amicus)

Case	Organizational Participation
Koppinger v. City of Fairmont (1976)	MCLU (sponsor)
People v. Ford (1989)	MPBA (party)
People v. New Horizons, Inc. (1980)	CDL (amicus)
Pierce v. City and County of Denver (1977)	MPBA (sponsor)
Rothschild v. Richland County Board of Adjustment (1992)	American Family Law Center (sponsor)
State v. Alexander (1979)	MCLU (amicus)
State v. Blecker (1978)	ACLU of New Jersey (sponsor)
State v. Carmel (1979)	ACLU of New Jersey (sponsor)
State v. Davidson (1992)	MCLU/ACLU Arts Censorship Project (amicus) Morality in Media (amicus) National Family Legal Foundation (amicus)
State v. J.O. (1976)	ACLU of New Jersey (sponsor)
State v. Watkins (1972)	ACLU (sponsor)
State v. Watkins (1973)	ACLU (sponsor)
Tattered Cover v. Tooley (1985)	MC (party)

Key:

ABA	American Booksellers Association
ACLU	American Civil Liberties Union
ALA	American Library Association
CDL	Citizens for Decency through Law
CPDA	Council for Periodical Distributors Association
IPDA	International Periodical Distributors Association

MC	Media Coalition
MCLU	Minnesota Civil Liberties Union
MPBA	Mountains and Plains Booksellers Association

Appendix C

Methodological Appendix

UNIVERSE OF CASES

To identify the universe of cases, the principal search mechanism was a series of Westlaw topical searches. For each of the five state appellate court systems (the intermediate appellate courts and state court of last resort) and for the U.S. Supreme Court, the following searches were conducted:

"To (148) & Date (aft 1959)." This search identified the universe of eminent domain cases between 1960 and 1994.

"To (281) & Date (aft 1959)." This search identified the universe of obscenity cases between 1960 and 1994.

A variety of other sources supplemented the Westlaw searches. To help identify amicus curiae participation, the following Lexis searches were conducted for the intermediate appellate and high courts of each state and the U.S. Supreme Court: "amicus or amici and obscenity and date aft 1959" and "amicus or amici and eminent domain or inverse condemnation or regulatory taking! and date aft 1959." In addition, cases were identified in law review articles and interest group files. The supplemental searches verified the validity of the principal Westlaw search and, in a few instances, added cases to the population.

The searches yielded a total of 1,236 eminent domain cases in the five state court systems and 71 in the U.S. Supreme Court. For obscenity law, the searches produced a population of 161 cases in the five state court systems and 128 in the Supreme Court (42 of which were summary reversals).

INTERVIEWS

During the period of January to September 1995, I conducted a total of twenty-four interviews. Most lasted 45 minutes to one hour, though some were finished in about 30 minutes. In most instances, I recorded the interviews and, as soon as possible thereafter, transcribed them. When interviewees preferred not to be recorded, I took notes and wrote them up soon afterward. The quotations taken from these interviews are accurate within a word or two of what the group officials or attorneys said. While most interviews were face-to-face, in some instances I was unable to meet group officials personally and had to rely on telephone conversations or written correspondence. Information taken from these sources is duly noted in the text. Finally, to achieve candor and best assure valid data, I offered confidentiality to all group officials. While most did not object to being quoted, some interviewees requested not to be personally identified.

As is typical in elite interviewing, I conducted open-ended, semistructured interviews with group officials and attorneys active in litigation. This type of interview allowed me to test hypotheses and seek comparative information, while at the same time continuing to develop and refine hypotheses based on the perspectives of group officials (Hammer and Wildavsky 1989; Dexter 1970). Recognizing that elites often are sources of bias, in as many situations as possible I rely on multiple respondents and/or support interview evidence with data from other sources (see McFarland 1994; Epstein 1989b).

Given this study's focus on interest group litigation, I sought to interview those with the most knowledge about litigation activities, namely, general counsel or staff attorneys. I also sought to interview each group's executive director, to gain a better understanding of the importance of litigation vis-à-vis other political and nonpolitical activities. For many organizations, this was not possible. For instance, the state affiliates of many groups do not have staff attorneys or a litigation department. Nevertheless, discussion with other group officials, especially those active on takings or obscenity issues, proved informative.

Table of Cases

520 East 81st St. Associates v. Lenox Hill Hospital, 555 N.Y.S.2d 697 (N.Y.A.D. 1 Dept. 1990)
ABA et al. v. Hudnut, 598 F.Supp. 1316 (1984), 771 F.2d 323 (1985)
ABA et al. v. Webb, 329 S.E.2d 495 (Ga. 1985)
ABA v. Rendell, 481 A.2d 919 (Pa. Super. 1984)
Action for Children's Television v. FCC, 11 F.3d 170 (1993)
Albright v. State, 501 N.E.2d 488 (Ind. App. 1986)
Alexander v. City of Minneapolis, 531 F.Supp. 1162 (1982)
Alexander v. City of Minneapolis, 928 F.2d 278 (1991), 713 F.Supp 1296 (1989)
Alexander v. City of St. Paul, 227 N.W.2d 370 (Minn. 1975)
Alexander v. U.S., 509 U.S. 544 (1993)
Alexander v. Virginia, 413 U.S. 836 (1973)
American Film Distributors v. State, 413 N.E.2d 1091 (Ind. App. 1981)
Antoine v. California Coastal Commission, 10 Cap. Rptr.2d 471 (Cal. App. 1992)
API v. New Jersey Dept. of Envtl. Protection, 554 A.2d 3 (N.J. Super. 1989)
Arcara v. Cloud Books, Inc., 478 U.S. 697 (1986)
Armstrong v. U.S., 364 U.S. 40 (1960)
Ashlock v. District Court, 717 P2d 483 (Colo. 1986)
Aspen Wilderness Workshop v. Colorado Water Conservation Board, 901 P.2d 1251 (Colo. 1995)
Associated Builders & Contractors v. Baca, 769 F.Supp. 1537 (1991)
Austin v. State, 528 N.E.2d 792 (Ind. App. 1988)
Azul Pacifico, Inc. v. City of Los Angeles, 948 F.2d 575 (1991)
Bantam Books v. Sullivan, 372 U.S. 58 (1963)
Barnes v. Glen Theatre, Inc., 501 U.S. 560 (1991)
Barrick Gold Exploration, Inc. v. Hudson, 823 F.Supp. 1395 (1993)
Batch v. Town of Chapel Hill, 387 S.E.2d 655 (N.C. 1990)
Beard v. South Carolina Coastal Council, 403 S.E.2d 620 (S.C. 1991)
Berggren v. Town of Duluth, 304 N.W.2d 24 (Minn. 1981)
Berman v. Parker, 348 U.S. 26 (1954)

Bernzen v. City of Boulder, 525 P.2d 416 (Colo. 1974)
Blatnik v. Ketola, 587 F.2d 379 (1978)
Board of Education of Union Beach v. New Jersey Education Association, 247 A.2d 867 (N.J. 1968)
Bock v. Westminster Mall Company, 819 P.2d 55 (Colo. 1991)
Bolger v. Youngs Drug Product Corp., 463 U.S. 60 (1983)
Brick v. Board of Education, 305 F.Supp. 1316 (1969)
Brown v. Board of Education, 347 U.S. 483 (1954)
Buechel v. State Dept. of Ecology, 884 P.2d 910 (Wash. 1994)
Butler v. Michigan, 352 U.S. 380 (1957)
Cain v. Commonwealth, 437 S.W.2d 769 (Ky. 1969)
California v. Krivda, 409 U.S. 33 (1972)
California v. LaRue, 409 U.S. 109 (1972)
Carlin Communications, Inc. v. F.C.C., 749 F.2d 113 (1984)
Central Baptist Theological Seminary v. City of New Brighton, 487 N.W.2d 528 (Minn. App. 1992)
Chaplinsky v. New Hampshire, 315 U.S. 568 (1942)
Chicago, B. & Q.R.R. v. City of Chicago, 166 U.S. 226 (1897)
City and County of Denver v. Bergland, 517 F.Supp. 155 (1981)
City of Colorado Springs v. Board of City Commrs. of Eagle, 895 P.2d 1105 (Colo. App. 1994)
City of Duluth v. Sarette, 283 N.W.2d 533 (Minn. 1979)
City of Duluth v. Wendling, 237 N.W.2d 79 (Minn. 1975)
City of Newport v. Iaobucci, 479 U.S. 92 (1986)
City of Renton v. Playtime Theatres, Inc., 475 U.S. 41 (1986)
City of Thorton v. Farmers Reservoir & Irrigation Co., 575 P.2d 382 (Colo. 1978)
Clajon Production Corp. v. Petera, 70 F.3d 1566 (1995), 854 F.Supp. 843 (1994)
Clemson University v. First Provident Corp., 197 S.E.2d 914 (S.C. 1973)
Cohen v. California, 403 U.S. 15 (1971)
Colorado Civil Rights Commission v. Travelers Insurance Co., 759 P.2d 1358 (Colo. 1988)
Colorado River Water Conservation District v. Colorado Water Conservation Board, 594 P.2d 570 (Colo. 1979)
Commonwealth v. Holmes, 17 Mass. 336 (1821)
Commonwealth v. Wasson, 842 S.W.2d 487 (Ky. 1992)
Cooper v. State, 540 N.E.2d 1216 (Ind. 1989)
County of Freeborn v. Bryson, 210 N.W.2d 290 (Minn. 1973)
County of Pine v. State, 280 N.W.2d 625 (Minn. 1979)
Crema v. New Jersey Dept. of Envtl. Protection, 442 A.2d 630 (N.J. Super. 1982), 463 A.2d 910 (N.J. 1983), 471 A.2d 422 (N.J. Super. 1984)
Crim v. State, 294 N.E.2d 822 (Ind. App. 1973)
Crow-New Jersey 32 Limited Partnership v. Township of Clinton, 718 F.Supp. 378 (1989)
Cryan v. Hamar Theatres, Inc., 419 U.S. 1085 (1974)
CSX Transp., Inc. v. Clark, 646 N.E.2d 1003 (Ind. App. 1995)
Davis-Kidd Booksellers, Inc. v. McWherter, 866 S.W.2d 520 (Tenn. 1993)
Dodd v. Hood River County, 59 F.3d 852 (1995), 855 P.2d 608 (Or. 1993), 836 P.2d 1373 (Or. App. 1992)
Doe v. City of Minneapolis, 898 F.2d 612 (1990)

Doe v. Smith, 527 N.E.2d 177 (Ind. 1988)
Dolan v. City of Tigard, 854 P.2d 437 (Or. 1993), 512 U.S. 374 (1994)
Dominus Rex v. Curll, 2 Stra. 789 (1727)
Dworkin v. Hustler Magazine, Inc., 867 F.2d 1188 (1989)
Ely-Moose Lake Wilderness Canoe Trips and Outfitters, Inc. v. U.S., No. 588-79L (U.S. Court of Claims slip opinion) (1981)
Energy Research Foundation v. Waddell, 367 S.E.2d 419 (S.C. 1988)
Essex County Welfare Board v. Cohen, 299 F.Supp. 176 (1969)
Evans v. Romer, 854 P.2d 1270 (Colo. 1993)
Fair Share Organization v. Kroger Company, 176 N.E.2d 205 (Ind. App. 1961)
Fallini v. Hodel, 963 F.2d 275 (1992)
Fay v. Noia, 372 U.S. 391 (1963)
F.C.C. v. Florida Power Corp., 480 U.S. 245 (1987)
F.C.C. v. Pacifica Foundation, 438 U.S. 726 (1978)
First English Evangelical Lutheran Church v. County of Los Angeles, 482 U.S. 304 (1987)
Floodwood-Fine Lakes Citizens Group v. Minnesota Envtl. Quality Council, 287 N.W.2d 390 (Minn. 1979)
Florida Rock Industries v. U.S., 18 F.3d 1560 (1994), 791 F.2d 893 (1986)
Flynt v. Ohio, 451 U.S. 619 (1981)
Fordyce v. State, 569 N.E.2d 357 (Ind. App. 1991)
Fort Wayne Books v. Indiana, 489 U.S. 46 (1989), 539 N.E.2d 948 (Ind. 1989)
Fox Film Corporation v. Muller, 296 U.S. 207 (1935)
Freedman v. Maryland, 380 U.S. 51 (1965)
Frejlach v. Butler, 573 F.2d 1026 (1978)
FW/PBS, Inc. v. City of Dallas, 648 F.Supp. 1061 (1986), 896 F.2d 864 (1990)
Gallagher v. Indiana State Election Board, 598 N.E.2d 510 (Ind. 1992)
Garlin v. State, 325 N.E.2d 515 (Ind. App. 1975)
Get Away Club, Inc. v. Coleman, 969 F.2d 664 (1992)
Glasheen v. City of Austin, 840 F.Supp. 62 (1993)
Glosemeyer v. Missouri-Kansas-Texas Railroad, 879 F.2d 316 (1989)
Goedecke v. State, 603 P.2d 123 (Colo. 1979)
Golden Gate Hotel Association v. City and County of San Francisco, 18 F.3d 1482 (1994)
Graham v. Estuary Properties, Inc., 399 So.2d 1374 (Fla. 1981)
Grand Land Co. v. Township of Bethlehem, 483 A.2d 818 (N.J. Super. 1984)
Green v. Castle Concrete Co., 509 P.2d 588 (Colo. 1973)
Guimont v. Clarke, 854 P.2d 1 (Wash. 1993)
Hadacheck v. Sebastian, 239 U.S. 394 (1915)
Hawaii Housing Authority v. Midkiff, 467 U.S. 229 (1984)
Heart of Atlanta Motel, Inc. v. U.S., 379 U.S. 241 (1964)
Heller v. New York, 413 U.S. 483 (1973)
Hendrickson v. State, 127 N.W.2d 165 (Minn. 1964)
Hodel v. Irving, 481 U.S. 704 (1987)
Hodel v. Virginia Surface Mining and Reclamation Association, 452 U.S. 264 (1981)
Hosack v. Smiley, 276 F.Supp. 876 (1967)
Humane Society of the U.S. v. State Fish and Game Council, 322 A.2d 841 (N.J. Super. 1974), 362 A.2d 20 (N.J. 1976)
In re City of Aurora, 799 P.2d 33 (Colo. 1990)

In re Discharge of Bruce W. Johnson, 180 N.W.2d 184 (Minn. 1970)
In re Egg Harbor Associates, 464 A.2d 1115 (N.J. 1983)
In re Hauptly, 312 N.E.2d 857 (Ind. 1974)
In re Lawrance, 579 N.E.2d 32 (Ind. 1991)
In re Mental Commitment of M.P., 510 N.E.2d 645 (Ind. 1987)
In re Nelson, 515 P.2d 1129 (Colo. 1973)
In re Plan for Orderly Withdrawal, 591 A.2d 1005 (N.J. Super. 1991)
In re Title, 877 P.2d 848 (Colo. 1994)
In re Township of Berkeley, 519 A.2d 901 (N.J. Super. 1986)
In the Matter of the Application for Water Rights, 891 P.2d 952 (Colo. 1995)
Jacobellis v. Ohio, 378 U.S. 184 (1964)
Jacobucci v. District Court in and for Jefferson, 541 P.2d 667 (Colo. 1975)
Jafay v. Board of City Commissioners of Boulder City, 848 P.2d 892 (Colo. 1993)
Jenkins v. Georgia, 418 U.S. 153 (1974)
Johnson v. Louisiana, 406 U.S. 356 (1972)
Kaplan v. California, 413 U.S. 115 (1973)
Keystone Bituminous Coal Assn. v. DeBenedictis, 480 U.S. 470 (1987)
Knudtson v. City of Coates, 519 N.W.2d 166 (Minn. 1994)
Koelfgen v. Jackson, 355 F.Supp. 243 (1972)
Koppinger v. City of Fairmont, 248 N.W.2d 708 (Minn. 1976)
Kosydar v. Wolman, 353 F.Supp 744 (1972)
Laux v. Chopin Land Associates, 550 N.E.2d 100 (Ind. App. 1990), 546 N.E.2d 115 (1989)
Leech v. ABA, 582 S.W.2d 738 (Tenn. 1979)
Liles v. Oregon, 425 U.S. 963 (1976)
Littoral Development Co. v. San Francisco Bay Conservation Commission, 33 Cal. App. 4th 211 (1995)
Lockary v. Kayfetz, 917 F.2d 1150 (1990), 587 F.Supp. 631 (1984)
Lordi v. UA New Jersey Theatres, Inc., 259 A.2d 734 (N.J. Super. 1969)
Loretto v. Teleprompter Manhattan CATV Corp., 458 U.S. 419 (1982)
Loveladies Harbor, Inc. v. U.S., 28 F.3d 1171 (1994)
Lucas v. South Carolina Coastal Council, 404 S.E.2d 895 (S.C. 1991), 505 U.S. 1003 (1992)
Lujan v. Colorado State Board of Education, 649 P.2d 1005 (Colo. 1982)
Lykken v. Vavreck, 366 F.Supp. 585 (1973)
MacDonald, Sommer & Frates v. County of Yolo, 477 U.S. 340 (1986)
Manocherian v. Lenox Hospital, 643 N.E.2d 479 (N.Y. 1994)
Manual Enterprises v. Day, 370 U.S. 478 (1962)
Marcus v. Search Warrant, 367 U.S. 717 (1961)
Margola Associates v. City of Seattle, 854 P.2d 23 (Wash. 1993)
Memoirs v. Massachusetts, 383 U.S. 413 (1966)
Metrolina Family Practice v. Sullivan, 767 F.Supp. 1314 (1989)
Michigan v. Long, 463 U.S. 1032 (1983)
Miller Brothers v. Dept. of Natural Resources, 513 N.W.2d 217 (Mich. 1994)
Miller v. California, 413 U.S. 15 (1973)
Minnesota Public Interest Research Group v. Minnesota Envtl. Quality Council, 237 N.W.2d 375 (Minn. 1975)
Minnesota Public Interest Research Group v. White, 257 N.W.2d 762 (Minn. 1977)
M.J. Brock & Sons v. City of Davis, 401 F.Supp. 354 (1975)

Monroe v. Pape, 365 U.S. 167 (1961)
Morality in Media of Western New York, Inc. v. City of Buffalo Common Council, 470 N.Y.S.2d 995 (N.Y. Super. 1984)
Morehart v. County of Santa Barbara, 872 P.2d 143 (Cal. 1994)
Mountain States Legal Foundation v. Apache County, 706 P.2d 1246 (Ariz. App. 1985)
Mountain States Legal Foundation v. Clark, 740 F.2d 792 (1984)
Mountain States Legal Foundation v. Espy, 833 F.Supp. 808 (1993)
Mountain States Legal Foundation v. Hodel, 799 F.2d 1423 (1986)
Mugler v. Kansas, 123 U.S. 623 (1887)
National Association of Property Owners v. U.S., 499 F.Supp. 1223 (1980)
National Railroad Passenger Corp. v. Boston and Maine Corp., 503 U.S. 407 (1992)
National Wildlife Federation v. Cotter Corp., 665 P.2d 598 (Colo. 1983), 646 P.2d 393 (Colo. App. 1981)
Nectow v. City of Cambridge, 277 U.S. 183 (1928)
New Jersey Builders Association v. Dept. of Environmental Protection, 404 A.2d 320 (N.J. Super. 1979)
New State Ice Co. v. Liebmann, 285 U.S. 262 (1932)
New York State Liquor Authority v. Bellanca, 452 U.S. 714 (1981)
New York Times v. Sullivan, 376 U.S. 254 (1964)
New York v. Ferber, 458 U.S. 747 (1982)
Nollan v. California Coastal Commission, 483 U.S. 825 (1987)
Noranda Explorations Inc. v. Ostrom, 335 N.W.2d 596 (Wis. 1983)
Oakwood at Madison, Inc. v. Township of Madison, 371 A.2d 1192 (N.J. 1977)
Ohlson v. Phillips, 304 F.Supp. 1152 (1969)
Olson v. U.S., 292 U.S. 246 (1934)
Osborne v. Ohio, 495 U.S. 103 (1990)
Owens v. Kohlmeyer, 381 N.E.2d 1097 (Ind. App. 1978)
Pacific Transportation Co. v. City of Los Angeles 922 F.2d 498 (1990)
Paris Adult Theatre v. Slaton, 413 U.S. 49 (1973)
Passmore v. Birkins, 311 F.Supp. 588 (1969)
Penn Central Transportation Co. v. New York City, 438 U.S. 104 (1978)
Pennsylvania Coal Co. v. Mahon, 260 U.S. 393 (1922)
Penthouse v. McAuliffe, 702 F.2d 925 (1983)
People ex. rel. Tooley v. Seven Thirty Five East Colfax, 697 P.2d 348 (Colo. 1985)
People v. Drake, 748 P.2d 1237 (Colo. 1988)
People v. Emmert, 597 P.2d 1025 (Colo. 1979)
People v. Ford, 773 P.2d 1059 (Colo. 1989)
People v. Gibson, 521 P.2d 774 (Colo. 1974)
People v. Hildebrandt, 544 P.2d 384 (Colo. 1976)
People v. New Horizons, Inc., 616 P.2d 106 (Colo. 1980)
People v. Pozo, 746 P.2d 523 (Colo. 1987)
People v. Rister, 803 P.2d 483 (Colo. 1990)
People v. Wiener, 35 Cal. Rptr.2d 321 (1994)
Pierce v. City and County of Denver, 565 P.2d 1337 (Colo. 1977)
Pinnock v. International House of Pancakes Franchisee, 844 F.Supp. 574 (1993)
Plessy v. Ferguson, 163 U.S. 537 (1896)
Pope v. Illinois, 481 U.S. 497 (1987)
Preseault v. I.C.C., 494 U.S. 1 (1990)
Provenzano v. U.S., 379 U.S. 947 (1964)

Ptasynski v. U.S., 550 F.Supp. 549 (1982)
Rank v. Krug, 142 F.Supp. 1 (1956)
Redrup v. New York, 386 U.S. 767 (1967)
Regina v. Hicklin, 3 QB 360 (1868)
Reno v. American Civil Liberties Union, 117 S.Ct. — (1997).
Rent Stabilization Assn. of New York, Inc. v. Higgins, 630 N.E.2d 626 (N.Y. 1993), 562 N.Y.S. 2d 962 (N.Y.A.D. 1990)
Reserve Mining Co. v. Minnesota Pollution Control Agency, 200 N.W.2d 142 (Minn. 1972)
Reserve Mining Company v. Herbst, 256 N.W.2d 808 (Minn. 1977)
Roaden v. Kentucky, 413 U.S. 496 (1973)
Robinson v. Cahill, 287 A.2d 187 (N.J. Super. 1972)
Robinson v. City of Seattle, 830 P.2d 318 (Wash. 1992)
Roe v. Wade, 410 U.S. 113 (1973)
Roman v. Sharper, 250 A.2d 745 (N.J. 1969)
Rothschild v. Richland County Board of Adjustment, 420 S.E.2d 853 (S.C. 1992)
Roth v. U.S., 354 U.S. 476 (1957)
Rowan v. U.S. Post Office Dept., 397 U.S. 728 (1970)
Saliba v. State, 475 N.E.2d 1181 (Ind. App. 1985)
San Antonio v. Rodriguez, 411 U.S. 1 (1973)
San Diego Gas & Electric Co. v. San Diego, 450 U.S. 621 (1981)
Schneider v. City of Ramsey, 800 F.Supp. 815 (1992)
Seawall Associates v. City of New York, 542 N.E.2d 1059 (N.Y. 1989)
Sedelbauer v. State, 455 N.E.2d 1159 (Ind. App. 1983)
Seventy-Two Fifty Corporation v. Adams, 799 P.2d 917 (Colo. 1990)
Shatto v. McNulty, 509 N.E.2d 897 (Ind. App. 1987)
Shelter Creek Development Corp. v. City of Oxnard, 838 F.2d 375 (1988)
Sierra Club v. Kiawah Resort Associates, 456 S.E.2d 397 (S.C. 1995), 1994 S.C. LEXIS 166 (1994)
Sierra Club v. Watt, 608 F.Supp. 305 (1985)
Sintra, Inc. v. City of Seattle, 829 P.2d 765 (Wash. 1992)
Smith v. California, 361 U.S. 147 (1959)
South Carolina Farm Bureau v. Scott, 262 S.E.2d 739 (S.C. 1980)
South Carolina Wildlife Federation v. South Carolina Coastal Council, 371 S.E.2d 521 (S.C. 1988)
Southern Burlington County NAACP v. Mt. Laurel, 456 A.2d 390 (N.J. 1983)
South Harrison v. Board of Chosen Freeholders of Gloucester, 510 A.2d 42 (N.J. Super. 1986)
Sparks v. Douglas County, 904 P.2d 738 (Wash. 1995)
Stanley v. Georgia, 394 U.S. 557 (1969)
State Board of Education v. Board of Education of Netcong, 270 A.2d 412 (N.J. 1970)
State Dairy Commission of South Carolina v. Pet, Inc., 324 S.E.2d 56 (S.C. 1984)
State ex rel. Firestone v. Parke Circuit Court, 621 N.E.2d 1113 (Ind. 1993)
State v. Alexander, 281 N.W.2d 349 (Minn. 1979)
State v. Blecker, 382 A.2d 400 (N.J. Super. 1978)
State v. Bonynge, 450 N.W.2d 331 (Minn. App. 1990)
State v. Carmel, 404 A.2d 1227 (N.J. Super. 1979)
State v. Carroll, 587 A.2d 260 (N.J. 1991)
State v. Christopher, 170 N.W.2d 95 (Minn. 1969)

State v. Dailey, 169 N.W.2d 746 (Minn. 1969)
State v. Davidson, 481 N.W.2d 51 (Minn. 1992)
State v. DeSantis, 323 A.2d 489 (N.J. 1974)
State v. Edwards, 177 N.W.2d 40 (Minn. 1970)
State v. Freedom from Religion Foundation, 898 P.2d 1013 (Colo. 1995)
State v. Hartman, 136 N.W.2d 543 (Minn. 1965)
State v. Henry, 732 P.2d 9 (Or. 1987)
State v. J.O., 355 A.2d 195 (N.J. 1976)
State v. Kam, 748 P.2d 372 (Hawaii 1988)
State v. Miller et al., 159 N.W.2d 895 (Minn. 1968)
State v. Minnesota Dept. of Natural Resources, 1994 Minn. LEXIS 568 (Minn.App. 1994) (unpublished)
State v. Sappenfield, 505 N.E.2d 504 (Ind. App. 1987)
State v. Target Stores, 156 N.W.2d 908 (Minn. 1968)
State v. Watkins, 203 S.E.2d 429 (S.C. 1973), 191 S.E.2d 135 (S.C. 1972)
State v. White, 464 N.W.2d 585 (Minn.App. 1990)
State v. Witherall, 174 N.W.2d 329 (Minn. 1970)
Stone v. Powell, 428 U.S. 465 (1976)
Stono River Environmental Protection Assn. v. South Carolina Dept. of Health and Environmental Control, 406 S.E.2d 340 (S.C. 1991)
Stupak-Thrall v. U.S., 70 F.3d 881 (1995), 843 F.Supp. 327 (1994)
Submission of Interrogatories on Senate Bill 93-74, 852 P.2d 1 (Colo. 1993)
Suess Builders Co. v. City of Beaverton, 656 P.2d 306 (Or. 1982)
Sumner v. Mata, 449 U.S. 539 (1981)
Switz v. Kingsley, 182 A.2d 841 (N.J. 1962)
Tampa-Hillsborough City Expressway Auth. v. A.G.W.S. Corp., 640 So.2d 54 (Fla. 1994)
Tattered Cover v. Tooley, 696 P.2d 780 (Colo. 1985)
Times-Film v. Chicago, 365 U.S. 43 (1961)
Township of Bass River v. Hogwallow Inc., 442 A.2d 1055 (N.J. Super. 1982)
Triple G Landfills v. Board of Commissioners, 977 F.2d 287 (1992)
UMBA v. City of Minneapolis, 602 F.Supp. 1361 (1985), 780 F.2d 1389 (1985)
University of Colorado v. Derdeyn, 863 P.2d 929 (Colo. 1993)
Urban Council on Mobility v. Minnesota Dept. of Natural Resources, 289 N.W.2d 729 (Minn. 1980)
U.S. v. 12 Reels of Super 8mm Film, 413 U.S. 123 (1973)
U.S. v. Carolene Products, 304 U.S. 144 (1938)
U.S. v. City and County of Denver, 656 P.2d 1 (Colo. 1982)
U.S. v. Jenks, 22 F.3d 1513 (1994)
U.S. v. Leon, 468 U.S. 897 (1984)
U.S. v. One Book Called "Ulysses," 5 F.Supp. 182 (1933), 72 F.2d 705 (1934)
U.S. v. Orito, 413 U.S. 139 (1973)
U.S. v. Reidel, 402 U.S. 351 (1971)
U.S. v. Riverside Bayview Homes, Inc., 474 U.S. 121 (1985)
Utah v. Andrus, 486 F.Supp. 995 (1979)
Vasquez v. Glassboro Service Association., 387 A.2d 1198 (N.J. Super. 1978)
Village of Euclid v. Ambler Realty, 272 U.S. 365 (1926)
Virginia v. ABA et al., 484 U.S. 383 (1988)
Webster v. Reproductive Health Services, 492 U.S. 490 (1989)

Welsh v. Sells, 193 N.E.2d 359 (Ind. 1963)
Whitney Benefits v. U.S., 926 F.2d 1169 (1991)
Whitney v. Heckler, 780 F.2d 963 (1986)
Williamson County Regional Planning Commission v. Hamilton Bank, 473 U.S. 172 (1985)
Wolff v. City of Monticello, 803 F.Supp. 1568 (1992)
Wyoming Trucking Assn. Inc. v. Bentsen, 1995 U.S. Dist. LEXIS 2357 (1995) (unpublished)
Yee v. City of Escondido, 503 U.S. 519 (1992)
Young v. American Mini Theatres, 427 U.S. 50 (1976)
Younger v. Harris, 401 U.S. 37 (1971)
Yunker v. Porter City Sheriff's Merit Board, 382 N.E.2d 977 (Ind. App. 1978)

Works Cited

Abrahamson, Shirley S. 1985. Criminal law and state constitutions: The emergence of state constitutional law. *Texas Law Review* 63 (March): 1141-93.

Abrahamson, Shirley S., and Diane S. Gutman. 1987. The new federalism: State constitutions and state courts. *Judicature* 71 (August–September): 88-99.

Ackerman, Bruce A. 1977. *Private property and the Constitution*. New Haven: Yale University Press.

Alumbaugh, Steve, and C. K. Rowland. 1990. The links between platform-based appointment criteria and trial judges' abortion judgments. *Judicature* 74 (October–November): 153-62.

Ayer, Donald. 1992. Straying from the right religion. *Legal Times*, 27 July: S39.

Bates, Steven, Executive Director, American Civil Liberties Union of South Carolina. 1995. Interview with author, 17 July, Columbia, South Carolina.

Baum, Lawrence. 1994. *American courts: Process and policy*. 3d ed. Boston: Houghton Mifflin.

——.1988. Measuring policy change on the U.S. Supreme Court. *American Political Science Review* 82 (September): 905-12.

——.1977. Judicial impact as a form of policy implementation. Chap. 5 in *Public law and public policy*, ed. Carl Van Horn, Washington: Congressional Quarterly Press.

——.1976. Implementation of judicial decisions: An organizational analysis. *American Politics Quarterly* 4 (January): 86-114.

Bauman, Gus. 1983. The Supreme Court, inverse condemnation and the Fifth Amendment: Justice Brennan confronts the inevitable in land use controls. *Rutgers Law Journal* 15 (Summer): 15-99.

Beasley, Dorothy Toth. 1996. Federalism and the protection of individual rights: The American state constitutional perspective. In *Federalism and rights*, ed. Ellis Katz and G. Alan Tarr, 101-21. London: Rowman & Littlefield.

Beavers, Staci L., and Jeffrey S. Waltz. 1997. An altered state of civil liberties: Factors encouraging their expression under state constitutional law. Paper presented at the Annual Meeting of the Midwest Political Science Association, Chicago.

Beiser, Edward N. 1973. The Rhode Island Supreme Court: A well-integrated political system. *Law and Society Review* 8 (Winter): 167-86.

Bell, Jane, Staff Attorney, American Civil Liberties Union of Colorado. 1995. Interview with author, 15 August, Denver.

Bentley, Arthur. 1908. *The process of government*. Cambridge, Mass.: Belknap Press of Harvard University.

Berger, Michael M. 1992. Late-breaking news about takings law. In *Eminent domain and land valuation litigation*, American Law Institute–American Bar Association Course of Study, 2-41. Fort Lauderdale, Fla.: American Law Institute.

Black, Donald. 1973. The mobilization of the law. *Journal of Legal Studies* 2 (January): 125-49.

Blaesser, Brian W. 1988. Closing the federal courthouse door on property owners: The ripeness and abstention doctrines in Section 1983 land use cases. *Hofstra Property Law Journal* 2 (Fall): 73-163.

Bowen, Lauren. 1994. Interest groups and the courts: An analysis of sexual harassment policy. Paper presented at the Annual Meeting of the American Political Science Association, New York.

Boyer, Paul S. 1968. *Purity in print: The vice society movement and book censorship in America*. New York: Scribner's.

Brace, Paul, and Melinda Gann Hall. 1995. Studying courts comparatively: The view from the American states. *Political Research Quarterly* 48 (March): 5-29.

——.1990. Neo-institutionalism and dissent in state supreme courts. *Journal of Politics* 52 (February): 54-70.

Brennan, William J., Jr. 1986. The Bill of Rights and the states: The revival of state constitutions as guardians of individual rights. *New York University Law Review* 61 (October): 535-53

——.1977. State constitutions and the protection of individual rights. *Harvard Law Review* 90 (January): 489-504.

Brest, Paul, and Ann Vandenberg. 1987. Politics, feminism, and the Constitution: The anti-pornography movement in Minneapolis. *Stanford Law Review* 39 (February): 607-61.

Burling, James S. 1995. Written testimony for the Task Force on Property Rights of the Committee on Resources, United States House of Representatives, 17 May.

Caira, Mark. 1992. State constitutional takings jurisprudence. *Rutgers Law Journal* 23 (Summer): 792-818.

Caldeira, Gregory A. 1985. The transmission of legal precedent: A study of state supreme courts. *American Political Science Review* 79 (March): 178-93.

——.1983. On the reputation of state supreme courts. *Political Behavior* 5, no. 4: 83-108.

Caldeira, Gregory A., and John R. Wright. 1990. Amicus curiae before the Supreme Court: Who participates, when, and how much? *Journal of Politics* 52 (August): 782-806.

——.1988. Interest groups and agenda setting in the Supreme Court of the United States. *American Political Science Review* 82 (December): 1109-27.

Callies, David L. 1994. Nexus redux on required land dedications. *Land Use Law and Zoning Digest* 46:3-4.

Canavan, Francis. 1984. *Freedom of expression: Purpose as limit*. Durham, N.C.: Carolina Academic Press.

Canon, Bradley C., and Lawrence Baum. 1981. Patterns of tort law innovations: An application of diffusion theory to judicial doctrines. *American Political Science Review* 75 (December): 975-87.

Casper, Jonathan. 1972. *The politics of civil liberties*. New York: Harper & Row.

Chemerinsky, Erwin. 1988. Parity reconsidered: Defining a role for the federal judiciary. *UCLA Law Review* 36 (December): 233-327.

Christianson, Ray, Colorado Farm Bureau Federation. 1995. Interview with author, 15 August, Denver.

Clark, Peter B., and James Q. Wilson. 1961. Incentive systems: A theory of organizations. *Administrative Science Quarterly* 6 (September): 129-66.

Cobb, Roger, and Charles Elder. 1983. *Participation in American politics: The dynamics of agenda building*. 2d ed. Baltimore: Johns Hopkins University Press.

Collins, Ronald. 1985. Reliance on state constitutions: Some random thoughts. In *Developments in state constitutional law*, ed. Bradley McGraw, 1-50. St. Paul: West Publishing.

——.1981. Commentary: Reliance on state constitutions—away from a reactionary approach. *Hastings Constitutional Law Quarterly* 9 (Fall): 1-19.

Collins, Ronald K.L, Peter J. Galie, and John Kincaid. 1986. State high courts, state constitutions, and individual rights litigation since 1980: A judicial survey. *Publius* 16 (Summer): 141-62.

Comment. 1981. Civil rights for the propertied class: The development of inverse condemnation in the federal courts. *Tulane Law Review* 55 (April): 897-935.

Corn, David. 1990. Dirty bookkeeping. *New Republic*, 2 April, 14-16.

Cortner, Richard C. 1975. *The Supreme Court and civil liberties policy*. Palo Alto, Calif.: Mayfield.

——.1968. Strategies and tactics of litigants in constitutional cases. *Journal of Public Law* 17: 287-307.

Cowan, Ruth B. 1976. Women's rights through litigation: An examination of the American Civil Liberties Union Women's Rights Project. *Columbia Human Rights Law Review* 8 (Spring–Summer): 373-412.

D'Alemberte, Talbot. 1996. Rights and federalism: An agenda to advance the vision of Justice Brennan. In *Federalism and rights*, ed. Ellis Katz and G. Alan Tarr, 123-38. London: Rowman & Littlefield.

Daynes, Byron W. 1988. Pornography: Freedom of expression or societal degradation? In *Social regulatory policy: Moral controversies in American politics*, ed. Raymond Tatalovich and Byron Daynes, 41-73. Boulder, Colo.: Westview Press.

Dexter, Lewis Anthony. 1970. *Elite and specialized interviewing*. Evanston: Northwestern University Press.

Douglass, Charles G., III. 1978. State judicial activism—the new role for the state bill of rights. *Suffolk University Law Review* 12 (Fall): 1123-50.

Downs, Donald A. 1989. *The new politics of pornography*. Chicago: University of Chicago Press.

——.1987. The Attorney General's commission and the new politics of pornography. *American Bar Foundation Research Journal* 1987 (Fall): 641-80.

——.1985. *Nazis in Skokie: Freedom, community, and the First Amendment*. Notre Dame, Ind.: University of Notre Dame Press.

Duerksen, Christopher J., and Richard J. Roddewig. 1994. *Takings law in plain English*. Washington, D.C.: American Resources Information Network.

Dworkin, Andrea. 1981. *Pornography*. New York: Putnam.

Eid, Sandra, Legislative Coordinator, Rocky Mountain Chapter of Sierra Club. 1995. Interview with author, 16 August, Denver.

Elazar, Daniel J. 1984. *American federalism: A view from the states*. 3d ed. New York: Harper & Row.

Emerson, Kirk. 1996. State property rights legislation: A policy development perspective. Paper presented at the Joint International Congress of the Association of Collegiate Schools of Planning and the Association of European Schools of Planning, Toronto.

Emerson, Kirk, and Charles R. Wise. 1995. Statutory approaches to regulatory takings: State property rights legislation issues and implications for public administrators. Paper presented at the Annual Meeting of the American Political Science Association, Chicago.

Emmert, Craig F. 1988. Judicial review in state supreme courts: Opportunity and activism. Paper presented at the Annual Meeting of the Midwest Political Science Association, Chicago.

Encyclopedia of Associations. Various years. Detroit: Gale Research Company.

Engdahl, David. 1969. Requiem for *Roth*. *Michigan Law Review* 68 (December): 185-236.

Engel, Kirsten. 1989. Taking risks: Executive Order 12,360 and environmental, health, and safety regulation. *Vermont Law Review* 14 (Summer): 213-45.

Ennis, Bruce. 1980. ACLU: 60 years of volunteer lawyering. *ABA Journal* 66 (September): 1080-83.

Epstein, Lee. 1994. Exploring the participation of organized interests in state court litigation. *Political Research Quarterly* 47 (June): 335-51.

——.1992. A longitudinal examination of the participation of organized interests in state court litigation. Paper presented at the Annual Meeting of the Law and Society Association, Philadelphia.

——.1991. Courts and interest groups. In *The American Courts: A Critical Assessment*, ed. John B. Gates and Charles A. Johnson, 335-71. Washington, D.C.: Congressional Quarterly Press.

——.1989a. A comparative analysis of the evolution, rules, and usage of amicus curiae briefs in the U.S. Supreme Court and state courts of last resort. Paper presented at the Annual Meeting of the Southwestern Political Science Association, Little Rock, Arkansas.

——.1989b. Interviewing U.S. Supreme Court justices and interest group attorneys. *Judicature* 73 (December–January): 196-98.

——.1985. *Conservatives in court*. Knoxville: University of Tennessee Press.

Epstein, Lee, and Joseph F. Kobylka. 1992. *The Supreme Court and legal change: Abortion and the death penalty*. Chapel Hill: University of North Carolina Press.

Epstein, Lee, Joseph F. Kobylka, and Joseph Stewart, Jr. 1995. A theory of interest groups and litigation. *Research in Law and Policy Studies* 4: 113-38.

Epstein, Lee and C. K. Rowland. 1991. Debunking the myth of interest group invincibility in the courts. *American Political Science Review* 85 (March): 205-17.

Epstein, Richard A. 1992. *Yee v. City of Escondido*: The Supreme Court strikes out again. *Loyola of Los Angeles Law Review* 26 (November): 3-22.

——.1985. *Takings: Private property and the power of eminent domain*. Cambridge, Mass.: Harvard University Press.

Esler, Michael. 1995. The impact of the Supreme Court in the new judicial federalism. Paper presented at the Annual Meeting of the American Political Science Association, Chicago.

——.1994. State supreme court commitment to state law. *Judicature* 78 (July–August): 25-32.

Fino, Susan P. 1987a. Judicial federalism and equality guarantees in state supreme courts. *Publius* 17 (Winter): 51-67.

——.1987b. *The role of state supreme courts in the new judicial federalism*. Westport, Conn.: Greenwood Press.

Fischman, Robert L. 1991. Global warming and property interests: Preserving coastal wetlands as sea levels rise. *Hofstra Law Review* 19 (Spring): 565-602.

Friedelbaum, Stanley H. 1987. Reactive response: The complementary role of federal and state courts. *Publius* 17 (Winter): 33-50.

Galanter, Marc. 1974. Why the "haves" come out ahead: Speculations on the limits of legal change. *Law and Society Review* 9 (Fall): 95-160.

Galie, Peter J. 1988. State courts and economic rights. *Annals of the American Academy of Political and Social Sciences* 496 (March): 76-87.

Gallagher, Kari Anne. 1992. *Yee v. City of Escondido*: Will mobile homes provide an open road for *Nollan* analysis? *Notre Dame Law Review* 67, no. 3: 821-49.

Gardner, James A. 1992. The failed discourse of state constitutionalism. *Michigan Law Review* 90 (February): 761-837.

Gibson, James L., and Richard D. Bingham. 1985. *Civil liberties and Nazis*. New York: Praeger.

Glick, Henry R. 1991. Policy making and state supreme courts. In *The American courts: A critical assessment*, ed. John B. Gates and Charles A. Johnson, 87-118. Washington, D.C.: CQ Press.

——.1978. The promise and performance of the Missouri Plan: Judicial selection in the fifty states. *University of Miami Law Review* 32 (June): 509-41.

——.1971. *Supreme courts in state politics: An investigation of the judicial role*. New York: Basic Books.

Goldman, Sheldon. 1993. Bush's judicial legacy: The final imprint. *Judicature* 76 (April–May): 282-97.

Gray, Virginia. 1973. Innovation in the states: A diffusion study. *American Political Science Review* 67 (December): 1174-85.

Greenberg, Jack. 1994. *Crusaders in the courts: How a dedicated band of lawyers fought for the civil rights revolution*. New York: Basic Books.

——.1977. *Judicial process and social change*. St. Paul: West.

Gustafson, Peter, Legislative Coordinator, South Carolina Farm Bureau. 1995. Interview with author, 17 July, Columbia, South Carolina.

Hagman, Donald G. 1975. *Urban planning and land development control law*. St. Paul: West.

Hakman, Nathan. 1966. Lobbying the Supreme Court: An appraisal of political science "folklore." *Fordham Law Review* 35, no. 1: 15-50.

Hall, Melinda Gann, and Paul Brace. 1992. Electoral politics and strategic voting in state supreme courts. *Journal of Politics* 54 (May): 427-46.

Hamilton, Alexander, James Madison, and John Jay. 1961. *The federalist papers*, ed. Clinton Rossiter. New York: New American Library.

Hammer, Dean, and Aaron Wildavsky. 1989. The open-ended, semistructured interview: An (almost) operational guide. In *Craftways: On the organization of scholarly work*, ed. Aaron Wildavsky, 57-101. New Brunswick, N.J.: Transaction.

Harris, Cheri, Staff Attorney, Indiana Civil Liberties Union. 1995. Interview with author, 21 February, Indianapolis.

Hertzberg, Henrick. 1986. Big boobs. *New Republic*, 14 and 21 July, pp. 21-24.

Horowitz, Morton J. 1977. *The transformation of American law, 1780-1860*. Cambridge, Mass.: Harvard University Press.

Howard, A. E. Dick. 1976. State courts and constitutional rights in the day of the Burger Court. *Virginia Law Review* 62 (June): 873-944.

Ivers, Gregg. 1995. *To build a wall: American Jews and the separation of church and state*. Charlottesville: University of Virginia Press.

Jackson, Jerry, and Lyle D. Albaugh. 1988. A critique of the takings executive order in the context of environmental regulation. *Environmental Law Reporter* 18:10,463.

Jacobs, Harvey M. 1995. The anti-environmental "wise use" movement in America. *Land Use Law and Zoning Digest* 47:3-8.

Jacobsohn, Gary Jeffrey. 1996. Contemporary constitutional theory, federalism, and the protection of rights. In *Federalism and rights*, ed. Ellis Katz and G. Alan Tarr, 29-55. London: Rowman & Littlefield.

Jennings, Garry. 1994. The amicus curiae brief in state courts from 1950 to 1964: A comparative perspective. Paper presented at the Annual Meeting of the Midwest Political Science Association, Chicago.

Jerman, Trish, Former Executive Director, South Carolina Wildlife Federation. 1995. Interview with author, 18 July, Columbia, South Carolina.

Johnson, Charles A., and Bradley C. Canon. 1984. *Judicial policies: Implementation and impact*. Washington, D.C.: CQ Press.

Kalven, Harry. 1960. The metaphysics of the law of obscenity. *Supreme Court Review* 1960: 1-45.

Katz, Al. 1969. Privacy and pornography: *Stanley v. Georgia*. *Supreme Court Review* 1969: 203-17.

Kaye, Judith S. 1987. Dual constitutionalism in practice and principle. *St. John's Law Review* 61 (Spring): 399-429.

Kennedy, Sheila, Executive Director, Indiana Civil Liberties Union. 1995. Interview with author, 21 February, Indianapolis.

Key, V. O. 1961. *Public opinion and American democracy*. New York: Knopf.

Kilwein, John C., and Richard A. Brisbin, Jr. 1997. Policy convergence in a federal judicial system: The application of intensified scrutiny doctrines by state supreme courts. *American Journal of Political Science* 41 (January): 122-48.

King, Gary, Robert O. Keohane, and Sidney Verba. 1995. The importance of research design in political science. *American Political Science Review* 89 (June): 475-81.

——. 1994. *Designing social inquiry: Scientific inference in qualitative research*. Princeton: Princeton University Press.

Kluger, Richard. 1976. *Simple justice: The history of* Brown v. Board of Education *and black America's struggle for equality*. New York: Vintage.

Kobylka, Joseph F. 1991. *The politics of obscenity: Group litigation in a time of legal change*. Westport, Conn.: Greenwood Press.

——. 1987. A Court-created context for group litigation: Libertarian groups and obscenity. *Journal of Politics* 49 (November): 1061-78.

Krislov, Samuel. 1963. The amicus curiae brief: From friendship to advocacy. *Yale Law Journal* 72 (March): 694-721.

Kritzer, Herbert M. 1994. Interpretation and validity assessment in qualitative research: The case of H. W. Perry's Deciding to Decide. *Law and Social Inquiry* 19: 687-724.

Latzer, Barry. 1991a. The hidden conservatism of the state court revolution. *Judicature* 74 (January–February): 190-97.

——. 1991b. *State constitutions and criminal justice*. Westport, Conn.: Greenwood Press.

Lawrence, Susan E. 1989. Legal services before the Supreme Court. *Judicature* 72 (February–March): 266-73.

Lazarus, Richard J. 1993. Putting the correct "spin" on Lucas. *Stanford Law Review* 45 (May): 1411-32.

Lee, A. James, and Burton A. Weisbrod. 1978. Public interest law in education. In *Public interest law: An economic and institutional analysis*, ed. Burton Weisbrod, 313-48. Berkeley: University of California Press.

Linde, Hans A. 1985. E pluribus—constitutional theory and state courts. In *Developments in state constitutional law*, ed. Bradley McGray, 273-305. St. Paul: West.

——. 1980. First things first: Rediscovering the state's bill of rights. *University of Baltimore Law Review* 9 (Spring): 379-96.

Lunney, Glynn S., Jr. 1992. A critical reexamination of the takings jurisprudence. *Michigan Law Review* 90 (June): 1892-1965.

MacKinnon, Catharine. 1985. Pornography, civil rights, and speech. *Harvard Civil Rights–Civil Liberties Review* 20 (Winter): 1-70.

——. 1984. Not a moral issue. *Yale Law and Policy Review* 2 (Spring): 321-45.

Maltz, Earl M., Robert F. Williams, and Michael Araten. 1989. Selected bibliography on state constitutional law. *Rutgers Law Journal* 20 (Summer): 1093-1113.

Manwaring, David. 1962. *Render unto Caesar: The flag salute controversy*. Chicago: University of Chicago Press.

Marzulla, Roger J., Former Executive Director, Mountain States Legal Foundation. 1995. Interview with author, 15 March, Washington, D.C.

Marzulla, Roger J., and Nancie G. Marzulla. 1991. Regulatory takings in the United States Claims Court: Adjusting the burdens that in fairness and equity ought to be borne by society as a whole. *Catholic University Law Review* 40 (Spring): 549-69.

McCann, Michael W. 1994. *Rights at work*. Chicago: University of Chicago Press.

McFarland, Andrew S. 1994. Interviewing interest group personnel: The little village in the world. In *Representing interests and interest group representation*, ed. William Crotty, Mildred A. Schwartz, and John C. Green, 46-56. Lanham, Maryland: University Press of America.

McGuire, Kevin T., and Barbara Palmer. 1995. Issue fluidity on the U.S. Supreme Court. *American Political Science Review* 89 (September): 691-702.

Meeker, James W. 1986. *State supreme court litigants and their disputes*. New York: Garland.

Meiklejohn, Alexander. 1961. The First Amendment is an absolute. *Supreme Court Review* 1961: 245-66.

Meltsner, Michael. 1973. *Cruel and unusual: The Supreme Court and capital punishment*. New York: Random House.

Meltz, Robert. 1993. Takings decisions of the U.S. Supreme Court: A chronology. *Congressional Research Service Report* 93-164.

Michaelman, Frank. 1967. Property, utility, and fairness: Comments on the ethical foundations of "just compensation" law. *Harvard Law Review* 80: 1165-1258.

Miles, Matthew B., and A. Michael Huberman. 1984. *Qualitative data analysis*. Thousand Oaks, Calif.: Sage.

Moe, Terry. 1981. Toward a broader view of interest groups. *Journal of Politics* 43 (May): 531-43.

——. 1980. *The organization of interests*. Chicago: University of Chicago Press.

Moore, Michael, Executive Director, Minnesota Civil Liberties Union. 1995. Interview with author, 5 July, Minneapolis.

Morrison, Alan B., ed. 1996. *Fundamentals of American law*. New York: New York University School of Law Foundation.

Murphy, Paul L. 1979. *World War I and the origins of civil liberties in the United States*. New York: Norton.

Murphy, Walter. 1959. Lower court checks on Supreme Court power. *American Political Science Review* 53 (December): 1017-31.

National Law Journal. 1983. The ACLU on the rebound: Should civil liberties have a wider agenda? *National Law Journal* 5, September, 1, 8-9.

Neier, Aryeh. 1979. *Defending my enemy*. New York: Dutton.

Neubauer, David W. 1991. *Judicial process: Law, courts, and politics in the United States*. Pacific Grove, Calif.: Brooks/Cole.

Neuborne, Burt. 1985. State constitutional protection of free speech and establishment clause values. In *Recent developments in state constitutional law*, by the Practising Law Institute, 205-29. New York: Practising Law Institute.

——. 1977. The myth of parity. *Harvard Law Review* 90 (April): 1105-31.

Neuhaus, Richard J. 1984. *The naked public square: Religion and democracy in America*. Grand Rapids, Mich.: Eerdmans.

Note. 1985. The origins and original significance of the Just Compensation Clause of the Fifth Amendment. *Yale Law Journal* 94 (January): 694-716.

——. 1949. The public use limitation on eminent domain: An advance requiem. *Yale Law Journal* 58 (March): 599-614.

O'Brien, David M. 1995. *Constitutional law and politics, volume 2: Civil rights and civil liberties*. 2d ed. New York: Norton.

O'Connor, Karen. 1980. *Women's organizations' use of the Court*. Lexington, Mass: Lexington Books.

O'Connor, Karen, and Lee Epstein. 1989. *Public interest law groups: Institutional profiles*. Westport, Conn.: Greenwood Press.

——. 1982. Amicus curiae participation in U.S. Supreme Court litigation: An appraisal of Hakman's "folklore." *Law and Society Review* 16, no. 2: 311-20.

O'Connor, Sandra Day. 1989. Our judicial federalism. *Intergovernmental Perspective* 15 (Summer): 8-12.

——. 1985. Trends in the relationship between the federal and state courts. In *Views from the bench: The judiciary and constitutional politics*, ed. Mark W. Cannon and David M. O'Brien, 244-51. Chatham, N.J.: Chatham House.

Obscenity Law Bulletin. 1989. 95% of population now lives under *Miller*-type test. *Obscenity Law Bulletin* 13: 1.

Obscenity Law Project. 1977. An empirical inquiry into the effects of *Miller v. California* on the control of obscenity. *New York University Law Review* 52 (October): 810-939.

Olson, Mancur. 1965. *The logic of collective action*. Cambridge, Mass.: Harvard University Press.

Olson, Susan. 1990. Interest-group litigation in federal district court: Beyond the political disadvantage theory. *Journal of Politics* 52 (August): 854-82.

——. 1984. *Clients and lawyers*. Westport, Conn.: Greenwood Press.

——. 1981. The political evolution of interest group litigation. In *Governing through courts*, ed. Richard A. L. Gambitta, Marlyn L. May, and James C. Foster, 234-49. Beverly Hills, Calif.: Sage.

Pacelle, Richard L., Jr. 1991. *The transformation of the Supreme Court's agenda: From the New Deal to the Reagan administration*. Boulder, Colo.: Westview Press.

Peltason, Jack. 1961. *Fifty-eight lonely men: Southern federal judges and school desegregation*. New York: Harcourt, Brace and World.

——. 1955. *Federal courts in the political process*. New York: Random House.

Pendley, William Perry. 1994. *It takes a hero: The grassroots battle against environmental oppression*. Bellevue, Wash.: Free Enterprise Press.

Petracca, Mark P. 1992. The rediscovery of interest group politics. In *The politics of interests: Interest groups transformed*, ed. Mark Petracca, 3-31. Boulder, Colo.: Westview Press.

Pinello, Daniel R. 1995. *The impact of judicial-selection methods on state supreme court policy: Innovation, reaction, and atrophy*. Westport, Conn.: Greenwood Press.

Pivar, David J. 1973. *Purity crusade: Sexual morality and social control*. Westport, Conn.: Greenwood Press.

Porter, Mary Cornelia. 1982. State supreme courts and the legacy of the Warren Court: Some old inquiries for a new situation. In *State supreme courts: Policymakers in the federal system*, ed. Mary Porter and G. Alan Tarr, 3-21. Westport, Conn.: Greenwood Press.

Porter, Mary Cornelia, and G. Alan Tarr, ed. 1982. *State supreme courts: Policymakers in the federal system*. Westport, Conn.: Greenwood Press.

President's Commission on Obscenity and Pornography. 1970. *Report*. New York: Bantam Books.

Rakove, Jack N. 1991. Parchment barriers and the politics of rights. In *A culture of rights: The Bill of Rights in philosophy, politics, and law—1791 and 1991*, ed. Michael J. Lacey and Knud Haakonssen, 98-143. New York: Woodrow Wilson International Center for Scholars and Cambridge University Press.

Randolph, Carman F. 1991. *The law of eminent domain in the United States*. Littleton, Colo.: Fred B. Rothman & Co.

Rapaczynski, Andrezej. 1985. From sovereignty to process: The jurisprudence of federalism after *Garcia*. In *The Supreme Court Review: 1985*, ed. Philip Kurland, Gerhard Casper, and Dennis J. Hutchinson, 341-419. Chicago: University of Chicago Press.

Rembar, Charles. 1968. *The end of obscenity*. New York: Simon & Schuster.

Richardson, Richard, and Kenneth N. Vines. 1970. *The politics of federal courts: Lower courts in the United States*. Boston: Little, Brown.

Roberts, Thomas F. 1995. Ripeness and forum selection in Fifth Amendment takings litigation. *Journal of Land Use and Environmental Law* 11 (Fall): 37-73.

——. 1992. Fifth Amendment claims in federal court: The compensation requirement and principles of res judicata. *The Urban Lawyer* 24 (Summer): 479-513.

Rosenthal, Alan. 1993. *The third house: Lobbyists and lobbying in the states.* Washington, D.C.: Congressional Quarterly Press.

Rubenfeld, Jeb. 1993. Usings. *Yale Law Journal* 102 (March): 1077-1163.

Rubin, Eva. R. 1987. *Abortion, politics, and the courts.* Revised ed. Westport, Conn.: Greenwood Press.

Sackman, Julius L., ed. 1964. *Nichols's the law of eminent domain.* Revised 3d ed. New York: Bender.

Salisbury, Robert H. 1969. An exchange theory of interest groups. *Midwest Journal of Political Science* 13 (February): 1-32.

Schattschneider, E. E. 1960. *The semisovereign people: A realist's view of democracy in America.* New York: Holt, Rinehart, and Winston.

Schauer, Frederick F. 1976. *The law of obscenity.* Washington, D.C.: Bureau of National Affairs.

Scheingold, Stuart A. 1974. *The politics of rights.* New Haven: Yale University Press.

Scheppele, Kim Lane, and Jack L. Walker, Jr. 1991. The litigation strategies of interest groups. In *Mobilizing interest groups in America: Patrons, professions, and social movements*, ed. Jack Walker, 157-83. Ann Arbor: University of Michigan Press.

Schlozman, Kay Lehman, and John Tierney. 1986. *Organized interests and American democracy.* New York: Harper & Row.

Schuck, Peter. 1983. *Suing government: Citizen remedies for official wrongs.* New Haven: Yale University Press.

Schwartz, Arthur, Attorney. 1995. Interview with author, 14 August, Denver.

Seby, Paul, Staff Attorney, Mountain States Legal Foundation. 1995. Interview with author, 14 August, Denver.

Sheehan, Reginald S., William Mishler, and Donald R. Songer. 1992. Ideology, status, and the differential success of direct parties before the Supreme Court. *American Political Science Review* 86 (June): 464-71.

Siegan, Bernard H. 1980. *Economic liberties and the Constitution.* Chicago: University of Chicago Press.

Singer, James W. 1979. Liberal public interest law firms face budgetary, ideological challenges. *National Journal*, 2052-56.

Smith, Brett, Conservation Coordinator, Sierra Club of Minnesota. 1995. Interview with author, 6 July, Minneapolis.

Smith, Loren. 1991. Forward. *Catholic University Law Review* 40 (Spring): 509-12.

Solimine, Michael E., and James L. Walker. 1983. Constitutional litigation in federal and state courts: An empirical analysis of judicial parity. *Hastings Constitutional Law Quarterly* 10 (Winter): 213-53.

Songer, Donald. 1988. Alternative approaches to the study of judicial impact: *Miranda* in five state courts. *American Politics Quarterly* 16 (October): 425-44.

Songer, Donald R., and Ashlyn Kuersten. 1995. The success of amici in state courts. *Political Research Quarterly* 48 (March): 31-42.

Songer, Donald R., and Reginald S. Sheehan. 1993. Interest group success in the courts: Amicus participation in the Supreme Court. *Political Research Quarterly* 46 (June): 339-54.

——. 1992. Who wins on appeal? Upperdogs and underdogs in the United States Court of Appeals. *American Journal of Political Science* 36 (February): 235-58.

Sorauf, Frank J. 1976. *The wall of separation: Constitutional politics of church and state*. Princeton: Princeton University Press.

Stoebuck, William B. 1972. A general theory of eminent domain. *Washington Law Review* 47 (August): 553-608.

Strossen, Nadine. 1995. *Defending pornography: Free speech, sex, and the fight for women's rights*. New York: Scribner's.

Sugameli, Glen P. 1993. Takings issues in *Lucas v. South Carolina Coastal Council*: A decision full of sound and fury signifying nothing. *Virginia Environmental Law Journal* 12 (Spring): 439-504.

Sullivan, Edward J. 1988. The rise of state constitutional limits on planning and zoning powers. Chap. 8 in *Proceedings of the institute on planning, zoning, and eminent domain*, ed. Janice R. Moss. New York: Bender.

Tarr, G. Alan, and Mary Cornelia Aldis Porter. 1988. *State supreme courts in state and nation*. New Haven: Yale University Press.

Tarrow, Sidney. 1995. Bridging the quantitative-qualitative divide in political science. *American Political Science Review* 89 (June): 471-74.

Thomas, Clive S., and Ronald J. Hrebenar. 1990. Interest groups in the states. In *Politics in the American states*, 5th ed. Virginia Gray, Herbert Jacob, and Robert B. Albritton, 123-58. Glenview, Ill.: Scott, Foresman.

Tocqueville, Alexis de. 1954. *Democracy in America*. Vol. 1. New York: Vintage Books.

Tribe, Laurence H. 1980. The puzzling persistence of process-based constitutional theories. *Yale Law Journal* 89 (May): 1063-80.

Truman, David B. 1951. *The governmental process*. New York: Knopf.

Tushnet, Mark V. 1987. *The NAACP's legal strategy against segregated education, 1925-1950*. Chapel Hill: University of North Carolina Press.

Twist, Steven J., and Len L. Munsil. 1989. The double threat of judicial activism: Inventing new "rights" in state constitutions. *Arizona State Law Journal* 21 (Winter): 1005-65.

Ulmer, S. Sidney. 1982. Issue fluidity in the U.S. Supreme Court: A conceptual analysis. In *Supreme Court activism and restraint*, ed. Stephen C. Halpern and Charles M. Lamb, 319-50. Lexington, Mass.: D.C. Heath.

Vose, Clement E. 1981. Interest groups and litigation. Paper presented at the Annual Meeting of the American Political Science Association, New York.

——. 1972. *Constitutional change*. Lexington, Mass: Lexington Books.

——. 1966. Interest groups, judicial review and local government. *Western Political Quarterly* 19 (March): 85-100.

——. 1959. *Caucasians only: The Supreme Court, the NAACP, and the restrictive covenant cases*. Berkeley: University of California Press.

——. 1958. Litigation as a form of pressure group activity. *Annals of the American Academy of Political and Social Science* 319 (September): 20-31.

——. 1957. National Consumers' League and the Brandeis Brief. *Midwest Journal of Political Science* 1 (November): 267-90.

——. 1955. NAACP strategy in the restrictive covenant cases. *Western Reserve Law Review* 6 (Winter): 101-45.

Walker, Jack L., Jr. 1991. *Mobilizing interest groups in America: Patrons, professions, and social movements*. Ann Arbor: University of Michigan Press.

——. 1969. The diffusion of innovation among the American states. *American Political Science Review* 63 (September): 880-89.

Walker, Samuel. 1990. *In defense of American liberties: A history of the ACLU*. New York: Oxford University Press.

Waples, Richard A., Legal Director, Indiana Civil Liberties Union. 1995a. Interview with author, 12 September, Indianapolis.

——. 1995b. Recent developments under the Indiana Constitution. *Indiana Law Review* 28, no. 4: 1067-88.

Wasby, Stephen L. 1995. *Race relations litigation in an age of complexity*. Charlottesville: University of Virginia Press.

——. 1988. *The Supreme Court in the federal judicial system*. 3d ed. Chicago: Nelson-Hall.

——. 1984. How planned is "planned litigation"? *American Bar Foundation Research Journal* 1, no. 1: 83-138.

——. 1983. Interest groups in courts: Race relations litigation. In *Interest group politics*, ed. Allan J. Cigler and Burdett A. Loomis, 251-73. Washington, D.C.: Congressional Quarterly Press.

——. 1976. *Continuity and change: From the Warren Court to the Burger Court*. Pacific Palisades, Calif.: Goodyear.

Watson, Richard A., and Randal G. Downing. 1969. *The politics of the bench and the bar*. New York: Wiley.

Watts, Tim J. 1991. *State constitutional law development: A bibliography*. Monticello, Ill.: Vance Bibliographies.

Wenk, Marsha, Staff Attorney, American Civil Liberties Union of New Jersey. 1995. Interview with author, 1 March, Newark.

Wenner, Lettie. 1984. *The environmental decade in court*. Bloomington: Indiana University Press.

West, Robin. 1987. The feminist-conservative anti-pornography alliance and the 1986 attorney general's pornography report. *American Bar Foundation Research Journal* 1987 (Fall): 681-712.

Wheeler, Stanton, Bliss Cartwright, Robert A. Kagan, and Lawrence M. Friedman. 1987. Do the "haves" come out ahead? Winning and losing in state supreme courts, 1870-1970. *Law and Society Review* 21, no. 3: 403-45.

Wilkes, Donald E., Jr. 1974. The new federalism in criminal procedure: State court evasion of the Burger Court. *Kentucky Law Journal* 62, no. 2: 421-51.

Williams, Robert F. 1984. In the Supreme Court's shadow: Legitimacy of state rejection of Supreme Court reasoning and result. *South Carolina Law Review* 35 (Spring): 353-404.

Wilson, James Q. 1973. *Political organizations*. New York: Basic Books.

Wold, John T. 1974. Political orientations, social backgrounds, and role perceptions of state supreme court judges. *Western Political Quarterly* 27 (June): 239-48.

Yackle, Larry. 1994. *Reclaiming the federal courts*. Cambridge, Mass.: Harvard University Press.

Yin, Robert K. 1989. *Case study research: Design and methods*. Newbury Park, Calif.: Sage.

Zemans, Frances. 1983. Legal mobilization: The neglected role of the law in the political system. *American Political Science Review* 77 (September): 690-702.

Index

About the Author

DONALD J. FAROLE, Jr. is Assistant Professor of Political Science at the University of North Carolina at Greensboro. His research interests include state courts, rights litigation, and judicial agendas.

ISBN 0-275-96067-6
90000>
EAN
9 780275 960674
HARDCOVER BAR CODE